GLENCOE MATH

BUILT TO THE COMMON CORE

CCSS

COMMON CORE PERFORMANCE TASKS

AUTHORS
Carter • Cuevas • Day • Malloy
Kersaint • Reynosa • Silbey • Vielhaber

Mc
Graw
Hill
Education

Bothell, WA • Chicago, IL • Columbus, OH • New York, NY

Contents

Performance Tasks

Chapter 1

Performance Task

On the Road with Mr. Sanford

Truck driver, Mr. Sanford, drives semi-trailer trucks for A-1 Fleet Company. He generally drives 8 hours per day and works 5 days per week. His truck has a gas tank that holds 210 gallons of gasoline.

Write your answers on another piece of paper. Show all your work to receive full credit.

Part A

In the first week of December, A-1 pays Mr. Sanford a one-time holiday bonus of $500 plus his usual $22.50 per hour. Find Mr. Sanford's December earnings for 1, 2, 3, and 4 weeks. Determine whether the amount of money he earns during that time is proportional to the number of hours he drives by graphing on the coordinate plane. Explain your reasoning.

Part B

If Mr. Sanford can drive 1,890 miles on one tank of gasoline, how many miles on average could he drive using 3 gallons of gasoline?

Part C

During an 8-hour shift, Mr. Sanford was able to drive 520 miles. Write and solve a proportion to find how many hours it will take at this rate for him to drive 1,495 miles. How many 8-hour shifts does this represent?

Performance Task   (continued)

Mr. Sanford records his drive time and distance for one day of driving in the table shown.

Distance d (miles)	60	120	180	240	300	360	420	480
Time t (hours)	1	2	3	4	5	6	7	8

Part D

Graph the data in the table. Find the slope of the line, and explain what the slope represents as it relates to this problem.

Part E

B-2 Fleet Company, another truck driving company, is offering Mr. Sanford $2.00 more per hour but only allows 7-hour shifts per day. Mr. Sanford thinks he should take the job at B-2 because he would make more money per hour. His wife disagrees and says Mr. Sanford would make less money at B-2 because he would be working less total hours during a year.

Which company would you recommend Mr. Sanford work for based on annual earnings driving 1 shift per day, 5 days per week, 52 weeks per year? Explain why this is the better choice.

Performance Task

Chapter 2

Rock Concert

RickRock Productions is trying to put together a concert. They have already spent $20,000 as a non-refundable deposit to reserve the outdoor location, and they are looking over a short list of bands they may hire to perform.

The concert location has three different ways they can arrange the space:

Seating arrangement #1: 25,000 seats

Seating arrangement #2: 15,000 seats and room for 20,000 on the grass

Seating arrangement #3: 5,000 seats and room for 30,000 on the grass

Regular seat tickets cost $85 and tickets for the grass area cost $65. The location's owners get the $20,000 deposit, rental fee, and 3.4% of all ticket sales. The owners keep all the parking fees and provide security for the concert.

Write your answers on another piece of paper. Round answers to the nearest hundredth when necessary. Show all your work to receive full credit.

Part A

Which seating arrangement would produce the greatest revenue for the RickRock producer? What is the percent of increase from the least revenue to the greatest? Explain what the percent increase represents in this situation.

Part B

RickRock will also need insurance for the concert. They usually pay a $450,000 bond to the insurance company. If no damages are reported, the money will be refunded less a 1.5% fee. If the insurance has to cover damages, the amount of the damages will be subtracted from the bond before it is refunded. The 1.5% fee still applies to the entire amount of the bond. What percent of the $450,000 insurance bond would be refunded if the concert-goers do $18,592 in damages?

Performance Task *(continued)*

RickRock is considering several bands for their concert. The chart shows the costs for the bands.

Band	Guaranteed Fee	Percent of Ticket Sales	Special Demands
Steel Spiders	$250,000	8.5%	$10,000 limousine $5,000 food $20,000 staff
Sir X-Z	$300,000	9%	$10,000 personal trainer $4,000 food
Lady BeeBop	$280,000	8.75%	$15,000 makeup $300 bottled water $20,000 wardrobe
Guitars & Pickups	$325,000	9.2%	$1,000 kennel for dogs $7,500 cow rental $2,000 barbeque

Part C

The table shows the fees and demands from each band. Find the cost for each band for seating arrangement 2. Which is the most costly band to bring in for a concert?

Part D

A survey of music lovers in the city tells RickRock's producer that the bands he is thinking of hiring vary in popularity. He has calculated the percent of tickets each band would sell.

If you were the RickRock producer, which band would you hire? Which seating arrangement would you choose? Including another $75,000 in general expenses and $600,000 in concert location rental, how much will it cost to produce this concert? What percent of the ticket income does the profit represent? Explain your choices.

Band	Percent of Ticket Sales
Guitars & Pickups	100%
Sir X-Z	98%
Lady BeeBop	97.6%
Steel Spiders	97.2%

Performance Task

Chapter 3

Spinner Challenge

The spinner challenge is a game in which each player gets to spin the spinner four times each turn. The player then moves a marker forward or backward on the board by the sum of the four spins. The first player to move forward exactly 100 spaces is declared the winner. If a player would move past 100 on a turn, that turn is forfeited.

Write your answers on another piece of paper. Show all your work to receive full credit.

Part A

Give three examples of a player's turn (4 spins) that would result in moving backward 6 spaces. Write an addition sentence for each of the three possible turns.

Part B

Player 1 spins 9, −8, −10, and 7 on his first turn. Graph each move on a separate number line to show where the marker would be after each spin. For each graph, clearly indicate where his marker starts, how many spaces and in which direction he moves, and where his marker is at the end of each spin.

Explain the difference between the expressions $|9| + |−8| + |−10| + |7|$ and $|9 − 8 − 10 + 7|$ in terms of the placement of the marker.

Part C

A player spins −18 on the first spin of a turn. Write an expression that shows what he would need to spin on the other three spins of his turn to get a net movement of zero spaces.

Part D

Describe a way to win the game in exactly four turns if a player never spins the same number twice in a row. Write addition expressions for each of the four turns to support your answer. Show that the sum of the four turns is exactly 100.

Performance Task (continued)

POINTS _____

After the fourth turn, there is a bonus round in which all spins are multiplied by −2. The same spinner is used during the bonus round.

Part E

During the bonus round, Player 1 wants to move forward at least 20 spaces. Write an expression to represent a possible combination for Player 1's four spins during this bonus round. Explain how Player 1 will know whether his four spins during the bonus round will result in a forward move of at least 20 spaces.

Part F

Player 2 moves 15 spaces during the bonus round. Player 1 claims that Player 2 must have miscalculated his total. Is Player 1 correct? Explain why or why not.

Performance Task

Chapter 4

Summer Job

Noah works for a lawn-care business during the summer to make some extra money. The following table shows how many acres he mows per day.

Day	Acres Mowed
Monday	$\frac{1}{2}$
Tuesday	$2\frac{1}{2}$
Wednesday	$1\frac{1}{3}$
Thursday	$\frac{5}{4}$
Friday	$\frac{16}{5}$
Saturday	$3\frac{1}{7}$

Write your answers on another piece of paper. Show all your work to receive full credit. Unless otherwise stated, use only fractions. Answers should be shown as mixed numbers when possible.

Part A

Noah wants to calculate how many acres he mowed on Monday and Friday combined. However, his calculator will only compute in decimals. Convert the fractions to decimals and show how many acres Noah mowed on Monday and Friday combined.

Part B

Noah is getting gasoline from the company and believes he will need to use more of it on Friday than on any other day. Sort the days by acres mowed from least to greatest and argue whether Noah's opinion is correct or incorrect.

Performance Task (continued)

Part C

The lawn-care company is considering only delivering gasoline to Noah twice a week to save time. Explain which half of the week (Monday through Wednesday or Thursday through Saturday) would require more gasoline.

Part D

It is Saturday, and Noah has mowed $\frac{2}{7}$ acre at one property and $1\frac{3}{4}$ acres at a second property. However, it begins to rain, so Noah decides to finish the rest of the properties on Sunday. How many acres will he be mowing on Sunday?

Part E

When Noah comes in to work on Thursday, he finds out that one of the other employees got sick and will not be working for the next few days. The company asks him to mow the sick employee's properties in addition to his own properties. This means that Noah will have to mow $1\frac{1}{3}$ times as many acres on Thursday, $2\frac{1}{2}$ times as many acres on Friday, and $1\frac{5}{16}$ times as many acres on Saturday. Explain how many total acres Noah will now have to mow over the next three days.

Noah knows he will not have enough time to do all the mowing himself, so he asks his brother to mow half of the number of acres. How many acres will Noah's brother mow?

Part F

As a special project, the company asks Noah to mulch one flower bed in the front yard of each of three different customers' properties. The first property has a $20\frac{1}{2}$-foot-long bed of flowers, the second property has a $3\frac{1}{4}$-foot-long bed of flowers, and the third property has a $9\frac{3}{7}$-foot-long bed of flowers. Each bag of mulch covers a bed of flowers 1 yard long. The company will deliver the mulch if Noah tells them how many bags are needed at each property. How many bags of mulch should be delivered to each location?

Performance Task

Chapter 5

Cell City

Cell City wants to drive up sales. So they decide to start paying each employee $5.50 for each cell phone sale they make, in addition to their normal base salary. Marcus, for example, has a base salary of $20 per day. Roberta and Danielle each have a base salary of $90 per week. Assume a workweek is five days when determining your answers.

Write your answers on another piece of paper. Show all your work to receive full credit.

Part A

Danielle is trying to budget her bills. She needs to know how much she will make over the next three months so she can determine if she will be able to afford a new motorcycle. Write a linear expression for this, using x as the number of cell phones she sells per day. Assume a month is four weeks.

If Danielle sold 5 cell phones per day for each of the first two months and 7 per day for the third month, will she make enough for the motorcycle if it costs $3,000? Explain.

Part B

Marcus and Roberta want to use their combined week's earnings to purchase a big screen TV that costs $400. They each sell the same number of cell phones per day. Write a linear expression representing their combined income after one week, using x as the number of phones each of them sells per day.

Marcus thinks that if they each sell 4 cell phones per day, they would be able to purchase the TV. Roberta disagrees. Decide who is correct. Explain.

Part C

Marcus talks to management about a different way to pay employees. He insists it would be fairer for employees to get a percentage of their total sales dollars, plus their base pay. Using a percentage of your choice, create your own linear expression for this situation, using x to represent total sales and b to represent an employee's base pay. Using your expression, determine how much Marcus would make if he had $200 in sales on a particular day.

What effect could Marcus's suggestion have on employee pay? Explain.

Performance Task (continued)

POINTS _____

Cell City offers three cell phone plans.

Plan	Monthly Fee	Text Message Charges
A	$29.25	$0.12 per text message
B	$95.20	Unlimited text messages
C	$49.95	$0.05 per text message

All plans offer unlimited calling and 2 GB of data per month. Long distance calls are included. Customers who exceed the 2 GB of data per month will be charged an additional $15 for every 1 GB of additional data.

Part D

Cho has recently moved to the area and wants to know which plan is best for her. She typically sends and receives about 500 text messages each month and never goes beyond 2 GB of data. Using an algebraic expression to represent each plan, help Cho decide which plan would be best based on the number of text messages m she usually sends and receives.

Cho is concerned that since she is far away from friends and family, the number of text messages may increase dramatically. How would your recommendation change if the number of text messages doubles?

Part E

Cell City's customers are asking for a monthly plan with unlimited text messaging that allows more than 2 GB of data. Design a Plan D that Cell City can offer that includes additional levels of data usage. Cell City must pay the service provider $5 for every 1 GB of data that a customer uses, so the plan should allow Cell City to cover their costs while charging the customer less than the additional $15 per GB charged when they go over the 2 GB included in their monthly plan. Explain.

Explain how a customer who uses about 9 GB of data each month could benefit from this new plan.

Performance Task

Chapter 6

Bank Statement

Mario receives his bank statement and is trying to make sense of it, but he is having a hard time deciding what he wants to do with his money. The statement shows that Mario's checking account has a balance of $7,456.43, his savings account has a balance of $2,010.55, and his money market account has a balance of $2,378.09.

Write your answers on another piece of paper. Show all your work to receive full credit.

Part A

Mario wants the total of the three accounts to be $13,000. He thinks that he needs to deposit more than $1,200 to achieve this goal. Is Mario correct? Use an equation to support your answer.

Part B

Mario decides to donate most of his money market account evenly to five of his favorite charities, but he wants to leave at least $75 in the account. Write and solve an inequality to represent this situation. Let m represent the amount of money donated to each charity. What is the largest whole-dollar amount Mario can donate to each charity? How much money will Mario have left in his money market account after his donations? Justify.

Part C

Mario's brother Alphonso owes Mario $2,989.45, and he is considering giving Mario $45 every month for the next several years to pay this debt. Mario plans on putting this money into his money market account. Determine how many years it will take Alphonso to pay what he owes Mario. Include an equation as part of your explanation.

Performance Task (continued)

Mario wants to make a few long-term investments using his checking and savings accounts. He is interested in alternative-energy cars and has been looking at a variety of hybrid cars. The model he would like to purchase costs $19,080. Mario is also interested in buying a condo, and he has been preapproved for a $70,000 home loan.

Part D

When Mario goes to the car dealership to buy the car, he is told he needs to make a down payment in cash of at least 5% to qualify for special financing. His plan was to take the down payment out of his checking account, but he wants to make sure he keeps at least 85% of his current checking account balance in the account. Verify that Mario was able to purchase the car.

Part E

After purchasing the car, Mario moved $4,000 from his checking account into his savings account so he can buy a condo. He wants the down payment to be greater than 20% of his loan amount. If Mario has an extra $350 put into his savings account each month, at least how many months will he need to wait before he is able to consider purchasing a condo? Justify your answer. Sketch a number line illustrating your solution.

Part F

Mario is now in his first month living at the new condo. He now has the following monthly expenses: house payment, $700; car payment, $250; and phone bill, $80. His electric bill varies, and his water bill is usually around one fifth of his electric bill. Mario's monthly income is $1,450. If he wants to have at least $250 left over for groceries and other expenses, how high of an electric bill and water bill could Mario afford and why? Use an equation or an inequality to justify your answer.

Performance Task

Chapter 7

Geometry in Buildings

A lot of time and work go into creating a building. Several different teams of people must work together to design and construct buildings. This is true for Archer Construction Company, which specializes in large buildings. They are currently in the process of constructing a building that has several floors.

Write your answers on another piece of paper. Show all your work to receive full credit.

Part A

The construction workers will be building two straight hallways that will intersect in the center of the building, making angles *A*, *B*, *C*, and *D* reading clockwise. What observation can you make about angles *A* and *C*? Give a reason for your observation.

When drawing the blueprints for this intersection, the architects said angle *C* would be 70° and Angle *D* would be 105°. Argue why their measurements must be incorrect.

Part B

A team of construction workers is trying to make sense of the architect's blueprints. They see that an elevator shaft is drawn 7 inches tall. The construction workers read at the bottom of the blueprints "Scale: 2 inches = 9 feet." Help them determine the actual height of the elevator shaft.

Would doubling the left side of the scale equation (i.e., 4 inches = 9 feet) cause the elevator shaft to also double in height? Explain.

Part C

The construction team plans to install a wheelchair ramp. In the blueprints, it is represented as a right triangle *FGH* in which angle *G* is the right angle. They want angle *F* to be 5 times the sum of angle *H* and −2. Show what the measure of both angle *F* and angle *H* will be.

In general, what is the largest angle *F* could be that would allow triangle *FGH* to still be a right triangle?

Performance Task *(continued)*

The building is designed to look like a cube with a triangular prism sitting on top (as the roof). The width of the building is 32 feet. The total height of the building, including the roof, is 44 feet.

Part D

If the peak of the roof as viewed from the front is 120°, explain what the other two angles will be. Classify the triangle formed by the sides of the roof.

Even if the exact measure of the obtuse angle of the peak were not known, could one of the other angles also be obtuse? Why or why not?

Part E

The architect sketched a corner view of the building.

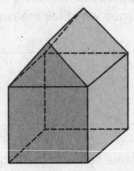

The building has two floors. The ceiling of the second floor represents a horizontal cross section of the building. What shape is this cross section?

The architect insists that the side view of the building is a rectangle that is not a square, but you know the part of the building without the roof is a cube. Is the architect correct? Explain. Describe the front and top views of the building.

Performance Task

Chapter 8

Home Sweet Home

Esperanza's family is getting ready to move into a two-story home that her parents built in another part of town. Her dad is a handyman, so they are doing a lot of the work themselves to save money. When viewed from the front, the house is 50 feet wide, 30 feet tall (not including the roof), and 45 feet deep. The garage door is 15 feet wide and 10 feet tall. Use 3.14 for π.

Write your answers on another piece of paper. Show all your work to receive full credit.

Part A

Esperanza's dad has a cement truck delivering cement for the driveway. The driveway is 8.5 feet wide and 60 feet long. The cement must fill the entire area to a depth of 6 inches. The cement truck carries 10 cubic yards of cement. Will that be enough cement to cover the entire driveway?

If any cement were left over, her father would like to use it for an addition on the side of the driveway where Esperanza and her family can park their bikes. The space is 4 feet wide, 6 feet long, and 6 inches deep. Will there be enough cement left to fill this area as well? Support your answers.

Part B

Esperanza's dad is ready to buy the carpet but is trying to determine how much it will cost. Both floors are going to be entirely carpeted except for the kitchen and two bathrooms. The dimensions of the kitchen floor are 20 feet by 18 feet and the dimensions of each bathroom are 8 feet by 7.5 feet. What is the square footage of area to be carpeted?

Carpet costs $2.49 per square foot plus a $900 installation charge. Write an equation that Esperanza's father can use to determine the total cost of carpeting the house. Then use your equation to determine how much he will spend to carpet the house.

Part C

As Esperanza was looking at the 45-foot-long side of the house that has the garage and the playroom upstairs, she was amazed at how many bricks were used just on that one wall. The wall is solid brick except for a window area in the playroom that is 5 feet tall by 8 feet wide. Each brick covers a 6-inch by 3-inch section of wall. How many bricks were used on that wall?

How could Esperanza estimate how many bricks were used for the entire house? What other information will she need to make her calculations as accurate as possible?

Performance Task *(continued)*

The space behind the house has a shed and a basketball court. Esperanza's father sketched out the area that will be the family's backyard.

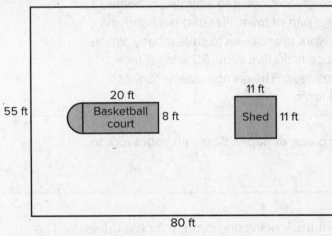

Part D

Esperanza asks how she can help, so her dad tells her that she can begin to landscape the backyard. She decides she will start by planting grass in the open areas surrounding the basketball court and the shed. If each bag of grass seed covers up to 1,500 square feet for a new lawn, how many bags of grass seed does she need?

Esperanza's father may clear some additional land to extend the backyard. If he doubles the length and width of the backyard, would the amount of grass seed needed also double? How many bags of grass seed would Esperanza need for this larger area? Justify your answer.

Performance Task

Chapter 9

College Basketball

Evan plays basketball for the university he attends. The following table displays his shot chart for the current season:

Type	Attempted	Made
2-pointer	40	25
3-pointer	31	13
Free throw	74	68

Write your answers on another piece of paper. Show all your work to receive full credit.

Part A

Basketball players are usually interested in their field goal statistics. A field goal is any shot that is not a free throw. Based on Evan's shot chart, what is the probability that he misses an attempted field goal?

Is this an example of theoretical or experimental probability? Explain your reasoning.

Part B

Evan is looking at his shot chart and is curious whether he will reach 200 points during the regular season. There are only three regular season games left. Based on his shot chart, will he statistically be able to hit this milestone if he attempts five of each type of shot per game? Validate your answer using ratios. (Free throws are worth 1 point each.)

Part C

Evan's team is down by 7 points in the final minutes, and the other players are losing hope. Evan tries to encourage his teammates and tells them to give him the ball. He says that if they keep the other team from scoring, he will attempt to win the game by making two 3-point shots and one 2-point shot.

Based on Evan's shot chart, do they have at least a 10% chance of Evan making a 3-point shot, another 3-point shot, and a 2-point shot in only three total attempts? Explain.

Would changing the order of shots change the probability of Evan making them? Justify your answers.

Performance Task (continued)

Part D

Evan's team wins the conference championship for the first time in eight years. To celebrate, a local newspaper wants to take a picture of the team. The newspaper photographer is quite the perfectionist and wants to get the perfect picture. She plans on having the players stand in a straight line. She lines up 10 of the players in a specific sequence that she likes but is having a hard time coming up with the order for the rest of the lineup. She announces that she will take a photo of each of the remaining possible lineups and that it will take 15 seconds per photo. However, Evan states that the extra photos will take too long because they have to leave for practice at 4:15 P.M. If it is currently 3:40 P.M., decide whether Evan is correct. Explain.

Part E

After practice, the team watches highlights of their conference championship game. The 4-minute highlight footage shows a 5-second video of each made shot. The coach announces that he will randomly select one of the highlights to be played at the sports banquet at the end of the semester. What are Evan's chances that one of his four made shots will be shown during the banquet?

Design a probability model that could be used to simulate this scenario. How is the theoretical probability of this scenario related to relative frequency in your simulation?

Chapter 10

Performance Task

For this Performance Task, your teacher will ask you to collect some data by conducting a survey and doing some research. Use the data collected to complete this task.

Data Time!

(1) Suppose you want to be more active and take part in intramural sports at school next year, but there are no sports you are interested in. Survey the students in your class to collect data on favorite sports in order to propose which intramural sports should be offered for all students next year.

(2) You will need to measure each student's arm span. Students being measured should be standing with their back to the wall and arms out to the sides, parallel to the floor. Use a measuring tape to measure from the tip of longest finger of one hand to the tip of the longest finger of the other hand. Record the measurements.

Write your answers on another piece of paper. Show all your work to receive full credit.

Part A

In order to help you view your data in different ways, create two different graphs to display the Favorite Sports data.

Write at least three questions that you can ask about your data. Answer those questions by reading the graphs you created. Indicate which graph you used to answer the question. Which graph was the easiest to read and provided the answers to your questions? Why?

Part B

You decide to use your Favorite Sports graph to model the *entire* seventh grade of your school. What are the top two favorite sports in your class? Use ratios to infer how many total students from your entire seventh grade would like each of the top three favorites. (Ask your teacher for an estimated number of seventh-graders in your school.)

One of your classmates believes that you can impress your teacher if you use this information to infer the top two favorite sports of all the students from seventh through twelfth grades. Is your sample biased? Explain. Provide an example of a biased and unbiased way you could pick a sample so you can make some predictions about all students in seventh through twelfth grade.

Performance Task (continued)

You are curious whether your data are similar to other schools. Some friends from another school took arm span measurements from their seventh-grade class. The following box plot illustrates the arm span of the students from their class:

Arm Spans of Seventh Grade Class at School A

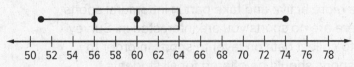

Part C

Draw a box plot representing the arm span of the students from your class.

Your friends believe there is a greater variation of arm spans in your class. Show why they are correct or incorrect by comparing their interquartile ranges and their medians. Write an inference you can draw about the arm span of students in your class compared to your friends' class.

Part D

Your friends tell you that their class has an average arm span of 64 inches. Explain why this does not accurately represent the arm span of any random student in their class. Show what number you would use when describing the arm span of the average student in your classroom.

Page PT1 On the Road with Mr. Sanford

CCSS Content Standard(s)	7.RP.1, 7.RP.2, 7.RP.2a, 7.RP.2b, 7.RP.2c, 7.RP.3, 7.NS.3, 7.EE.3
Mathematical Practices	MP1, MP2, MP6, MP8
Depth of Knowledge	DOK2, DOK3

Scoring Rubric

Part	Max Points	Scoring Rubric
A	3	**Full Credit:** 1 Week: Bonus ($500) + 40 hours(22.50) = $1,400 2 Weeks: Week 1 + 40(22.50) = $2,300 3 Weeks: Week 1 + Week 2 + 40(22.50) = $3,200 4 Weeks: Week 1 + Week 2 + Week 3 + 40(22.50) = $4,100 The sample graph is drawn as follows: **December Earnings** Not proportional: The graph does not pass through the origin. Partial Credit (1 point) will be given for correct earnings OR correct graph OR explanation about whether the relationship is proportional. No credit will be given for an incorrect answer.
B	1	**Full Credit:** 1,890 miles ÷ 210 gallons = 9 miles/gallon; an average of 9 miles per gallon; 3 gallons × 9 miles per gallon = 27 miles Mr. Sanford can drive an average of 27 miles on 3 gallons of gasoline. No credit will be given for an incorrect answer.
C	2	**Full Credit:** $\frac{\text{miles}}{\text{hours}}\ \frac{520}{8} = \frac{1,495}{h}$, $h = 23$ hours 23 ÷ 8 = 2.875; Mr. Sanford will need to work 3 shifts. Partial Credit will be given for writing and solving a correct proportion OR the correct the number of shifts Mr. Sanford needs to work. No credit will be given for an incorrect answer.
D	3	**Full Credit:** The graph is drawn as follows: The slope of the line is $\frac{60}{1}$ or 60, which means Mr. Sanford travels 60 miles per hour. Partial Credit (1 point) will be given for a correct graph OR the correct slope OR for a correct explanation about the slope. No credit will be given for an incorrect answer.
E	2	**Full Credit:** Recommend A-1 Fleet Company; Even though B-2 pays more per hour, Mr. Sanford is only able to work a 7-hour shift each day, so he would work less hours per year. Mr. Sanford would earn $2,210 more per year at A-1 company. His earnings at A-1 would be 22.5 × 8 × 5 × 52 = $46,800. His earnings at B-2 would be 24.5 × 7 × 5 × 52 = $44,590. $46,800 − $44,590 = $2,210 more per year working at A-1. Partial Credit will be given for creating a table OR recommending A-1 Fleet company with a correct explanation. No credit will be given for an incorrect answer.
TOTAL	11	

Performance Task Rubrics

Chapter 2 Performance Task Rubric

Page PT3 Rock Concert

CCSS Content Standard(s)	7.RP.2c, 7.RP.3, 7.EE.2, 7.EE.3
Mathematical Practices	MP 1, MP 2, MP 6, MP 4, MP 7
Depth of Knowledge	DOK2, DOK3, DOK4

Part	Max Points	Scoring Rubric
A	4	**Full Credit:** Seating #1: 25,000 × 85 = $2,125,000 Seating #2: (15,000 × 85) + (20,000 × 65) = $2,575,000 Seating #3: (5,000 × 85) + (30,000 × 65) = $2,375,000 Seating #2 would produce the greatest revenue. Percent of increase: 2,575,000 − 2,125,000 = 450,000 450,000 ÷ 2,125,000 = 0.2118, or 21.18% increase The percent of increase means for every $1 that seating #1 takes in, seating #2 takes in an additional 21.18% or $1.21. Partial Credit (2 points) will be given for indicating that seating #2 would produce the greatest revenue OR determining the percent of increase and explaining what it means for the given situation. No credit will be given for an incorrect answer.
B	1	**Full Credit:** 450,000 × 0.015 = $6,750 fee 450,000 − 6,750 − 18,592 = $424,658 refunded 424,658 ÷ 450,000 = 0.9437, or 94.37% of the bond refunded No credit will be given for an incorrect answer.
C	2	**Full Credit:** Steel Spiders 250,000 + 10,000 + 5,000 + 20,000 = $285,000 2,575,000 × 0.085 = 218,875; 218,875 + 285,000 = $503,875 Sir X-Z 300,000 + 10,000 + 4,000 + $314,000 2,575,000 × 0.09 = 231,750; 231,750 + 314,000 = $545,750 Lady BeeBop 280,000 + 15,000 + 300 + 20,000 = $315,300 2,575,000 × 0.0875 = 225,312.50; 225,312.50 + 315,300 = $540,612.50 Guitars & Pickups 325,000 + 1,000 + 7,500 + 2,000 = $335,500 2,575,000 × 0.092 = 236,900; 236,900 + 335,500 = $572,400 The most costly band is Guitars & Pickups for seating #2. Partial Credit will be given for correctly determining the cost for each band OR for indicating Guitars & Pickups as the most costly band. No credit will be given for an incorrect answer.
D	4	**Full Credit:** Sample answer: I would choose Guitars & Pickups because they would sell 100% of the tickets. The income would be $2,575,000. This means that there would be the greatest number of people at the concert which would benefit vendors and advertisers and could lead to more business in the future. Expenses: Deposit: $20,000; Location rental: $600,000; Percent of Ticket sales: $87,550; Band: $572,400; Insurance: $6,750; Damages: $18,592; General Expenses: $75,000; Total: $1,380,292 2,575,000 − 1,380,292 = $1,194,708 profit 1,194,7058 ÷ 2,575,000 = 0.4639, or 46.39% of the income. Partial Credit (2 points) will be given for band selection and correctly determining total profit and percent of income OR selection and explanation of band choice. No credit will be given for an incorrect answer.
TOTAL	11	

Chapter 3 Performance Task Rubric

Page PT5 Spinner Challenge

CCSS Content Standard(s)	7.NS.1a, 7.NS.1b, 7.NS.1c, 7.NS.1d, 7.NS.2a, 7.NS.3, 7.EE.3
Mathematical Practices	MP 1, MP 2, MP 3, MP 4, MP 6, MP 7, MP 8
Depth of Knowledge	DOK1, DOK2, DOK3

Part	Max Points	Scoring Rubric
A	1	**Full Credit:** Answers will vary. Sample answers: $-18 + 9 + 3 + 0 = -6$ $-10 + (-8) + 9 + 3 = -6$ $-18 + 7 + 3 + 2 = -6$ No credit will be given for an incorrect answer.
B	3	**Full Credit:** Spin 1: Start at 0 and move right 9; ends at 9. Spin 2: Start at 9 and move left 8; ends at 1. Spin 3: Start at 1 and move left 10; ends at −9. Spin 4: Start at −9 and move right 7; ends at −2. The expression $|9| + |-8| + |-10| + |7| = 9 + 8 + 10 + 7 = 34$ represents the total distance that the marker moves during the turn. The expression $|9 - 8 - 10 + 7| = |-2| = 2$ represents the final distance that the marker is from 0. Partial Credit of 1 point will be given for correctly drawn graphs of the player's spins OR 1 point for each correct absolute value expression explanation. No credit will be given for incomplete or incorrect answers.
C	1	**Full Credit:** Sample answer: $-18 + 9 + 7 + 2 = 0$ No credit will be given for an incorrect answer.
D	1	**Full Credit:** Sample answer: Turn 1: $9 + 7 + 9 + 7 = 32$ Turn 2: $9 + 7 + 9 + 7 = 32$ Turn 3: $9 + 7 + 9 + 7 = 32$ Turn 4: $9 + (-8) + 0 + 3 = 4$ $32 + 32 + 32 + 4 = 100$ No credit will be given for an incorrect answer.
E	1	**Full Credit:** Sample answer: $9 + 3 + (-18) + (-10) = -16$ $-16 \times -2 = 32$ The sum of the four spins must total −10 or less so that the product of the sum of those four spins and −2 would be greater than or equal to +20. No credit will be given for an incorrect answer.
F	1	**Full Credit:** Player 1 is correct. Sample explanation: Because the sum of all four spins is multiplied by −2, the total will be a multiple of 2. Since 15 is NOT a multiple of 2, Player 2 must have miscalculated. No credit will be given for an incorrect answer.
TOTAL	8	

Performance Task Rubrics

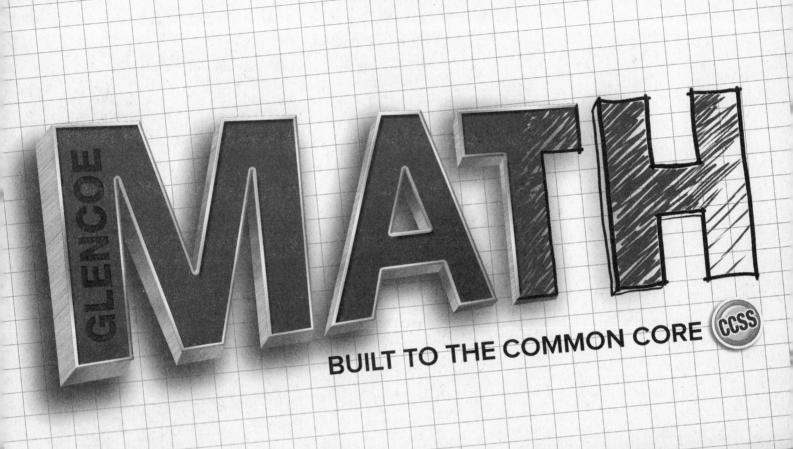

GLENCOE MATH

BUILT TO THE COMMON CORE (CCSS)

COMMON CORE PRACTICE MASTERS

AUTHORS
Carter • Cuevas • Day • Malloy
Kersaint • Reynosa • Silbey • Vielhaber

Mc
Graw
Hill
Education

Bothell, WA • Chicago, IL • Columbus, OH • New York, NY

connectED.mcgraw-hill.com

Send all inquiries to:
McGraw-Hill Education
8787 Orion Place
Columbus, OH 43240

ISBN: 978-0-02-143395-7
MHID: 0-02-143395-X

Printed in the United States of America.

1 2 3 4 5 6 7 8 9 QLM 19 18 17 16 15 14

Contents

Lesson 1 Multi-Step Problem Solving

Multi-Step Example

Makayla and her friends earn money by babysitting after school. At the end of one week, they deposit their weekly earnings at the bank. Which friend earns the most money per hour babysitting? **7.RP.2b,** **2**

Ⓐ Makayla   Ⓒ Jason

Ⓑ Gael   Ⓓ Cecilia

Name	Hours Worked	Deposit Amount ($)
Makayla	15	138.75
Gael	13	136.50
Jason	16	168.00
Cecilia	9	101.25

Use a problem-solving model to solve this problem.

1 Analyze

Read the problem. Circle the information you know. Underline what the problem is asking you to find.

2 Plan

What will you need to do to solve the problem? Write your plan in steps.

Step 1 Calculate the _____ for each person.

Step 2 Compare the unit rates to determine _____ earns the most.

3 Solve

Use your plan to solve the problem. Show your steps.

Makayla: $138.75 ÷ 15 = _____ per hour

Gael: $136.50 ÷ 13 = _____ per hour

Jason: $168 ÷ 16 = _____ per hour

Cecilia: $101.25 ÷ 9 = _____ per hour

_____ earns _____ per hour, which is the greatest unit rate.

So, the correct answer is _____ . Fill in that answer choice.

> **Read to Succeed!**
> Be sure to calculate each unit rate. Do not assume that a lower deposit amount will result in a lower unit rate.

4 Justify and Evaluate

How do you know your solution is accurate?

_____

_____

_____

Lesson 1 (continued)

Use a problem-solving model to solve each problem.

1 An automobile magazine compared the gas mileage for new cars. The distance traveled and amount of gasoline used for each car is shown in the table. Which car had the greatest gas mileage(miles per gallon)? **7.RP.2b, MP 2**

Car	Distance (mi)	Gasoline (gal)
Car A	650	20
Car B	426	12
Car C	515	15
Car D	280	8

Ⓐ Car A

Ⓑ Car B

Ⓒ Car C

Ⓓ Car D

2 The graph shows the amount of electricity used by one household over six months. If the cost per kilowatt hour usage is $0.12, approximately how much would it cost per day for the month of April? (*Hint:* There are 30 billable days in the month of April.) **7.RP.2b, MP 1**

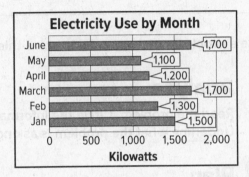

3 The graph shows the first 45 minutes of Darlene's bike trip. If she continues at a constant rate, how far will she travel in two hours? **7.RP.2, MP 7**

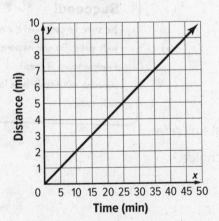

4 🔥**H.O.T. Problem** Kai can run 100 meters in 12.5 seconds and Josalin can run 150 meters in 20 seconds. If they both ran a 400-meter race at this rate, how many meters ahead would Kai cross the finish line before Josalin? **7.RP.2, MP 4**

Lesson 2 Multi-Step Problem Solving

Multi-Step Example

Carolina and her friends went kayaking over the weekend. The distance and time traveled is shown in the table. Which person kayaked at the greatest speed, in miles per hour? 7.RP.1, 1

Ⓐ Carolina

Ⓒ Bryan

Ⓑ Leslie

Ⓓ Javier

Person	Distance (mi)	Time (h)
Carolina	$3\frac{1}{2}$	$\frac{1}{2}$
Leslie	$5\frac{1}{4}$	$\frac{3}{4}$
Bryan	$4\frac{1}{2}$	$\frac{3}{4}$
Javier	$2\frac{1}{2}$	$\frac{1}{3}$

Use a problem-solving model to solve this problem.

1 Analyze

Read the problem. Circle the information you know.
Underline what the problem is asking you to find.

2 Plan

What will you need to do to solve the problem? Write your plan in steps.

Step 1 Calculate the _____ for each person.

Step 2 Compare the unit rates to determine _____ kayaks at the fastest rate, in miles per hour.

3 Solve

Use your plan to solve the problem. Show your steps.

Calculate each unit rate.

Carolina: $3\frac{1}{2} \div \frac{1}{2} =$ ____ mi/h   Leslie: $5\frac{1}{4} \div \frac{3}{4} =$ ____ mi/h

Bryan: $4\frac{1}{2} \div \frac{3}{4} =$ ____ mi/h   Javier: $2\frac{1}{2} \div \frac{1}{3} =$ ____ mi/h

Compare the unit rates to determine which person kayaked at the fastest rate.

Javier kayaked at a rate of ____ miles per hour, which is the fastest unit rate.

So, the correct answer is ____. Fill in that answer choice.

Read to Succeed!

Use the formula r = d ÷ t to help you calculate the unit rate for each person.

4 Justify and Evaluate

How do you know your solution is accurate?

_____

_____

_____

Lesson 2 *(continued)*

Use a problem-solving model to solve each problem.

1 Emma has been training for a bike race. She recorded her training times in the table below. Emma believes that if her average speed is above 15 miles per hour, then she has a good chance of winning the race. On which day(s) was Emma's average speed over 15 miles per hour? **7.RP.1, MP 2**

Day	Time (hr)	Distance (mi)
Monday	$1\frac{1}{2}$	27
Wednesday	$3\frac{1}{3}$	$63\frac{1}{3}$
Saturday	$2\frac{1}{2}$	35
Sunday	$\frac{3}{4}$	9

Ⓐ Monday only

Ⓑ Saturday only

Ⓒ Monday and Wednesday

Ⓓ All four days

2 The table shows the percent commission that a sales person earns based on monthly sales. Last month, Elijah's sales totaled $8,924. Including commission, how much did he earn last month? **7.RP.3, MP 1**

Sales	Commission
under $5,000	5%
$5,000 — $7,499	$9\frac{1}{2}$%
$7,500 — $9,999	$12\frac{1}{2}$%
$10,000 and higher	15%

3 A cheetah is one of the fastest land running animals. A cheetah can run $17\frac{1}{2}$ miles in $\frac{1}{4}$ hour. If a cheetah ran at this rate, how far would it travel in $1\frac{1}{2}$ hours? **7.NS.3, MP 2**

4 👍 **H.O.T. Problem** The distance between the two islands shown on the map is 210 miles. A ruler measures this distance on the map as $3\frac{1}{2}$ inches. How many miles would be represented by $1\frac{3}{4}$ inches on the map? **7.RP.1, MP 8**

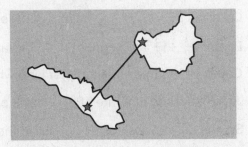

Lesson 3   **Multi-Step** Problem Solving

Multi-Step Example

The table shows the price of almonds at three different grocery stores. What is the cost, in dollars per pound, for the cheapest almonds? **7.RP.2b, MP 1**

Store	Weight (oz)	Price ($)
A	64	19.96
B	80	21.75
C	112	33.95

Use a problem-solving model to solve this problem.

Analyze

Read the problem. (Circle) the information you know.
Underline what the problem is asking you to find.

> **Read to Succeed!**
> When you are converting a smaller unit to a larger unit, you need to multiply.

2 Plan

What will you need to do to solve the problem? Write your plan in steps.

Step 1   Calculate each _____ and convert to an equivalent rate.

Step 2   Compare the unit rates to determine _____ per pound.

3 Solve

Use your plan to solve the problem. Show your steps.

Store A: $\dfrac{\$19.96}{64\text{ oz}} \cdot \dfrac{16\text{ oz}}{1\text{ lb}} = \dfrac{\$319.36}{64\text{ lb}} =$ _____

Store B: $\dfrac{\$21.75}{80\text{ oz}} \cdot \dfrac{16\text{ oz}}{1\text{ lb}} = \dfrac{\$348}{80\text{ lb}} =$ _____

Store C: $\dfrac{\$33.95}{112\text{ oz}} \cdot \dfrac{16\text{ oz}}{1\text{ lb}} = \dfrac{\$543.20}{112\text{ lb}} =$ _____

Compare the unit rates. _____ < _____ < _____

Store B sells the cheapest almonds for _____ per pound.

4 Justify and Evaluate

How do you know your solution is accurate?

_____

_____

_____

Lesson 3 *(continued)*

Use a problem-solving model to solve each problem.

1 The table shows the speeds of several runners on a track team. What is the speed, in feet per minute, of the fastest runner? 7.RP.3, **MP** 1

Runner	Distance (yd)	Time (s)
Imani	12	3
Jada	9	2
Tenesha	34	8

2 Lian used her garden hose to fill her 15,000-gallon swimming pool in 5 hours. She plans to graph the fill rate on a coordinate grid, showing the amount of water, in pints, on the *y*-axis and time, in minutes on the *x*-axis . What will be the *y*-value on the coordinate grid at 1 minute? (*Hint:* There are 8 pints in one gallon.) 7.RP.2, **MP** 8

3 Adam painted the rectangular wall shown below in 1 hour. On average, how many square feet did he paint per minute? 7.RP.3, **MP** 2

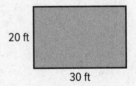

20 ft

30 ft

4 ✋**H.O.T. Problem** Use dimensional analysis to determine whether the rate 3,000 grams per week is 1,000 times faster than 3 kilograms per week. Explain. 7.RP.3, **MP** 3

_____
_____
_____
_____
_____

Lesson 4 Multi-Step Problem Solving

Multi-Step Example

Federico pays sales tax equal to $\frac{3}{50}$ of the retail price of his purchases. If the sales tax rate remains proportional, what is the total cost, in dollars, for a purchase amount of $84? 7.RP.2b, **MP** 2

Purchase Amount ($)	Sales Tax Amount ($)	Total Amount ($)
12	0.72	12.72
24	1.44	25.44
36	2.16	38.16
48	2.88	50.88

Use a problem-solving model to solve this problem.

 Analyze

Read the problem. Circle the information you know.
Underline what the problem is asking you to find.

 Plan

What will you need to do to solve the problem?
Write your plan in steps.

Read to Succeed!

To determine the sales tax amount, multiply the purchase amount by the fractional tax amount.

Step 1 Determine the _____ for his purchase of $84.

Step 2 Add the purchase amount and sales tax to determine the _____.

 Solve

Use your plan to solve the problem. Show your steps.

Determine the sales tax.

$\frac{3}{50} \times \$84 =$ _____

$\$84 +$ _____ $=$ _____   Add.

The total amount Federico will pay for a purchase of $84 is _____.

 Justify and Evaluate

How do you know your solution is accurate?

_____

_____

_____

_____

Lesson 4 *(continued)*

Use a problem-solving model to solve each problem.

1 Laurita is writing a research paper. If the relationship remains proportional, how many pages will she complete in 7 hours? **7.RP.2b, MP 2**

Time (hr)	Pages Completed
2	3
3	4.5

2 The table shows three membership options at a fitness center. Logan chooses the membership that represents a proportional relationship between the number of classes and the monthly cost. How much will he spend, in dollars, if he takes 12 classes in a month? **7.RP.2, MP 2**

Membership	Cost
Basic	$20 per class
Fit Plus	$60 per month plus $10 per class
Fit Extreme	$75 per month plus $30 enrollment fee

3 Carla donates 3% of her salary to charity each year. She makes $35,000 each year. If the relationship remains proportional, how much money will she have donated after 8 years? **7.RP.3 MP 1**

4 ☙ **H.O.T. Problem** The graph shows the distance of a race car over time. Is this relationship between distance and time proportional? Justify your answers. **7.RP.2a, MP 7**

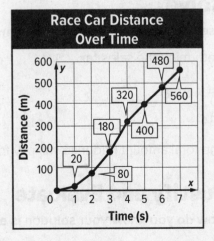

Race Car Distance Over Time

Lesson 5 Multi-Step Problem Solving

Multi-Step Example

The amount of time it takes a car to travel a certain distance is shown in the table. Choose the statement below that best describes the appearance of the graph of the relationship between time traveled and distance traveled. **7.RP.2, MP 4**

Time (min)	Distance (mi)
10	10
20	18
35	30
45	38

(A) a straight line that passes through the origin

(B) a curved line that passes through the origin

(C) a curved line that does not pass through the origin

(D) a straight line that does not pass through the origin

Use a problem-solving model to solve this problem.

 Analyze

Read the problem. Circle the information you know. Underline what the problem is asking you to find.

Read to Succeed!

Be sure to graph the ordered pairs on a coordinate plane to determine if the graph is a straight line.

 Plan

What will you need to do to solve the problem? Write your plan in steps.

Step 1 _____ ordered pairs on a coordinate plane.

Step 2 Analyze the _____ to describe the relationship shown.

 Solve

Use your plan to solve the problem. Show your steps.

Graph the ordered pairs (time, distance) on the coordinate plane. Then connect the ordered pairs with a line.

The line is _____ and _____ pass through the origin.

So, the correct answer is ____. Fill in that answer choice.

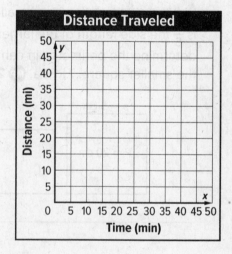

Distance Traveled

 Justify and Evaluate

How do you know your solution is accurate?

_____

_____

Lesson 5 *(continued)*

Use a problem-solving model to solve each problem.

1 Raisins are sometimes sold by the pound. The table below shows the cost for different weights of raisins. Choose the statement below that best describes the appearance of the graph of the relationship between weight and cost of raisins sold. **7.RP.2, MP 4**

Weight of Raisins (lb)	Cost ($)
1	4.60
2	9.20
4	18.40
5.5	25.30

ⓐ a straight line that passes through the origin

ⓑ a curved line that passes through the origin

ⓒ a curved line that does not pass through the origin

ⓓ a straight line that does not pass through the origin

2 Line A shows the distance traveled for five minutes by a giant tortoise. Line B shows the distance traveled for five minutes by a three-toed sloth. If each animal kept traveling at its same rate for one hour, how much farther would the sloth have traveled than the tortoise? **7.RP.2a, MP 4**

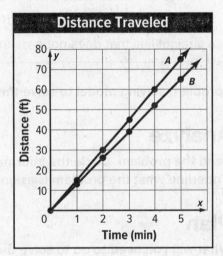

3. The relationship between the side length *s* of a square and the perimeter *P* of the square is a proportional relationship. Given that the side length of the smaller square is $\frac{4}{5}$ the side length of the larger square, determine the perimeter, in centimeters, of the smaller square. **7.RP.2a, MP 2**

$s = 5$ cm

$P = 20$ cm

4 ✋**H.O.T. Problem** Jarrod is comparing gym memberships. Gym A charges $38 per month for membership, with no annual fees. Gym B charges an annual fee of $15 and a monthly membership cost of $35. Which gym charges more for a yearly membership? By how much more? Justify your response. **7.RP.2a, MP 2**

_____

_____

_____

_____

_____

Lesson 6 Multi-Step Problem Solving

Multi-Step Example

Hugo can run 4 miles in 25 minutes. How many more miles can Hugo run in 90 minutes than in 25 minutes? Assume the situation is proportional and he always runs at the same rate. **7.RP.2, MP 1**

Distance (mi)	Time (min)
4	25
m	90

Ⓐ 10.2 miles   Ⓒ 14.4 miles

Ⓑ 10.4 miles   Ⓓ 18.4 miles

Use a problem-solving model to solve this problem.

 Analyze

Read the problem. Circle the information you know.
Underline what the problem is asking you to find.

 Plan

What will you need to do to solve the problem? Write your plan in steps.

Step 1 Calculate the _____ for Hugo's running rate. Then multiply the rate by 90 minutes to determine his distance.

Step 2 _____ the distances to determine how much _____ he runs in 90 minutes compared to 25 minutes.

③ Solve

Use your plan to solve the problem. Show your steps.
Calculate the unit rate.

4 ÷ 25 = _____ mile per minute
Determine how many miles he runs in 90 minutes.

90 × _____ = _____
Subtract to determine how much more he runs in 90 minutes.

_____ − 4 = _____

So, Hugo runs _____ miles more in 90 minutes. The correct answer is _____.
Fill in that answer choice.

> **Read to Succeed!** 👀
> Don't forget to subtract! The problem asks for how much more, which tells you to subtract the distances.

 Justify and Evaluate

How do you know your solution is accurate?

_____

_____

_____

Lesson 6 *(continued)*

Use a problem-solving model to solve each problem.

1 On average, Rai correctly answers 12 out of 18 questions in a trivia game. Assuming the situation is proportional, how many more questions is she likely to correctly answer if there are 36 questions in all? **7.RP.2, MP 2**

Correct answers	Total questions
12	18
?	36

Ⓐ 12 questions

Ⓑ 18 questions

Ⓒ 20 questions

Ⓓ 24 questions

2 Kareem needs a new car and is making a decision between the three cars listed below based on fuel efficiency. Determine which car has the best fuel efficiency in kilometers per gallon. (*Hint:* 1 km ≈ 0.62 mile) **7.RP.2c, MP 4**

Car	Miles	Gallons
Car A	248	10
Car B	210	10
Car C	225	12

_____

3 Aaron bought $\frac{1}{2}$ pound of cheese for $6. Assuming the situation is proportional, write and solve an equation to determine how many dollars *d* Aaron will pay for $3\frac{1}{2}$ pounds of cheese *c*. **7.RP.2, MP 4**

_____

4 ✋ **H.O.T. Problem** Taylor bought 12 more pencils this month than last month. Taylor paid $2.88 last month and $7.20 this month for the pencils. Assuming the situation is proportional, how many pencils did she buy this month? **7.RP.3, MP 2**

_____

Lesson 7   Multi-Step Problem Solving

Multi-Step Example

The table shows the number of feet walked, given a certain amount of footsteps. Choose the set of values that would yield a constant rate of change. 7.RP.2b, 2

Ⓐ $a = 12, b = 24, c = 36, d = 48$

Ⓑ $a = 12, b = 24, c = 36, d = 60$

Ⓒ $a = 12, b = 24, c = 48, d = 96$

Ⓓ $a = 12, b = 24, c = 46, d = 68$

Number of Footsteps	Distance Walked (ft)
5	a
10	b
15	c
25	d

Use a problem-solving model to solve this problem.

1 Analyze

Read the problem. Circle the information you know.
Underline what the problem is asking you to find.

2 Plan

What will you need to do to solve the problem? Write your plan in steps.

Step 1 Calculate the _____ using the values in the answer choices.

Step 2 Compare the _____ to determine a constant rate of change.

Read to Succeed!

Make sure you calculate the unit rate between each set of numbers.

3 Solve

Use your plan to solve the problem. Show your steps.

A: $\frac{12}{5} =$ ___ $\frac{24}{10} =$ ___ $\frac{36}{15} =$ ___ $\frac{48}{25} =$ ___

B: $\frac{12}{5} =$ ___ $\frac{24}{10} =$ ___ $\frac{36}{15} =$ ___ $\frac{60}{25} =$ ___

C: $\frac{12}{5} =$ ___ $\frac{24}{10} =$ ___ $\frac{48}{15} =$ ___ $\frac{96}{25} =$ ___

D: $\frac{12}{5} =$ ___ $\frac{24}{10} =$ ___ $\frac{46}{15} =$ ___ $\frac{68}{25} =$ ___

Compare the unit rates to determine which one has a constant rate of change.

Answer choice ____ is the only answer choice that has a constant rate of change.

So, the correct answer is ____. Fill in that answer choice.

4 Justify and Evaluate

How do you know your solution is accurate?

_____

_____

Lesson 7 *(continued)*

Use a problem-solving model to solve each problem.

1 The table compares number of apples purchased and the total cost. Choose which set of values would give a constant rate of change with a cost of $0.75 per apple. **7.RP.2b, MP 2**

Number of Apples	Cost ($)
4	a
6	b
10	c

Ⓐ $a = \$3.00, b = \$6.00, c = \$7.50$

Ⓑ $a = \$3.00, b = \$3.75, c = \$4.50$

Ⓒ $a = \$3.00, b = \$3.75, c = \$5.25$

Ⓓ $a = \$3.00, b = \$4.50, c = \$7.50$

2 Noah has been growing at a constant rate as shown in the graph below. What is his average rate of change in inches per month? **7.RP.2b, MP 7**

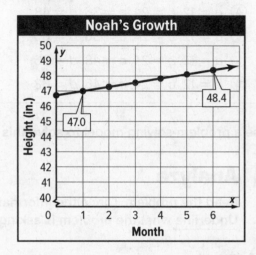

3 The table gives the distance traveled over a certain amount of time. What is the value of *a* that will result in a constant rate of change? **7.RP.2, MP 2**

Time (hr)	Distance (mi)
3	213
5	a
8	568

4 👍**H.O.T. Problem** The table below shows ordered pairs on a graph. Determine the missing value that will guarantee a constant rate of change. **7.RP.2d, MP 8**

x	y
a	30
a + 2	42
a + 3	?

Lesson 8 Multi-Step Problem Solving

Multi-Step Example

The table represents the rates at Jin's Internet Café for last year. This year, his rates will be $1\frac{1}{4}$ times greater to help pay his increase of rent costs. How much more will a customer pay to use the Internet for 6 hours? **7.RP.2b, MP 2**

Time (h) (x)	1	2	3	4
Cost ($) (y)	7	14	21	28

- Ⓐ $1.75
- Ⓒ $10.50
- Ⓑ $7.00
- Ⓓ $15.75

Use a problem-solving model to solve this problem.

1 Analyze

Read the problem. Circle the information you know.
Underline what the problem is asking you to find.

2 Plan

What will you need to do to solve the problem? Write your plan in steps.

Step 1 Determine the _____ for 6 hours of Internet usage.

Step 2 Multiply the cost by _____ and subtract the two costs.

3 Solve

Use your plan to solve the problem. Show your steps.

Determine the cost for 6 hours.

$7(6) = _____

Determine the increased cost for 6 hours. Then subtract.

_____ · $\left(1\frac{1}{4}\right)$ = _____

_____ − _____ = _____   Subtract.

The cost will be _____ greater.

So, the correct answer is _____. Fill in that answer choice.

> **Read to Succeed!**
> Interpret the slope in the table as the cost per hour for Internet usage. The slope shown in the table is $7 per hour.

4 Justify and Evaluate

How do you know your solution is accurate?

_____

_____

Lesson 8 (continued)

Use a problem-solving model to solve each problem.

1 The table represents the number of push-ups completed by Diego over the past 5 days. The next 5 days, he will increase the number of push-ups to be $2\frac{1}{2}$ times greater. How many more push-ups will he complete on day 5 after the increase compared to the number he completed on day 5 in the table below? **7.RP.2b,** **MP** 2

Day	1	2	3	4	5
Push-Ups	10	20	30	40	50

Ⓐ 50 push-ups

Ⓑ 75 push-ups

Ⓒ 100 push-ups

Ⓓ 125 push-ups

2 Mrs. Timken took her students on a hiking trip. She wants to avoid steep trails. On the steepest part of Evergreen Path, the path rises 12 feet over a horizontal distance of 60 feet. On Shady Glen Path, the path rises 18 feet over a horizontal distance of 45 feet. How much greater is the slope of the steeper path? Explain. **7.RP.2,** **MP** 1

_____

_____

3 The tables compare the number of bowling games and costs at two different bowling alleys. What is the difference in slopes? **7.RP.2,** **MP** 2

Number of Games	2	3	4
Cost ($)	9	10.50	12

Number of Games	2	3	5
Cost ($)	9	11	15

_____

4 **H.O.T. Problem** The slope of a line is −0.5. Two points on the line are (2, −1) and (6, a). What is the value of a? Use the graph to help you solve. **7.RP.2d,** **MP** 4

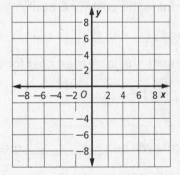

_____

Lesson 9   **Multi-Step** Problem Solving

Chapter 1

Multi-Step Example

The graph shows the distance a car travels over a certain amount of time. What is the ratio of kilometers traveled to the time in hours? (*Hint*: 1 mi ≈ 1.61 km) **7.RP.2b,** **1**

Ⓐ 40 kilometers per hour

Ⓑ 64.4 kilometers per hour

Ⓒ 80 kilometers per hour

Ⓓ 128.80 kilometers per hour

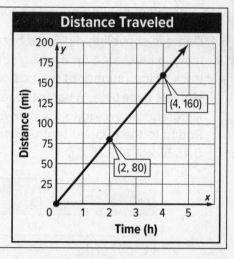

Distance Traveled

Use a problem-solving model to solve this problem.

1 Analyze

Read the problem. Circle the information you know.
Underline what the problem is asking you to find.

Read to Succeed!

Use the symbols y = kx to help you determine the ratios from the graph.

2 Plan

What will you need to do to solve the problem? Write your plan in steps.

Step 1   Use the graph to determine the constant of _____.

Step 2   Convert miles to _____.

3 Solve

Use your plan to solve the problem. Show your steps.

$\frac{80}{2} =$ ___ $\frac{160}{4} =$ ___   The rate of change is ____ miles per hour.

Convert miles to kilometers.

$\frac{40\ mi}{1\ h} \times \frac{1.61\ km}{1\ h} \approx$ _____

The car traveled about _____ kilometers per hour.

So, the correct answer is ____. Fill in that answer choice.

4 Justify and Evaluate

How do you know your solution is accurate?

_____

_____

Lesson 9 *(continued)*

Use a problem-solving model to solve each problem.

1 Dante is shoveling dirt in his backyard to make a level area for a swing set. He keeps track of the number of pounds of dirt he shovels over time. What is the ratio of kilograms shoveled to the time in minutes? Round to the nearest tenth. (*Hint*: 1 lb ≈ 0.4536 kg) **7.RP.2b, MP 1**

Time (min)	Dirt Shoveled (lb)
20	100
45	225

Ⓐ 2.3 kilograms per minute

Ⓑ 4.5 kilograms per minute

Ⓒ 5 kilograms per minute

Ⓓ 11.0 kilograms per minute

2 The table shows the wages Ramona earned for the number of hours she spent babysitting. If her wage is a direct variation of hours babysitting, how many hours does she need to babysit to earn $60? **7.RP.2, MP 2**

Hours Babysitting	Wage ($)
2	15
3	22.50
5	37.50

_____

3 Reynaldo needs to purchase cupcakes for the after-school picnic. The table shows the price of different numbers of cupcakes. How many cupcakes can Reynaldo purchase with $45? **7.RP.2, MP 1**

Number of Cupcakes	Price ($)
3	6.75
6	13.50
12	27.00

_____

4 👍 **H.O.T. Problem** Change one *y*-value in the table below so that it represents a direct variation. Explain your reasoning, and identify the constant of proportionality. **7.RP.2a, MP 3**

x	11	25	41	58
y	27.5	62.5	100	145

_____
_____
_____
_____
_____
_____

Lesson 1 Multi-Step Problem Solving

Multi-Step Example

The table shows how much Alfonso earns per week at his summer job. He wants to put 30% of his earnings into a savings account. How much should he deposit into a savings account? **7.RP.3, MP 1**

Ⓐ $360

Ⓑ $400

Ⓒ $1,200

Ⓓ $3,600

Week	Money Earned ($)
1	100
2	150
3	250
4	75
5	175
6	125
7	115
8	210

Use a problem-solving model to solve this problem.

 Analyze

Read the problem. Circle the information you know.
Underline what the problem is asking you to find.

 Plan

What will you need to do to solve the problem? Write your plan in steps.

Step 1 _____ the money Alfonso makes for all 8 weeks.

Step 2 Determine _____ of his earnings.

 Solve

Use your plan to solve the problem. Show your steps.

100 + 150 + 250 + 75 + 175 + 125 + 115 + 210 = _____ Add.

Determine 30% of _____. 0.3 × _____ = _____

Alfonso will need to put _____ into his savings account.

So, the correct answer is _____. Fill in that answer choice.

> **Read to Succeed!**
> Alfonso wants to save a percentage of his earnings. You can eliminate answer choice D, since the amount is more than he earns.

Justify and Evaluate

How do you know your solution is accurate?

_____

_____

_____

Lesson 1 *(continued)*

Use a problem-solving model to solve each problem.

1 Ella and her family normally pay $165 per month for electricity. The utility company is adding a 5% tax to help fund research for eco-friendly energy sources. How much tax will Ella's family pay for the entire year? **7.RP.3, MP 1**

    Ⓐ $990.00

    Ⓑ $99.00

    Ⓒ $66.00

    Ⓓ $8.25

2 The local newspaper asked people to vote for their favorite candidate for mayor. The results are shown. If 2,500 people voted, how many more people voted for Candidate B than Candidate C? **7.EE.3, MP 1**

Candidate	Percent of Vote
A	20
B	56
C	24

3 Mr. Jenkins buys a hat for $18 and a coat for $63. He has a coupon that allows him to get 15% off the total cost. He pays with four $20 bills. How much change should he receive, in dollars? **7.RP.3, MP 2**

4 ✋ **H.O.T. Problem** Rodrigo is at the mall shopping for new shoes. Two stores are offering a special deal on the pair of shoes he wants. How much is each store charging, and which is a better deal? **7.RP.3, MP 7**

Store	Original Cost	Percent Discount
A	$70	15
B	$85.50	40

Lesson 2   Multi-Step Problem Solving

Multi-Step Example

The students at Elgin Middle School voted on a new mascot. The principal found that 19% of each grade chose a tiger for a new mascot. About how many more 7th graders voted for a tiger than 8th graders? **7.RP.3, MP 2**

Grade	Number of Students
6	149
7	168
8	123

Ⓐ 4 students   Ⓒ 34 students

Ⓑ 10 students   Ⓓ 44 students

Use a problem-solving model to solve this problem.

1 Analyze

Read the problem. Circle the information you know. Underline what the problem is asking you to find.

2 Plan

What will you need to do to solve the problem? Write your plan in steps.

Step 1 Estimate _____ of 170 and 120.

Step 2 _____ to determine the difference.

3 Solve

Use your plan to solve the problem. Show your steps.

Estimate of 7th graders.   Estimate of 8th graders.

19% of $168 \approx 0.2 \times 170$ 19% of $123 \approx 0.2 \times 120$

$\approx$ _____ $\approx$ _____

_____ − _____ = _____   Subtract.

About _____ more 7th graders voted for a tiger than 8th graders.

So, the correct answer is _____. Fill in that answer choice.

> **Read to Succeed!**
> You can also estimate using an equivalent fraction to determine the number of students.

4 Justify and Evaluate

How do you know your solution is accurate?

_____

_____

_____

Lesson 2 *(continued)*

Use a problem-solving model to solve each problem.

1 Elena works on a farm that has three types of animals. There are a total of 47 animals. About how many more cows are there than chickens? **7.RP.3, MP 2**

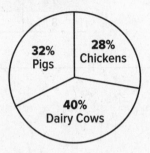

32% Pigs
28% Chickens
40% Dairy Cows

(A) 2 cows

(B) 5 cows

(C) 12 cows

(D) 564 cows

2 Brad borrowed money from his sister to buy a new video game that costs $62. He has paid back 78% of the cost of the game. About how much money does he still owe his sister, in dollars? **7.RP.3, MP 2**

_____

3 Dana buys the camping supplies shown below. About how many dollars does she spend if sales tax is 6%? **7.RP.3, MP 1**

Item	Cost ($)
Sleeping bag	29
Tent	52
Flashlight	18

_____

4 ✋ **H.O.T. Problem** The table shows the number of shots taken and the percent made by the top female basketball players. Estimate who made the most shots and about how many more shots were made than the next best player. **7.RP.3, MP 7**

Player	Shots Taken	Percent Made
Rosa	301	43
Domenica	384	52
Melinda	501	50

_____

_____

Lesson 3   Multi-Step Problem Solving

Multi-Step Example

The recommended caloric intake for boys ages 9–13 is 1,800 Calories per day. The table shows what percent of the Calories should be divided into different nutrients. How many daily Calories should *not* come from protein? **7.RP.3,** **2**

Nutrient	Percent of Daily Calories
Carbohydrates	45
Fat	20
Protein	35

Ⓐ 810

Ⓒ 1,170

Ⓑ 990

Ⓓ 1,440

Use a problem-solving model to solve this problem.

Analyze

Read the problem. Ⓒircle the information you know.
Underline what the problem is asking you to find.

Plan

What will you need to do to solve the problem? Write your plan in steps.

Step 1   Determine the percent of daily Calories that do *not come*

from _____.

Step 2   Write a _____ to determine the number of Calories.

Solve

Use your plan to solve the problem. Show your steps.

100% − 35% = _____   Subtract.

$$\frac{p}{1,800} = \frac{}{100}$$ Write the proportion.

$p =$ _____

The daily Calories that should *not* come from protein is _____.

So, the correct answer is __. Fill in that answer choice.

> **Read to Succeed!**
>
> You can add the percent of daily Calories that come from Carbohydrates and fat to determine the percent that does not come from protein.

Justify and Evaluate

How do you know your solution is accurate?

_____

_____

_____

Lesson 3 *(continued)*

Use a problem-solving model to solve each problem.

1 Carlos is saving up to buy two new books. He has saved 60% of the cost of one book that costs $18, and 30% of the cost of another book that costs $21. How much more does he need to save? **7.RP.3, MP 2**

Ⓐ $17.10

Ⓑ $18.20

Ⓒ $21.30

Ⓓ $21.90

2 Hasina entered a raffle 5 times and there are 125 entries. She decided to buy 15 more raffle tickets. By what percent does her chance of winning increase? Round to the nearest percent. **7.RP.3, MP 1**

_____

3 Rudy took a test and earned a 92%. Camilo earned an 88% on the same test. If Rudy answered 46 questions correctly, how many more questions did he answer correctly than Camilo? **7.RP.3, MP 7**

_____

4 ✋ **H.O.T. Problem** Alma bought a rocking chair for $266. She used a coupon to save some money. If she paid $226.10 for the chair, what percent discount did Alma get on the chair? **7.RP.3, MP 2**

_____

Lesson 4   **Multi-Step** Problem Solving

Multi-Step Example

Three friends work on a sales team. The table shows their sales for the month of January. What percent of the team's total sales was sold by Inali and Nigel? Express your answer as a decimal. **7.RP.2,** **1**

Employee	January Sales ($)
Inali	28,000
Nigel	32,000
Sydney	20,000

Use a problem-solving model to solve this problem.

1 Analyze

Read the problem. (Circle) the information you know.
Underline what the problem is asking you to find.

2 Plan

What will you need to do to solve the problem? Write your plan in steps.

Step 1   Determine the _____ and sales from Inali and Nigel.

Step 2   Determine the _____ of the total sales that was from Inali and Nigel.

> **Read to Succeed!**
> Inali and Nigel's sales are part of the total sales. Make sure you use the percent equation appropriately.

3 Solve

Use your plan to solve the problem. Show your steps.

Total sales: 28,000 + 32,000 + 20,000 = _____   Add.

Inali and Nigel: 28,000 + 32,000 = _____   Add.

Use the percent equation to determine the percent.

_____ = $n \cdot$ _____

$n =$ _____

Inali and Nigel sold _____ of the team's total sales.

4 Justify and Evaluate

How do you know your solution is accurate?

_____

_____

_____

Lesson 4   (continued)

Use a problem-solving model to solve each problem.

1 The table shows the distribution of entries for a science fair. The middle school consists of grades 6 through 8, and the high school consists of grades 9 through 12. What percent more of science projects are completed by middle school students than high school students? Express your answer as a decimal. **7.EE.3, MP 1**

Grade Level	Number of Science Projects
6	6
7	8
8	11
9	7
10	3
11	3
12	2

2 The circle graph shows the types of movies Abul watched last year. If he saw a total of 40 movies, how many more independent movies did he see than drama and action movies combined? **7.RP.3, MP 2**

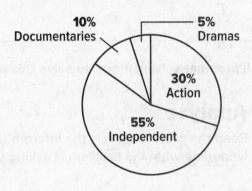

10%
Documentaries

5%
Dramas

30%
Action

55%
Independent

3 The low-fuel light in Sophia's car comes on when her fuel tank is 10% full. If she has used 18.2 gallons when the light comes on, how many gallons does her fuel tank hold? Round to the nearest tenth. **7.RP.3, MP 2**

4 👆**H.O.T. Problem** An art dealer sells art for two galleries. He makes 25% commission on sales at Gallery A and 35% commission on sales at Gallery B. Will the higher commission rate always result in a higher monthly commission income? Justify your reasoning. **7.RP.3, MP 6**

Lesson 5 Multi-Step Problem Solving

Multi-Step Example

The track and field coach records Ian's 400-meter race times during several practices. How much greater was the percent of change from practice 1 to practice 2 than from practice 2 to practice 3? Round to the nearest tenth. **7.EE.3,** **1**

Practice	Time (s)
1	63
2	60
3	58

Ⓐ 1.5%   Ⓒ 4.8%

Ⓑ 3.3%   Ⓓ 7.9%

Use a problem-solving model to solve this problem.

1 Analyze

Read the problem. Circle the information you know.
Underline what the problem is asking you to find.

2 Plan

What will you need to do to solve the problem? Write your plan in steps.

Step 1   Determine the _____ between each practice.

Step 2   _____ to determine how much greater the percent of change was between each practices.

3 Solve

Use your plan to solve the problem. Show your steps.

practice 1 to practice 2   practice 2 to practice 3

$\dfrac{63 - 60}{63}$ = _____ $\dfrac{60 - 58}{60}$ = _____

Write each as a percent, then subtract.

_____ − _____ = _____

Ian's percent of decrease was _____ greater between practice 1 and 2.

So, the correct answer is _____. Fill in that answer choice.

> **Read to Succeed!**
>
> Since his time is decreases, this situation represents a percent of decrease. Subtract to calculate the percent of decrease.

4 Justify and Evaluate

How do you know your solution is accurate?

_____

_____

_____

Lesson 5 *(continued)*

Use a problem-solving model to solve each problem.

1 The table shows Dashawna's science grade during four grading periods. How much greater was the percent change in her grade from grading period 1 to 2, than from grading period 2 to 3? Round to the nearest tenth. **7.EE.3, MP 1**

Grading Period	Grade
1	92%
2	96%
3	99%
4	96%

Ⓐ 1.0%

Ⓑ 1.2%

Ⓒ 3.1%

Ⓓ 4.3%

2 Earth follows an elliptical orbit around the Sun. At its nearest point on the orbit, it is about 147 million kilometers from the Sun. At its farthest point, it is about 152 million kilometers away. What is the percent change, rounded to the nearest tenth, from its nearest point to its farthest? **7.RP.3, MP 1**

_____

3 The graph below shows Alexa's bank account balance over the past four months. Between which months is the percent of increase the greatest? **7.EE.3, MP 2**

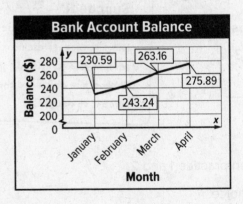

4 🖐 **H.O.T. Problem** Is the percent increase from *A* to *B* greater than or less than the percent decrease from *B* to *A*? Explain your answer. **7.RP.3, MP 6**

_____

_____

_____

_____

_____

_____

_____

Lesson 6   **Multi-Step** Problem Solving

Multi-Step Example

Takara orders the rib basket meal at a barbecue restaurant. She wants to leave an 18% tip. Sales tax is 6.5% at the restaurant. She also buys one bottle of barbecue sauce, plus tax. How much does Takara spend, in dollars? **7.RP.3,** **6**

Purchase	Price ($)
Rib basket	21
Barbecue sauce	15

Use a problem-solving model to solve this problem.

 Analyze

Read the problem. (Circle) the information you know.
Underline what the problem is asking you to find.

 Plan

What will you need to do to solve the problem? Write your plan in steps.

Step 1 Determine the _____ for just the meal.

Step 2 Determine the _____. Then add the tip, sales tax, and total bill.

> **Read to Succeed!**
> Takara only wants to leave a tip for the meal and not the bottle of sauce. Be sure to only determine the tip for the meal.

 Solve

Use your plan to solve the problem. Show your steps.

Tip: $21 × 0.18 = _____

Total Bill: $21 + $15 = _____

Sales Tax: $36 × 0.065 = _____

Add the tip, sales tax, and total bill.

_____ + _____ + _____ = _____

Takara spends _____ at the restaurant.

4 **Justify and Evaluate**

How do you know your solution is accurate?

_____

_____

_____

Lesson 6 (continued)

Use a problem-solving model to solve each problem.

1 Brian has $24 worth of pizzas delivered to his house for a $3 delivery fee. He pays 7% sales tax and a 15% tip, which are both calculated on the total price before the delivery fee. How much change does he receive, in dollars, if he pays with two $20 bills? **7.RP.3, MP 6**

2 Yoselin bought a broken antique table at a garage sale for $30. She plans to repair and paint it before reselling it. Her supplies will cost $45 plus 6% sales tax. She takes the amount that she spent on the table and increases the price by 100%. How much does she charge for the table, in dollars? Round to the nearest cent, if necessary. **7.EE.2, MP 2**

3 Two customers buy the same couch, but live in different states. The table shows the couch pricing information. What is the difference, in percent, between the sales tax in New Jersey and the sales tax in New York? **7.EE.3, MP 2**

Location	Price before tax	Price after tax
New York	$2,500	$2,600
New Jersey	$2,000	$2,140

4 ✋ **H.O.T. Problem** Umar sells personalized sports T-shirts at the City Sports Festival. Each shirt costs him $15 to make. The bar graph shows the number of shirts he sold last weekend. He charged a 50% markup on Friday and Saturday, and then lowered it to 30% on Sunday to increase sales. On which day did he make the most money? Justify your answers. **7.RP.3, MP 1**

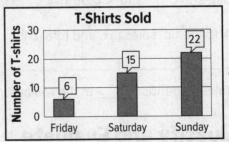

Lesson 7 Multi-Step Problem Solving

Multi-Step Example

At the end of the summer season, a garden store discounts all of its summer merchandise. The table shows the discounts for beach umbrellas. Which umbrella would be the least expensive to purchase after the discount and a 6% tax? **7.RP.3,** **2**

Ⓐ Umbrella A   Ⓒ Umbrella C

Ⓑ Umbrella B   Ⓓ Umbrella D

Umbrella	Original Price ($)	Percent Discount
A	75	30
B	68	20
C	85	40
D	80	35

Use a problem-solving model to solve this problem.

 Analyze

Read the problem. Circle the information you know.
Underline what the problem is asking you to find.

 Plan

What will you need to do to solve the problem?
Write your plan in steps.

Step 1   Determine the amount of _____ for each umbrella.

Step 2   Apply the _____ after the discount is applied.

> **Read to Succeed!**
> Calculate the amount of discount before applying the tax to determine the final price.

 Solve

Use your plan to solve the problem. Show your steps.

Discount: A: $75 × 0.7 = _____   B: $68 × 0.8 = _____

             C: $85 × 0.6 = _____   D: $80 × 0.65 = _____

Tax: A: $52.50 × 1.06 = _____   B: $54.40 × 1.06 = _____

             C: $51.00 × 1.06 = _____   D: $52.00 × 1.06 = _____

The least expensive umbrella is _____.

So, the correct answer is ____. Fill in that answer choice.

4 Justify and Evaluate

How do you know your solution is accurate?

_____

_____

_____

Lesson 7 (continued)

Use a problem-solving model to solve each problem.

1 The table shows the percent discount that a customer will save based on the original cost of an item. If Jeremy buys a $35 item and an $80 item, how much will he spend after the discount is applied to each item? 7.RP.3, **MP** 2

Original Cost	Percent Discount
Under $50	10
$50–$100	20
over $100	25

Ⓐ $95.50

Ⓑ $86.25

Ⓒ $19.50

Ⓓ $28.75

2 A pair of jeans that regularly cost $75 is on sale for 30% off. Javier has a coupon for an additional 15% off, which is calculated after the initial discount. How much will Javier pay for the jeans, in dollars? Round to the nearest cent. 7.RP.3, **MP** 6

_____

3 Christian was excited when he saw an ad for a local electronics store in the newspaper that was going out of business. Everything in the store was 40% off. He would like to purchase a new television that originally costs $1,250. How many months would it take him to pay for the television if he paid $75 each month? 7.EE.3, **MP** 2

_____

4 🔥 **H.O.T. Problem** Maria purchased a new jacket for $78.12. The original price of the jacket was discounted 20%, and Maria had to pay a 5% sales tax. What was the original price of the jacket? 7.RP.3, **MP** 1

_____

Lesson 8   **Multi-Step** Problem Solving

Multi-Step Example

Donte is buying a car that costs $8,000. He is deciding between a 3-year loan and a 4-year loan. Use the rates in the table to determine how much money he will save if he chooses the 3-year loan instead of the 4-year loan. **7.RP.3,** **MP** **1**

Time (y)	Simple Interest (%)
3	2.25
4	2.5
5	3

Ⓐ $20   Ⓒ $100

Ⓑ $60   Ⓓ $260

Use a problem-solving model to solve this problem.

 Analyze

Read the problem. (Circle) the information you know.
Underline what the problem is asking you to find.

 Plan

What will you need to do to solve the problem? Write your plan in steps.

Step 1   Determine the _____ for each loan.

Step 2   Subtract to determine how much _____ he will save.

 Solve

Use your plan to solve the problem. Show your steps.

Use the simple interest formula.

3 year loan: $I = 8,000 \cdot 0.0225 \cdot 3 =$ _____

4 year loan: $I = 8,000 \cdot 0.025 \cdot 4 =$ _____

_____ − _____ = _____   Subtract.

Donte would save _____ if he chooses a 3-year loan.

So, the correct answer is _____. Fill in that answer choice.

> **Read to Succeed!**
> Remember to change each percent to a decimal before calculating the simple interest.

 Justify and Evaluate

How do you know your solution is accurate?

_____

_____

_____

Lesson 8   (continued)

Use a problem-solving model to solve each problem.

1 Evan has $4,000 that he wants to put into a savings account until he leaves for college, which will be 6 years from now. How much more money will he have in his savings account if he chooses Bank B instead of Bank A? **7.RP.3, MP 1**

Bank	Interest Rate
Bank A	4.5%
Bank B	4.9%

Ⓐ $16

Ⓑ $96

Ⓒ $1,176

Ⓓ $1,080

2 Isabel has $1,500 to deposit into a savings account with a 3.2% interest rate. She wants to wait until she earns $240 in interest before withdrawing the money. How many years will she have to wait before she can withdraw the money? **7.EE.3, MP 8**

_____

3 A higher interest rate and a longer loan term lead to a higher amount of interest. Given the information in the table, what percent interest rate for Bank B would make the amount of interest from each bank the same? **7.EE.3, MP 2**

	Bank A	Bank B
Interest rate	4.2%	▪
Term	4 year	5 year
Principal	$4,000	$4,000

_____

4 🔥 **H.O.T. Problem** Alex is buying a car that costs $18,000. He will make a down payment of $2,000, and the tax rate is 7%. He is considering a 5-year loan with an interest rate of 6.2%. What is the total cost of the car including tax and interest over the life of the loan? **7.RP.3, MP 6**

_____

Lesson 1 **Multi-Step** Problem Solving

Multi-Step Example

Doug is playing a game and has a score of 6. He draws a card that reads, "Lose 10 points." What is his score now? *Preparation for* **7.NS.3,**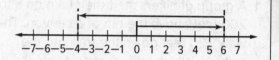

Ⓐ −10　　　　　　　Ⓒ 4

Ⓑ −4　　　　　　　Ⓓ 10

Use a problem-solving model to solve this problem.

Analyze

Read the problem. ⟨Circle⟩ the information you know.
Underline what the problem is asking you to find.

2 Plan

What will you need to do to solve the problem? Write your plan in steps.

Step 1 Identify the integer that represents Doug's score before he draws the "Lose 10 points" card.

Step 2 Represent "Lose 10 points" as a negative integer.

Step 3 Use |−10| to find Doug's new score.

> **Read to Succeed!**
> A number's absolute value is its distance from zero on the number line. Read |n| as "the absolute value of n."

3 Solve

Use your plan to solve the problem. Show your steps.

The integer _____ represents Doug's score. The integer _____

represents the points he loses. |−10| = _____.

Since this is a loss, count 10 spaces to the _____ of 6.

So, the integer _____ represents Doug's new score.

The correct answer is _____. Fill in that answer choice.

Justify and Evaluate

How do you know your solution is accurate?

_____

_____

_____

Lesson 1 (continued)

Use a problem-solving model to solve each problem.

1 A group of hikers start their hike on a trail 200 feet above the rim of a canyon. They walk 320 feet down the trail into the canyon. Which integer represents the hikers' elevation (in feet) below the rim of the canyon? *Preparation for* **7.NS.3,** **MP** **4**

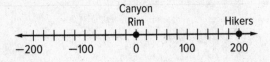

Canyon
Rim   Hikers

−200   −100   0   100   200

- (A) 520
- (B) 180
- (C) −120
- (D) −320

2 Rebecca recorded the temperature every 3 hours from 6:00 A.M. to 6 P.M. The table shows her results. Between which two consecutive time periods can the temperature change be represented as a negative integer? Explain your answer in terms of comparing integers. *Preparation for* **7.NS.3,** **MP** **6**

Time	Temperature (°F)
6:00 A.M.	−10
9:00 A.M.	−3
12:00 P.M.	7
3:00 P.M.	12
6:00 P.M.	8

_____

_____

_____

_____

_____

_____

3 The number line shows the position of a diver below the surface of the water. The diver descends another 8 feet. Write an absolute value expression that shows the total number of feet the diver descended. How many feet did the diver descend below the surface of the water? *Preparation for* **7.NS.3,** **MP** **4**

Diver   Sea level

−30   −20   −10   0   10

_____

_____

_____

_____

4 🖐 **H.O.T. Problem** If $|x| = 15$ and $|y| = 15$, do x and y have the same value? Support your reasoning. *Preparation for* **7.NS.3,** **MP** **3**

_____

_____

_____

_____

_____

_____

_____

_____

Lesson 2 **Multi-Step** Problem Solving

Multi-Step Example

Carlos is swimming at the beach. The number line shows his vertical movement in feet. Which expression is represented on the number line model? Describe his vertical movement in relation to the surface of the water. **7.NS.1b, MP 4**

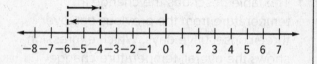

$$-8\ -7\ -6\ -5\ -4\ -3\ -2\ -1\ \ 0\ \ 1\ \ 2\ \ 3\ \ 4\ \ 5\ \ 6\ \ 7$$

Ⓐ $(-6) + (-4)$; He swam 6 feet down and then 4 feet down. He is 10 feet below the surface.

Ⓑ $0 + (-6)$; He swam 6 feet down and is 6 feet below the surface of the water.

Ⓒ $(-4) + (-2)$; He swam 4 feet down and then 2 feet down. He is 6 feet below the surface.

Ⓓ $(-6) + 2$; He swam 6 feet down and then 2 feet up. He is 4 feet below the surface.

Use a problem-solving model to solve this problem.

1 Analyze

Read the problem. Circle the information you know.
Underline what the problem is asking you to find.

2 Plan

What will you need to do to solve the problem? Write your plan in steps.

Step 1 Determine the direction and length of the red arrow.

Step 2 Determine the direction and length of the blue arrow.

3 Solve

Use your plan to solve the problem. Show your steps.

One arrow starts at 0 and goes to the left to _____. Then,

the other arrow goes to the right 2 units and ends at _____.

So, Carlos swims 6 feet down to −6, then 2 feet up to −4.

He is _____ feet _____ the surface. Choice ____ is correct.

Read to Succeed!

When an arrow goes to the right, it means adding or a positive number. When it goes to the left, then it means subtraction or a negative number.

4 Justify and Evaluate

How do you know your solution is accurate?

_____

Lesson 2 *(continued)*

Use a problem-solving model to solve each problem.

1 The table describes the change in temperature from the previous day over three consecutive days. Which expression shows the overall temperature change between Sunday and Wednesday? Express the temperature change as an integer. **7.NS.1b, MP 1**

Day	Change in Temperature (°F)
Monday	dropped 2°
Tuesday	dropped 5°
Wednesday	rose 3°

Ⓐ $(5) + (-2)$; 3°F

Ⓑ $(-2) + (-3) + 5$; 0°F

Ⓒ $(-2) + (-5) + 3$; -4°F

Ⓓ $(-2) + (-5) + (-3)$; -10°F

2 In golf, a score of 0 is called *par*. A score *over par* is represented with a positive integer, and a score *under par* is represented with a negative integer. The goal is to get the lowest score possible. Justin and Omar played three rounds of golf, with their scores for each round as shown in the table. What is the winning final score? Who wins the three rounds? **7.NS.1b, MP 1**

	Round 1	Round 2	Round 3
Justin	-2	0	3
Omar	2	-3	1

3 The table shows the transactions of Sierra's checking account during one week. What is her account balance at the end of the week? **7.NS.1b, MP 1**

Transaction	Amount
Beginning balance	$124
ATM withdrawal	$20
Deposit	$35
Bank card purchase	$12

4 🔥 **H.O.T. Problem** In a convenience store, a tray by the register contains leftover change. Customers can use this change for their purchases, or place their change in the tray for other customers to use. At the beginning of the day, there is 27¢ in the tray. At end of the day, there is 15¢ left in the tray. Only two customers used the change tray, and one of these customers added 6¢. How did the other customer use the tray? Justify your response. **7.NS.3, MP 2**

_____

_____

_____

_____

Lesson 3 Multi-Step Problem Solving

Multi-Step Example

On the first play of a football game, the quarterback ran with the football and gained 4 yards. On the next play, he lost 7 yards. The two plays are illustrated on the number line. Write a subtraction equation that represents the two consecutive plays and the net yardage. 7.NS.1, 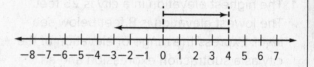 4

Ⓐ $-4 - 7 = -3$ yards

Ⓒ $7 - 3 = 4$ yards

Ⓑ $4 - 7 = -3$ yards

Ⓓ $3 - 7 = -4$ yards

Use a problem-solving model to solve this problem.

 Analyze

Read the problem. Circle the information you know. Underline what the problem is asking you to find.

 Plan

What will you need to do to solve the problem? Write your plan in steps.

Step 1 Determine the integer that represents the yards after the first play.

Step 2 Determine the integer that represents the yards after the second play.

> **Read to Succeed!**
> When a value is gained, it represents a positive integer. A loss represents a negative integer.

 Solve

Use your plan to solve the problem. Show your steps.

The quarterback gained 4 yards, so the first arrow ends at 4. He then lost 7 yards, so the second arrow goes to the left 7 units. The arrow ends at −3.

So, the subtraction equation is _____. Choice ____ is correct.

 Justify and Evaluate

How do you know your solution is accurate?

_____

_____

_____

Lesson 3 *(continued)*

Use a problem-solving model to solve each problem.

1 The highest elevation in a city is 25 feet. The lowest elevation is 8 feet below sea level. Express the range of elevation of the city as a subtraction expression and an addition expression. **7.NS.1c,** **MP** **4**

Ⓐ $25 - 8; 25 + (-8)$

Ⓑ $8 - 25; -25 + 8$

Ⓒ $-8 - (-25); -8 + 25$

Ⓓ $25 - (-8); 25 + 8$

2 Eratosthenes and Ptolemy were both mathematicians that made significant contributions in the areas of mathematics, as well as astronomy and geography. The time line below shows the estimated times they lived. Find the difference between the number of years they lived. **7.NS.1,** **MP** **1**

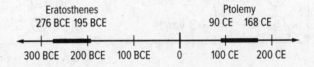

3 Kai is working on her budget. The table below is her budget for a month. Find the amount of money Kai has left over at the end of the month. Make three suggestions that change Kai's budget and allow her to save more money each month **7.NS.1d,** **MP** **3**

_____

_____

_____

_____

_____

_____

_____

Description	Amount ($)
Net pay	2,000
Cable TV	220
Car insurance	74
Cell phone	175
Credit card payment	125
Electric	135
Food	400
Gym membership	90
Rent	800
Savings	50

Lesson 4   **Multi-Step** Problem Solving

Multi-Step Example

Each time Min uses an ATM that belongs to a bank other than the one he has a checking account with, he is charged a fee. The number line shows his ATM fees for one month. Write a numerical expression that represents his ATM fees and explain the meaning. **7.NS.2, MP 4**

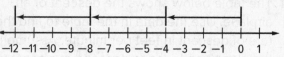

Ⓐ (−3)4; Min uses an ATM 4 times and is charged $3 for each use.

Ⓑ (−12)1; Min is charged $12 for 1 ATM use.

Ⓒ (−4)3; Min uses an ATM 3 times and is charged $4 for each use.

Ⓓ (−4)12; Min uses the ATM 12 times and is charged $4 for each use.

Use a problem-solving model to solve this problem.

Analyze

Read the problem. Circle the information you know.
Underline what the problem is asking you to find.

Plan

What will you need to do to solve the problem? Write your plan in steps.

Step 1   Determine the direction of the arrows.

Step 2   Determine the integer for each arrow.

Solve

Use your plan to solve the problem. Show your steps.

Since the arrows are going to the _____ the integers represented

are _____. There are three arrows that each represent ____.

(−4) • 3 = _____

So, Min used the ATM 3 times and was charged $4 each time.

The correct answer is ___. Fill in that answer choice.

> **Read to Succeed!**
> There are three groups of equal arrows. These three groups represent the three fees.

Justify and Evaluate

How do you know your solution is accurate?

_____

_____

Lesson 4   *(continued)*

Use a problem-solving model to solve each problem.

1 The table below shows the descent of an airplane. Use the data in the table to find the rate of descent in feet per minute. Assume the plane continues to descend at a constant rate. Write a multiplication expression that represents how far the plane has descended in 7 minutes and find the product. **7.NS.2, MP 7**

Distance (ft)	Minutes
−1,200	1
−2,400	2
−3,600	3
−4,800	4

Ⓐ (−1,200)7; −8,400 feet

Ⓑ (−2,400)7; −16,800 feet

Ⓒ (−1,400)7; −9,800 feet

Ⓓ (−1,371)7; −9,600 feet

2 Olivia is playing a trivia game where you gain points for each right answer and lose points for each wrong answer. Some questions are worth 3 points and some questions are worth 5 points. Olivia gets four 3-point questions right and three 3-point questions wrong. She gets three 5-point questions right and two 5-point questions wrong. How many points does she have? **7.EE.3, MP 2**

_____

3 Jose drives a limousine and he wants to calculate his profit at the end of the day. He spent money on gasoline but made money on trips. He bought 14 gallons worth of gasoline at $4 per gallon. He drove customers 75 miles and charged them a rate of $5 per mile. How much profit did he make, in dollars, at the end of the day? **7.EE.3, MP 4**

_____

4 🔥 H.O.T. Problem Tom multiplies 5 negative integers. Is the product positive, negative, or zero? Explain and include an example. Then write a general rule about the product of negative numbers. **7.NS.2a, MP 8.**

_____

_____

_____

Lesson 5 **Multi-Step** Problem Solving

Multi-Step Example

The table shows the distance and time for each phase of a submersible's trial run. Which expression represents the average speed throughout the trial run? **7.NS.2b,** **1**

Distance (m)	Time (sec)
−15	5
−30	6
+5	5
−50	10

Ⓐ 3 m/s

Ⓑ −3 m/s

Ⓒ −3.5 m/s

Ⓓ 3.5 m/s

Use a problem-solving model to solve this problem.

1 Analyze

Read the problem. Circle the information you know.
Underline what the problem is asking you to find.

2 Plan

What will you need to do to solve the problem? Write your plan in steps.

Step 1 Determine the speed for each phase of the trial run.

Step 2 Add the speeds and divide to find the average speed.

3 Solve

Read to Succeed!
To find the average, add the values and divide by the number of values.

Use your plan to solve the problem. Show your steps.

Phase 1: −15 ÷ 5 = −3   Phase 2: −30 ÷ 6 = −5

Phase 3: 5 ÷ 5 = 1   Phase 4: −50 ÷ 10 = −5

The average speed is $\dfrac{(-3) + (-5) + (1) + (-5)}{4}$ or −3.

So, the average speed of the submersible is ____ meters per second.

The correct answer is ____. Fill in that answer choice.

4 Justify and Evaluate

How do you know your solution is accurate?

_____

_____

Lesson 5 *(continued)*

Use a problem-solving model to solve each problem.

1 Dakota earns the money shown in the table. After buying 4 chairs, she has $30 left. How much did Dakota pay for each chair? **7.NS.2b, MP 1**

Job	Amount Earned
Babysitting	$120
Pet sitting	$65
Dog walking	$45

Ⓐ $22.50

Ⓑ $50

Ⓒ $47.50

Ⓓ $200

2 The table below shows the temperature for a town over 5 consecutive days. Use the data to find the average temperature. Then convert the average to degrees Fahrenheit using the formula below. **7.NS.3, MP 4**

$$F = \frac{9C + 160}{5}$$

Day	Temperature (C)
1	−19°C
2	−18°C
3	−15°C
4	−15°C
5	−18°C

_____

_____

3 Basir played a game, starting with a certain number of points. He lost 6 points each of the first three rounds. He gained 3 points and then gained 7 points the next two rounds. Then he lost 8 points each of two rounds. His final score is −9. How many points did he have in the beginning of the game? **7.NS.3, MP 2**

_____

4 🔥 **H.O.T. Problem** Susan divides two negative integers. She divides the quotient by a positive integer and multiplies the quotient by a negative integer. Is the result positive or negative? Explain. **7.NS.2, MP 8**

_____

_____

_____

_____

_____

Lesson 1   **Multi-Step** Problem Solving

Multi-Step Example

Thirty-six 7th graders were asked to choose their favorite color. The table shows the fraction of students that chose each color. What decimal shows the difference between the most and least popular colors? **7.NS.2d,** **8**

Color	Fraction
Red	$\frac{5}{18}$
Yellow	$\frac{1}{6}$
Blue	$\frac{4}{9}$
Green	$\frac{1}{9}$

Ⓐ $0.1\overline{6}$ Ⓒ $0.\overline{3}$

Ⓑ $0.\overline{1}$ Ⓓ $0.\overline{5}$

Use a problem-solving model to solve this problem.

1 Analyze

Read the problem. Ⓒircle **the information you know.**
Underline **what the problem is asking you to find.**

2 Plan

What will you need to do to solve the problem? Write your plan in steps.

Step 1   Express each fraction as a _____.

Step 2   Determine which decimal is the _____ and

which is the _____. Then subtract.

> **Read to Succeed!**
> Read the question carefully. Since it asks for the difference, you will need to subtract.

3 Solve

Use your plan to solve the problem. Show your steps.

Express each fraction as a decimal. Subtract the least from the greatest.

$\frac{5}{18} =$ _____ $\frac{1}{6} =$ _____ $\frac{4}{9} =$ _____ $\frac{1}{9} =$ _____

_____ − _____ or _____   Subtract.

There were _____ more of the students chose _____ as their favorite color

over _____. So, the correct answer is _____. Fill in that answer choice.

4 Justify and Evaluate

How do you know your solution is accurate?

_____

_____

_____

Lesson 1 (continued)

Use a problem-solving model to solve each problem.

1 The table shows the lengths of straws, in centimeters, that Jessica has available for an art project.

Straw	Length (cm)
Striped	12.5
White	10.75
Clear	13.35
Blue	11.3

She cut the white straw into two equal-size pieces. What mixed number represents the length of each piece of white straw after cutting? **7.NS.3,** 6

Ⓐ $6\frac{1}{4}$

Ⓑ $5\frac{13}{20}$

Ⓒ $5\frac{3}{8}$

Ⓓ $5\frac{1}{8}$

2 Roger made a square sign to place on his bedroom door shown below in the sketch. What is the decimal equivalent of the perimeter, in inches, of his sign? **7.NS.3,** 1

$8\frac{7}{8}$ in.

_____

_____

3 Destiny read $\frac{1}{4}$ of a book on the day she received it. The next day, she read $\frac{5}{8}$ of the book. On the third day, she finished reading the book. What decimal represents the fraction of the book Destiny read on the third day? **7.NS.3,** 2

_____

4 🖐 **H.O.T. Problem** Graph and label the fractions $-\frac{2}{3}$, $-\frac{3}{5}$, and $-\frac{5}{8}$ on the number line shown using their equivalent decimal value. Explain how you determined where to place each fraction. **7.NS.2d,** 2

_____

_____

_____

_____

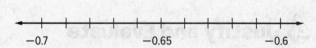

Lesson 2   Multi-Step Problem Solving

Multi-Step Example

The table shows the change in value for four stocks over one day. What is the difference between the greatest value change and the least value change expressed as a decimal? **7.EE.3,** **MP** 6

Stock	Value
MCD	+1.75%
THC	+0.65
BIG	$+\frac{7}{8}$
GES	$+1\frac{1}{4}$

Ⓐ 1.25   Ⓒ 1.1

Ⓑ 1.2325   Ⓓ 0.6

Use a problem-solving model to solve this problem.

 Analyze

Read the problem. Circle the information you know.
Underline what the problem is asking you to find.

 Plan

What will you need to do to solve the problem? Write your plan in steps.

Step 1   Express each number as a _____. Then compare.

Step 2   Determine which decimal is the _____ and

which is the _____. Then subtract.

 Solve

Use your plan to solve the problem. Show your steps.
Write each percent or fraction as a decimal. Then subtract.

$1.75\% =$ _____ $0.65 =$ _____ $\frac{7}{8} =$ _____ $1\frac{1}{4} =$ _____

_____ − _____ = _____   Subtract.

The difference between the greatest value change and least value

change is _____.

The correct answer is _____. Fill in that answer choice.

> **Read to Succeed!**
> Remember to move the decimal point two places to the left when changing the percent 1.75% to a decimal.

 Justify and Evaluate

How do you know your solution is accurate?

_____

_____

_____

Lesson 2   *(continued)*

Use a problem-solving model to solve each problem.

1 In Mr. Nguyen's class, 24 out of 30 students have a pet. In Ms. Young's class, 55% of students have a pet. Which statement below correctly compares the fraction of students who have a pet in Mr. Nguyen's class to the fraction of students who have a pet in Ms. Young's class? **7.EE.3, MP 6**

(A) $\dfrac{4}{5} = \dfrac{11}{20}$

(B) $\dfrac{4}{5} < \dfrac{11}{30}$

(C) $\dfrac{4}{5} > \dfrac{4}{55}$

(D) $\dfrac{4}{5} > \dfrac{11}{20}$

2 The circle graph below shows the favorite subjects of seventh-grade students in a gym class. There are 32 students in the class. How many more students chose Math than Social Studies and Language Arts? **7.EE.3, MP 2**

Favorite Subject

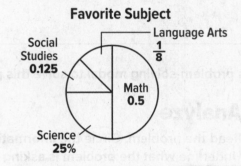

3 The table shows the amount of time Pablo practiced his saxophone over three days. Pablo realized he made an error by writing the reciprocal for the time spent on Monday. Once he corrects the error, what is the decimal equivalent of the number that would come first if the times were ordered from greatest to least? **7.EE.3, MP 1**

Day	Time (hr)
Monday	$\dfrac{4}{3}$
Tuesday	$\dfrac{7}{8}$
Wednesday	$\dfrac{5}{6}$

4 🔥 **H.O.T. Problem** Which of the following numbers is closest to 88% on the number line?

$$\dfrac{4}{5}, \dfrac{8}{9}, \dfrac{21}{25}$$

Write both the decimal and fraction form of the number. **7.NS.2d, MP 4**

Lesson 3 **Multi-Step** Problem Solving

Multi-Step Example

Rosa asked her classmates where they would like to take a vacation. The bar graph shows the fraction of the class that chose each option. What fraction more of the class prefer the beach than the other three vacations combined? **7.NS.3,** **1**

(A) $\frac{3}{8}$ (C) $\frac{5}{8}$

(B) $\frac{9}{16}$ (D) $\frac{5}{16}$

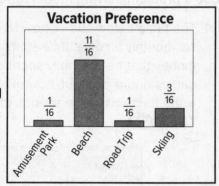

Vacation Preference

Use a problem-solving model to solve this problem.

Analyze

Read the problem. Circle the information you know.
Underline what the problem is asking you to find.

Plan

What will you need to do to solve the problem? Write your plan in steps.

Step 1   _____ the fractions for amusement park, road trip, and skiing.

Step 2   _____ the sum from the classmates that prefer the beach.

Solve

Use your plan to solve the problem. Show your steps.

$\frac{1}{16} + \frac{1}{16} + \frac{3}{16} =$ ____   Determine the sum.

____ − ____ = ____ or ____   Subtract to determine the difference.

There are ____ more of the class that prefer a beach vacation.

The correct answer is ____. Fill in that answer choice.

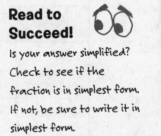

Read to Succeed!

Is your answer simplified? Check to see if the fraction is in simplest form. If not, be sure to write it in simplest form.

Justify and Evaluate

How do you know your solution is accurate?

_____

_____

_____

Lesson 3   (continued)

Use a problem-solving model to solve each problem.

1 The table below shows how Mason spends his monthly income. If he starts saving the money that he originally spent on video games and dining out, how much greater is the fraction that he spends than saves? **7.NS.3, (MP) 1**

Category	Fraction of Income
Clothing	$\frac{7}{15}$
Music	$\frac{2}{15}$
Video Games	$\frac{4}{15}$
Dining Out	$\frac{2}{15}$

(A) $\frac{1}{5}$ (B) $\frac{3}{2}$ (C) $\frac{3}{5}$ (D) $\frac{2}{5}$

2 The table shows two types of music notes and how many beats they represent. How many total beats are represented by an augmented eighth followed by two sixteenth notes and another augmented eighth note? **7.NS.3, (MP) 2**

Note	Symbol	Beats
Sixteenth Note	♪	$\frac{1}{4}$
Augmented Eighth Note	♪.	$\frac{3}{4}$

3 The table shows the time Jira spends as she gets ready for school. The tasks are listed in order of when she completes them. How many minutes does she spend getting ready before she brushes her teeth? **7.EE.3, (MP) 1**

Task	Time Spent (hours)
Shower	$\frac{2}{12}$
Get dressed	$\frac{1}{12}$
Eat breakfast	$\frac{3}{12}$
Brush teeth	$\frac{1}{12}$
Fix hair	$\frac{5}{12}$

4 ✋ **H.O.T. Problem** The table shows two data sets. Which set has a greater average? By how much greater? **7.NS.3, (MP) 6**

Data Set 1	$\frac{10}{11}$	$\frac{2}{11}$	$\frac{7}{11}$	$\frac{5}{11}$
Data Set 2	$\frac{9}{31}$	$\frac{1}{31}$	$\frac{3}{31}$	$\frac{1}{31}$

Lesson 4 Multi-Step Problem Solving

Multi-Step Example

Hakeem has a reading assignment to complete this week. He completes some of the assignment each day. By Wednesday night, he has completed two-thirds of his assignment. What fraction more of his assignment does Hakeem complete on Wednesday than on Tuesday?
7.EE.3, **MP** 2

Day	Total Fraction Completed
Monday	$\frac{1}{6}$
Tuesday	$\frac{1}{4}$
Wednesday	$\frac{2}{3}$

Ⓐ $\frac{5}{12}$

Ⓒ $\frac{1}{3}$

Ⓑ $\frac{1}{12}$

Ⓓ $\frac{1}{4}$

Use a problem-solving model to solve this problem.

Analyze

Read the problem. Circle the information you know.
Underline what the problem is asking you to find.

Plan

What will you need to do to solve the problem? Write your plan in steps.

Step 1 Determine the _____ completed on Wednesday and Tuesday.

Step 2 Determine how much more he completed _____.

Solve

Use your plan to solve the problem. Show your steps.

$\frac{2}{3} - \frac{1}{4} =$ ____ $\frac{1}{4} - \frac{1}{6} =$ ____

Determine how much more was completed on Wednesday.

____ – ____ = _____   Subtract.

He completed ____ more of the assignment on Wednesday.

The correct answer is _____. Fill in that answer choice.

Read to Succeed!

The fractions in the table are cumulative, meaning they are the total fraction he has completed. It is not the fraction he completes each day.

Justify and Evaluate

How do you know your solution is accurate?

_____

_____

_____

Lesson 4 *(continued)*

Use a problem-solving model to solve each problem.

1 Over three days, a veterinarian measures the difference between a cat's weight and the weight on its first visit. What is the net weight change of the cat's weight, in pounds, from the second visit to the fourth? **7.EE.3, MP 2**

Visit	Difference from Original Weight (lb)
Second	$-\frac{1}{2}$
Third	$-\frac{1}{5}$
Fourth	$-\frac{3}{10}$

Ⓐ $\frac{1}{5}$

Ⓑ $\frac{1}{10}$

Ⓒ $-\frac{1}{5}$

Ⓓ $-\frac{1}{10}$

2 How many units greater is the perimeter of Triangle *B* than the perimeter of Triangle *A*? **7.NS.3, MP 1**

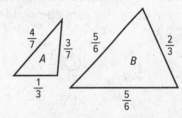

3 The table shows the fraction of each soccer game that Zoe spent playing goalie. On average, how much of one game did Zoe spend playing goalie? Express your answer as a decimal. **7.NS.1d, MP 1**

Game	Fraction of Game as Goalie
1	$\frac{1}{4}$
2	$\frac{5}{8}$
3	$\frac{1}{2}$
4	$\frac{5}{8}$

4 🔥 **H.O.T. Problem** The circle graph shows how Elena handles her monthly income. What fraction more does she spend or give to charity than she saves? **7.NS.3, MP 1**

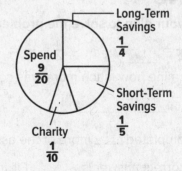

Lesson 5   Multi-Step Problem Solving

Multi-Step Example

The table shows the makeup of the cheese tray at the DeSilva family reunion. If the family eats $6\frac{5}{6}$ pounds of the cheese, how many pounds of cheese remain on the tray? **7.NS.3,** **1**

Type of Cheese	Amount (lb)
Cheddar	$3\frac{1}{2}$
Provolone	$2\frac{1}{2}$
Swiss	$2\frac{1}{4}$

Ⓐ 1 pound

Ⓒ $1\frac{1}{2}$ pound

Ⓑ $1\frac{5}{12}$ pound

Ⓓ $2\frac{7}{12}$ pound

Use a problem-solving model to solve this problem.

Analyze

Read the problem. Circle **the information you know.**
Underline **what the problem is asking you to find.**

2 Plan

What will you need to do to solve the problem? Write your plan in steps.

Step 1   Determine the amount of cheese on the tray by _____ the mixed numbers.

Step 2   _____ the weight of cheese that was eaten from the original amount on the cheese tray.

3 Solve

Use your plan to solve the problem. Show your steps.
Determine the amount of cheese on the tray. Then subtract.

$3\frac{1}{2} + 2\frac{1}{2} + 2\frac{1}{4} =$ ____   Add.

____ − ____ = ____   Subtract.

There were ____ pounds remaining on the cheese tray.

The correct answer is ____. Fill in that answer choice.

> **Read to Succeed!**
> When subtracting the mixed numbers, be sure to rename them using the LCD before trying to subtract.

4 Justify and Evaluate

How do you know your solution is accurate?

_____

_____

_____

Lesson 5   (continued)

Use a problem-solving model to solve each problem.

1 The table shows Lily's length from the time she was born. How many more inches did she grow during the first month than during her second month? **7.NS.3, MP 1**

Age	Length (in.)
Birth	$19\frac{3}{4}$
1 Month	$22\frac{1}{4}$
2 Month	$23\frac{1}{4}$

Ⓐ $\frac{3}{4}$ inch

Ⓑ $1\frac{1}{4}$ inches

Ⓒ $1\frac{1}{2}$ inches

Ⓓ $3\frac{1}{2}$ inches

2 The side measures for two sides of a triangle are shown. What is the measure, in inches, of side A if the perimeter of the triangle is 180 inches? **7.NS.3, MP 4**

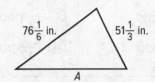

3 Farid's family took a road trip. The circle graph shows the part of an hour that each family member drove. What fraction more of an hour did his parents drive than the rest of the family combined? **7.NS.3, MP 1**

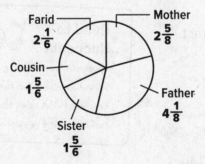

4 ✋**H.O.T. Problem** A point is plotted on a coordinate grid at $-7\frac{2}{3}$, $-11\frac{1}{2}$. A second point is plotted 9 units to the right and $2\frac{2}{3}$ units down. What are the coordinates of the second point? Is it in a different quadrant than the first point? Explain your reasoning. **7.NS.3, MP 2**

_____

_____

_____

_____

_____

_____

Lesson 6   **Multi-Step** Problem Solving

Multi-Step Example

The thermometer shows the temperature in Badger, Minnesota, at 10 P.M. The temperature decreased by $\frac{1}{3}$ of its absolute value by 4 A.M. What is the final temperature, to the nearest degree Fahrenheit? **7.EE.3, MP 1**

Ⓐ −4   Ⓒ −15

Ⓑ −8   Ⓓ −19

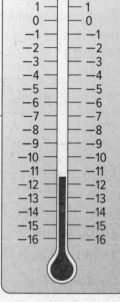

Use a problem-solving model to solve this problem.

 Analyze

Read the problem. Ⓒircle the information you know. Underline what the problem is asking you to find.

 Plan

What will you need to do to solve the problem? Write your plan in steps.

Step 1   Determine _____ of the absolute value of _____.

Step 2   Then _____ the product from the current temperature.

 Solve

Use your plan to solve the problem. Show your steps.

Determine the product. Then subtract from the current temperature.

$11\frac{1}{2} \times \frac{1}{3} =$ _____

_____ − _____ = _____   Subtract.

The final temperature was about _____ degrees Fahrenheit.

The correct answer is _____. Fill in that answer choice.

Read to Succeed!

The final temperature decreased, which means the absolute value of the final temperature will be greater than the absolute value of the original temperature.

 Justify and Evaluate

How do you know your solution is accurate?

_____

_____

_____

Lesson 6 *(continued)*

Use a problem-solving model to solve each problem.

1 Jin took a 15-hour flight to Korea. He slept for $\frac{1}{3}$ of the flight. The table shows how Jin spent his time when he was awake. How many minutes did he spend talking? **7.EE.3, MP 1**

Activity	Fraction of Time Awake
Reading	$\frac{1}{2}$
Eating	$\frac{1}{6}$
Talking	$\frac{1}{3}$

Ⓐ 100 minutes

Ⓑ 180 minutes

Ⓒ 200 minutes

Ⓓ 300 minutes

2 The table shows the number of miles for each segment of a triathlon. Lina trained on a team of 5 people. Each person completed each segment of the race. How many total yards did her team swim? **7.EE.3, MP 6**

Activity	Distance (miles)
Swim	$2\frac{2}{5}$
Bike ride	112
Run	$26\frac{1}{5}$

3 Rectangle 1 has a length of $2\frac{1}{2}$ inches and a width of $\frac{1}{3}$ inch. Rectangle 2 is created by multiplying each side by a factor of $1\frac{1}{2}$. Determine how many more square inches the new area is than the original area. **7.EE.3, MP 2**

4 🔥**H.O.T. Problem** The circle graph shows the breakdown of Seth's math grade. His quiz grade consists of 6 quizzes, each worth equal amounts. He missed $\frac{1}{10}$ of the possible points on his first quiz. What fraction of his overall grade do the missed points represent? Which is worth a greater fraction of his grade, Quizzes and Homework or Quizzes and Tests? Explain. **7.NS.3, MP 1**

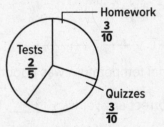

Lesson 7   Multi-Step Problem Solving

Multi-Step Example

The students listed in the table each made a pitcher of lemonade. About how many more liters did Serena make than Kyle? **7.RP.3, MP 6**

(A) 0.89 liter

(B) 1.4 liters

(C) 3.37 liters

(D) 11.37 liters

Person	Capacity
Serena	3 gal
Morgan	3,500 mL
Charity	13 quarts
Kyle	8 L

Use a problem-solving model to solve this problem.

Analyze

Read the problem. Circle **the information you know.**
Underline **what the problem is asking you to find.**

Plan

What will you need to do to solve the problem? Write your plan in steps.

Step 1   Convert 3 gallons to _____.

Step 2   _____ the amount Kyle made from the amount of liters.

Solve

Use your plan to solve the problem. Show your steps.
Convert gallons to liters.

$3 \text{ gal} \cdot \dfrac{3.79 \text{ L}}{1 \text{ gal}} \approx$ _____ liters

Subtract the amount in liters of Kyle's pitcher from Serena's pitcher amount in liters.

_____ − 8 = _____

Serena made about _____ liters more than Kyle.

So, the correct answer is _____. Fill in that answer choice.

Read to Succeed!

You may need to refer to the conversion chart in your book to help you convert between measurement systems.

Justify and Evaluate

How do you know your solution is accurate?

_____

_____

_____

Lesson 7 *(continued)*

Use a problem-solving model to solve each problem.

1 Kofi and Vanessa each measured the length of their hands. In centimeters, about how much longer is Vanessa's hand compared to Kofi's? **7.RP.3,** **MP** **6**

Student	Length of Hand
Kofi	7 in.
Vanessa	19 cm

Ⓐ 1.22 cm

Ⓑ 1.5 cm

Ⓒ 12 cm

Ⓓ 17.78 cm

2 Three tables are going to be combined together in a row to make one long table. About how many feet long will the new table be? **7.RP.3,** **MP** **6**

Table	Length
A	4.5 feet
B	2.7 meters
C	2 yards

_____

3 In a sauce recipe, 2 cups of ketchup are added for every 1 cup of tomato sauce. If 2.25 cups of tomato sauce are added, about how many milliliters of ketchup should be added? Round to the nearest whole number. **7.RP.3,** **MP** **6**

_____

4 👆 **H.O.T. Problem** A suitcase weighing 50 pounds contains clothes, towels, and shoes. The weight distribution is shown in the circle graph below. About how much do the clothes weigh in kilograms? Round to the nearest hundredth. **7.RP.3,** **MP** **6**

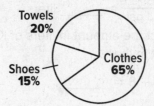

_____

Lesson 8 **Multi-Step** Problem Solving

> ### Multi-Step Example
>
> William has $15\frac{3}{5}$ quarts of paint. He equally divided the paint into 3 two-gallon
> containers. How many gallons of paint are in each container? Express your answer
> as a decimal. 7.EE.3, MP 1

Use a problem-solving model to solve this problem.

Analyze

Read the problem. Circle the information you know.
Underline what the problem is asking you to find.

Plan

What will you need to do to solve the problem? Write your plan in steps.

> **Read to Succeed!**
> Every gallon has 4 quarts. Since you're converting from a smaller unit (quarts) to a larger unit (gallons), your answer needs to be a smaller number, so you will need to divide.

Step 1 Convert quarts to _____ by dividing by 4.

Step 2 Then divide the quotient by ____ to determine how many gallons are in each container.

Solve

Use your plan to solve the problem. Show your steps.
Convert quarts to gallons.

$15\frac{3}{5} \div 4 = $ _____

Divide by 3 to determine the amount in each container.

_____ $\div 3 = $ _____

Each container holds _____ gallons of paint.

Justify and Evaluate

How do you know your solution is accurate?

_____

_____

_____

Lesson 8 (continued)

Use a problem-solving model to solve each problem.

1 A family-sized container of macaroni holds sixteen $\frac{3}{4}$-cup servings. A chef prepares meals using $1\frac{1}{3}$ cups in each bowl. How many bowls can the chef prepare from one family-sized container? **7.EE.3, MP 1**

_____

2 The side length of Cube 1 is $2\frac{1}{2}$ inches. Cube 2 has a side length of 5 inches. How many times larger is the volume of Cube 2? **7.EE.3, MP 1**

_____

3 The table shows how much Rita paid for beans at the local market. How much more per pound will it cost to buy the most expensive beans per pound than the cheapest beans per pound? **7.NS.3, MP 2**

Type	Weight (lb)	Cost ($)
Black beans	4	6
Lentil beans	$3\frac{1}{8}$	4
Kidney beans	$6\frac{1}{4}$	11

_____

4 ✋ **H.O.T. Problem** Compare the mean of the data below with and without the outlier, which is the extremely high data value. Which mean represents the majority of the data more closely? Explain. **7.NS.2c, MP 2**

_____

_____

_____

_____

Lesson 1   Multi-Step Problem Solving

Multi-Step Example

Nelson has $65.00 to spend on some polo shirts and a jacket. One store has the shirts he likes on sale for $8.98 and a denim jacket he likes for $25.00. Write an algebraic expression that represents the cost of any number of shirts and the jacket. Use the expression to decide if Nelson has enough money to buy 4 shirts and the jacket. *Preparation for 7.EE.1,* 4

Use a problem-solving model to solve this problem.

1 Analyze

Read the problem. (Circle) the information you know.
Underline what the problem is asking you to find.

2 Plan

What will you need to do to solve the problem? Write your plan in steps.

Step 1   Write an _____ expression that represents the cost of the purchases.

Step 2   Evaluate the expression for ____ shirts and the jacket, and compare the cost to _____.

> **Read to Succeed!**
> To determine if Nelson has enough money, you need to find a value for s that will make the total less than $65.

3 Solve

Use your plan to solve the problem. Show your steps.

Algebraic expression: _____   Let *s* represent the number of shirts.

Replace *s* with _____. 8.98(4) + 25 = _____ + 25 = _____ or $_____.

_____ is _____ $65.00, so Nelson has enough money to buy 4 shirts and the jacket.

4 Justify and Evaluate

How do you know your solution is accurate?

_____

_____

_____

Lesson 1 *(continued)*

Use a problem-solving model to solve each problem.

1 Sonja has read 222 pages of a 350-page book. She needs to complete the book in 8 days. Write and simplify an expression to find the number of pages *p* that she must read per day to finish in 8 days. If Sonja skips reading on day 3, how does it affect the number of pages she needs to read on days 4–8? Explain your reasoning.
Preparation for **7.EE.1, MP 4**

_____

_____

_____

_____

_____

_____

2 Cho has a piece of fiberboard that measures 24 centimeters by 36 centimeters. She will cut it into rectangles like the one shown below for an art project. If the area of Triangle I is 48 square centimeters, what is the greatest number of rectangles Cho can cut out of the piece of fiberboard?
Preparation for **7.EE.1 MP 4**

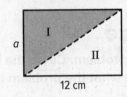

_____

3 Write a real-world problem that can be represented by the expression $49 + 8w$.
Preparation for **7.EE.1, MP 4**

_____

_____

_____

_____

4 🔥 **H.O.T. Problem** Richard evaluated the expressions below. He says that if $y = 6$, the value of each of the expressions will be the same. His math partner says he is wrong. Who is correct? Support your answer.
Preparation for **7.EE.1, MP 3**

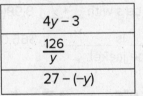

_____

_____

_____

_____

_____

Lesson 2 **Multi-Step** Problem Solving

Multi-Step Example

A pet store orders a 144-box case of two new dog treats—Arffs and Yums. The table shows the total number of boxes of each brand sold at the end of each week. If the patterns continue for each brand, what will be the total number of boxes sold after 10 weeks?
Preparation for 7.EE.1, **MP** 7

Weeks	Arffs	Yums
1	12	8
2	24	16
3	36	24

(A) 80 (B) 120 (C) 144 (D) 200

Use a problem-solving model to solve this problem.

1 Analyze

Read the problem. Circle the information you know.
Underline what the problem is asking you to find.

2 Plan

What will you need to do to solve the problem? Write your plan in steps.

Step 1 Write algebraic expressions that can be used to find the number of boxes of each brand sold at the

end of _____ of weeks.

Step 2 Use the expressions to find how many of each brand are sold after ____ weeks. Add the numbers.

Read to Succeed!

Find the relationship between the numbers in the first and second, and the first and third columns. Use that relationship to write the algebraic expressions.

3 Solve

Use your plan to solve the problem. Show your steps.

If n is the number of weeks: Arffs sold = _____ and Yums sold = ____.

$12n = 12 \times$ ____ = 120 boxes of Arffs after 10 weeks.

$8n = 8 \times$ ____ = 80 boxes of Yums after 10 weeks.

Since $120 + 80 =$ _____, the store will have sold 200 total boxes of treats after

10 weeks. So, the correct answer is ____. Fill in that answer choice.

4 Justify and Evaluate

How do you know your solution is accurate?

_____

_____

_____

Lesson 2 *(continued)*

Use a problem-solving model to solve each problem.

1 Laura and Shani have a summer business making bracelets. The table below shows the number of bracelets they each can make in 4 days. Patrice helps them. She can make bracelets faster than Laura can but slower than Shani. Assuming that they all work at a constant rate, which could be a number of bracelets that Patrice can make in 8 days? *Preparation for 7.EE.1,* **MP** **7**

Days	1	2	3	4
Laura	9	18	27	36
Shani	12	24	36	48

Ⓐ 42

Ⓑ 72

Ⓒ 88

Ⓓ 96

2 Kamal is drawing columns of squares to make a design. The first column he draws has 2 squares, the second has 4 squares, and the third has 6 squares. He continues the pattern until he has 8 columns. Represent the number of squares in each column on the graph below. *Preparation for 7.EE.1,* **MP** **7**

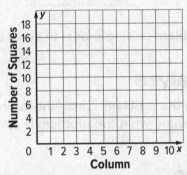

How many squares does Kamal draw? If he shades every third square, what fraction of the squares will be shaded? Explain your reasoning.

_____

_____

_____

3 Marta has a travel and lunch budget of $45 a week. Lin's budget is $40. Both spend *x* dollars each school day to ride the bus to school. Marta spends $20 a week on lunches, while Lin spends $17. Write an expression for each student's expenses. Who has the most money left at the end of the week? Justify your answer. *Preparation for* **7.EE.1,** **MP** **4**

_____

_____

_____

_____

_____

4 🖐 **H.O.T. Problem** Write five terms for an arithmetic sequence and describe the relationship between the terms. *Preparation for 7.EE.1,* **MP** **1**

_____

_____

_____

_____

NAME_____ DATE _____ PERIOD _____

Lesson 3   **Multi-Step** Problem Solving

Multi-Step Example

Janelle wants to buy a set of 24 colored drawing pencils. The table shows the brands and prices available at a local art store. Better quality pencils always cost more, but Janelle doesn't want to buy the most expensive pencils, so she uses the mean of the prices as a guide. Which brand did she buy? If this cost is 40% of her art supply budget, what is her total budget? **7.EE.1,** **2**

Brand	Cost ($)
Artistica	15
Classic Colors	22
Prism Natural	25
Prism Plus	20
True Color	18

Use a problem-solving model to solve this problem.

1 Analyze

Read the problem. Circle the information you know.
Underline what the problem is asking you to find.

2 Plan

What will you need to do to solve the problem? Write your plan in steps.

Step 1   Find the mean of the cost of the _____.

Step 2   Determine which brand she bought. Use this information to find her total _____.

Read to Succeed!
If Janelle uses the mean as a guide, it suggests that she chooses the price that is the exact mean or the price that is closest to the mean.

3 Solve

Use your plan to solve the problem. Show your steps.

15 + 22 + 25 + 20 + 18   Use the Associative Property to reorder the addends.

= (15 + ____) + (22 + ____) + 20   Use mental math to add and to divide.

= 40 + 40 + 20 = _____ ÷ 5 = ____ spent on _____

40% = 0.____. $20 ÷ 0.4 = _____

So, Janelle bought Prism Plus pencils for $_____, and her art budget is $_____.

4 Justify and Evaluate

How do you know your solution is accurate?

_____

_____

_____

Course 2 · Chapter 5 Expressions   **65**

Lesson 3 *(continued)*

Use a problem-solving model to solve each problem.

1 Neil and Jamie went shopping at a biking discount store. Neil bought a can of bike cleaner, two pairs of shorts, a wrist brace, and a pair of sunglasses. Jamie bought the same items as Neil plus two other items. If he spent about 18% more money than Neil, what other items did he buy? Support your reasoning. **7.EE.2,** MP **2**

Item	Cost ($)
Bike cleaner	12
Biking shorts	20
Sunglasses	8
Tire-pressure gauge	18
Wrist brace	9
Water bottles	6

_____

_____

_____

_____

2 Darla recorded and displayed the daily high and low temperatures on Monday through Saturday of one week. During the previous week, the difference between the average daily high and the average daily low was 8°F. Is this week's difference an increase over the previous week, a decrease, or is it the same? Support your answer. **7.EE.1,** MP **2**

	M	Tu	W	Th	F	S
High (°F)	65	67	65	70	72	63
Low (°F)	52	56	56	54	54	58

_____

_____

_____

_____

_____

3 Rashida plans to build a fence around an irregularly shaped piece of land. The cost of the fencing, excluding the poles, is $38 per 20 linear feet for plain chain link and $120 per 20 linear feet for vinyl-coated chain link. How much more will it cost to use the vinyl-coated fencing for Rashida's project? **7.EE.1,** MP **7**

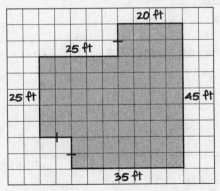

4 ✋**H.O.T. Problem** A student simplifies the expression as shown. He says he uses only the Commutative Property of Multiplication. Is the student correct? Support your position. **7.EE.1,** MP **2**

$$12a(5)$$
$$= 12 \cdot a \cdot 5$$
$$= (12 \cdot 5) \cdot a$$
$$= 60a$$

_____

_____

_____

_____

_____

_____

Lesson 4 **Multi-Step** Problem Solving

Multi-Step Example

Dawit wants to buy some vintage comic books at a local shop and have them shipped to his cousin who resells them online. He buys two that are in excellent condition, four that are in good condition, and two that are in fair condition. The tax rate on the comic books is 8.25%, and the shipping cost is $5.00. What is the total cost of buying and shipping the comic books? **7.EE.2, MP 2**

Vintage Comic Books Costs ($)	
Poor	2.00
Fair	4.00
Good	10.00
Excellent	18.00
Like new	26.00

Ⓐ $90.83   Ⓒ $96.34

Ⓑ $95.93   Ⓓ $100.26

Use a problem-solving model to solve this problem.

 Analyze

Read the problem. ⟨Circle⟩ the information you know.
Underline what the problem is asking you to find.

 Plan

What will you need to do to solve the problem? Write your plan in steps.

Step 1 Write and simplify an expression to find the cost of the comic books.

Step 2 Add the _____ and the _____.

 Read to Succeed!

Notice that the tax rate is on the comic books alone, not on the comic books and the shipping.

 Solve

Use your plan to solve the problem. Show your steps.

2(____) + 4(____) + 2(____)

2(____ + ____) + 4(____) = ____ Use the Distributive Property to rewrite the expression.

84 × _____ = _____ + $5.00 shipping = $_____   Find the tax on the cost.
                                                       Add the tax and the shipping.

So, the correct answer is ____. Fill in that answer choice.

Justify and Evaluate

How do you know your solution is accurate?

_____

_____

_____

Lesson 4 (continued)

Use a problem-solving model to solve each problem.

1 The Puccio's have an urban farm and they sell the produce at the farmers' market. Every fall they order bulk seeds and small seed packets to plant in the early spring. The table shows what they ordered one fall. If the shipping rate is $3 per $50 ordered, which is the total cost of the seeds? **7.EE.1, MP 2**

Variety	Packages Ordered
Carrots	2 @ $19.99
Collards	3 @ $19.99
Radishes	4 @ $3.49
Snow peas	10 @ $3.49
Spinach	3 @ $19.99
Sugar snap peas	10 @ $3.49

Ⓐ $242.18

Ⓑ $243.18

Ⓒ $243.68

Ⓓ $258.68

2 Kip works 65 hours a month at four part-time jobs. He works 20 hours at one company and is paid $300. He works 15 hours at his second job and is paid $8 an hour. He is paid $12 an hour at his third job. He works 15 hours at his fourth job and is paid $10.50 an hour. Complete the table to help you find his total monthly income from the four jobs. Kip puts 18% of his pay in a savings account to pay for taxes and unexpected expenses. What is his income after he deposits the 18% into savings? Round your answer to the nearest cent. **7.EE.1, MP 2**

Job	Hours	Rate (hr)	Total ($)
1			
2			
3			
4			

3 Yasmin bought a case of 144 beach hats. She bought them for $7 per hat and sold them for $10 per hat. Write an expression that shows her profit. Use the Distributive Property to evaluate the expression. Find the number of cases of hats Yasmin needs to buy and sell to earn $1,200 in profit. **7.EE.1, MP 2**

_____

_____

_____

_____

4 ♨ **H.O.T. Problem** Towanda used algebra tiles to model an expression. Write the expression she modeled. Use the Distributive Property to rewrite the expression, and then simplify. What is true about the value of the three expressions? Support your reasoning. **7.EE.2, MP 3**

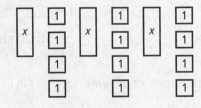

_____

_____

Lesson 5 Multi-Step Problem Solving

Multi-Step Example

A store is having a closeout sale on two models of televisions. The table shows each model, its discount, and the number available for sale. Which expression can be used to find the total sales for all of the televisions? **7.EE.2, MP 4**

Model	A	B
Discount	40%	25%
Available	15	18

Ⓐ $(0.6a)(0.75b)$

Ⓒ $15(0.4a) + 18(0.25b)$

Ⓑ $(1.4a) + (1.25b)$

Ⓓ $15(0.6a) + 18(0.75b)$

Use a problem-solving model to solve this problem.

 Analyze

Read the problem. Circle the information you know. Underline what the problem is asking you to find.

 Plan

What will you need to do to solve the problem? Write your plan in steps.

Step 1 Select variables to represent each model.

Step 2 Determine the percent of the original cost that the buyer will pay for each model.

Step 3 Write the expression for each model. Then, add.

Read to Succeed!

The cost of each television is discounted, so the buyer will pay less than 100% of the original cost.

 Solve

Use your plan to solve the problem. Show your steps.

Use the variable _____ to represent the original cost for Model A and _____ to represent the original cost for Model B.

Find the percent that the buyer will pay for each model.

Model A: 100% − 40% = _____%. Model B: 100% − 25% = _____%.

Total sales for Model A: _____   Total sales for Model B: _____

Total sales for all the televisions: _____ + _____.

So, the correct answer is _____. Fill in that answer choice.

 Justify and Evaluate

How do you know your solution is accurate?

_____

_____

Lesson 5 *(continued)*

Use a problem-solving model to solve each problem.

1 The tax rate in Todd's city is 6.75%. The tax rate in Anita's city is 8.25%. They both spend $36 on Blu-Rays at a national chain store. Three of the following expressions can be used to determine how much more Anita pays for her purchase. Which expression *cannot* be used? **7.EE.2,** **4**

Ⓐ 36(0.015)

Ⓑ 36(1.0825 − 1.0675)

Ⓒ 36 − (0.825 − 0.675)

Ⓓ (36)(0.0825) − (36)(0.0675)

2 Jon has the parallelogram below. He wrote the expression $A = \dfrac{2m + 2(2n)}{8}$ to use to find the area of any of the smaller congruent triangles within it. Is his expression correct? Support your answer. **7.EE.2,** MP **4**

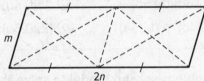

_____

_____

_____

_____

_____

3 Cecilia drew a circle graph to show how she spends her leisure time on weekends. Write an expression to use to find how much time she spends relaxing with family and friends, where *t* is equal to her total leisure time. If she has 16 hours of leisure time, how much time does she spend relaxing with family and friends? Round your answer to the nearest half hour. Show your work. **7.EE.1,** MP **6**

_____

_____

_____

_____

_____

4 👍 **H.O.T. Problem** Kenji says that the following expressions are equivalent. Is he correct? If not, explain the possible error in thinking. **7.EE.1,** MP **3**

$5x(x − 7)$
$5x^2 − 35x$
$5x(x) − 5x(7x)$

_____

_____

_____

_____

Lesson 6   **Multi-Step** Problem Solving

Multi-Step Example

The Drama Club is selling tickets for their latest production. They are also accepting additional cash donations. They plan to save 20% of the money from all ticket sales and donations for their spring trip. Ticket sales and donations from adults are represented by (92a + 109), and ticket sales and donations from students are represented by (34m + 13). If adult tickets cost $9 and student tickets cost $5, how much money will the Drama Club have available for their spring trip. **7.EE.1,** **MP** 6

Ⓐ $224   Ⓒ $937

Ⓑ $896   Ⓓ $1,120

Use a problem-solving model to solve this problem.

 Analyze

Read the problem. (Circle) the information you know.
Underline what the problem is asking you to find.

2 Plan

What will you need to do to solve the problem? Write your plan in steps.

Step 1   Write an algebraic expression that represents total adult and student ticket sales and donations.

Step 2   Find _____% of the total ticket sales and donations.

Read to Succeed!

Read the question carefully. The Drama Club can only use 20% of total ticket sales and donations for their spring trip.

3 Solve

Use your plan to solve the problem. Show your steps.

(92a + 109) _____ (34m + 13)

(92 × _____ + 109) + (34 × _____ + 13)   Substitute the values of a and m.

937 + 183 = _____   Simplify.

0.2(_____) = $_____ saved.   Find 20% of the sum.

The correct answer is _____. Fill in that answer choice.

4 Justify and Evaluate

How do you know your solution is accurate?

_____

_____

_____

Lesson 6   *(continued)*

Use a problem-solving model to solve each problem.

1 Alberto gets an allowance of $10 a week. His older brother gets a $15 allowance a week. They also are paid *c* dollars for each household chore they do. One week, Alberto does 8 chores and his brother does 3. They would like to combine their weekly money to buy a video game. Which linear expression in simplest form represents their total earnings for that week? **7.EE.1, MP 2**

Ⓐ $(10 + 8c)(15 + 3c)$

Ⓑ $10(8c) + 15(3c) = 80c + 45c$

Ⓒ $10 + 15 + c + 8 + 3 = 31 + c$

Ⓓ $(10 + 8c) + (15 + 3c) = 25 + 11c$

2 Lakisha has a triangular flower garden. She wants to put a small fence around it to keep her dogs out. The fencing she likes costs $4.25 per foot. Write and simplify a linear expression to represent the cost of the fencing. **7.EE.1, MP 4**

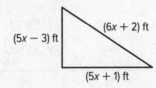

$(5x - 3)$ ft · $(6x + 2)$ ft · $(5x + 1)$ ft

_____

_____

_____

_____

3 Larry and some friends are playing a game. Two of the rules for the game are shown. **7.EE.1, MP 2**

Move	Score	Bonus
Capture	*x* points	+ 10 points if done in one move
Rescue	*y* points	+ 5 points if done in one move

Larry has two captures, one of which took one move, and two rescues, both of which took one move. If $x = 2$ and $y = 2x$, how many points did he score? Support your answer by writing and simplifying an expression.

_____

_____

_____

4 ♨ **H.O.T. Problem** If *x* is an integer, will the linear expression $(x + 1) + (x - 1)$ always simplify to a positive value for *x*? If your answer is no, include a counterexample. **7.EE.1, MP 3**

_____

_____

_____

Lesson 7　Multi-Step Problem Solving

Multi-Step Example

Bonnie owns a T-shirt shop. She tracks the sales of plain T-shirts and T-shirts with a design each week to be sure she has enough stock. If $t = 25$, the sales of T-shirts with a design total how much more than the sales of plain T-shirts? **7.EE.1, MP 1**

Sales in One Week		
Style	Cost ($)	Number Sold
Plain	12	$5t - 4$
Design	15	$8t + 3$

Ⓐ $780 more

Ⓒ $1,230 more

Ⓑ $984 more

Ⓓ $2,050 more

Use a problem-solving model to solve this problem.

 Analyze

Read the problem. Circle the information you know.
Underline what the problem is asking you to find.

 Plan

What will you need to do to solve the problem? Write your plan in steps.

> **Step 1**　_____ the expressions that represent the number of T-shirts sold.
>
> Evaluate the difference using $t =$ _____.

> **Step 2**　_____ the product by $_____.

Read to Succeed!

The answer to the question represents the difference between the total sales of T-shirts with and without a design. Careful: The variable t is not a dollar amount.

 Solve

Use your plan to solve the problem. Show your steps.

$(8t + 3) - (5t - 4)$

$\;8t + 3$

$\underline{(+) - 5t + 4}$　　　　The additive inverse of $5t - 4$ is $(-5t + 4)$.

_____ more design T-shirts

$3(\underline{}) + 7 = (\underline{})$　　Substitute the value given for t. Simplify.

$(\$\underline{})(\underline{}) = \$\underline{}$.　　Multiply the cost by the number of shirts.

So, _____ is the correct answer. Fill in that answer choice.

Justify and Evaluate

How do you know your solution is accurate?

_____

_____

_____

Lesson 7 *(continued)*

Use a problem-solving model to solve each problem.

1 The table shows the attendance at a home football game, where $a = 250$. About what percent more of the crowd at the game were home fans than were visitors? **7.EE.1, MP 1**

Team	Attendance
Home	$8a + 3$
Visitors	$6a - 5$

Ⓐ 15%

Ⓑ 25%

Ⓒ 33%

Ⓓ 57%

2 The perimeter of the triangular reception room shown is $12x + 4$ feet. Find the missing side length in terms of x. If $x = 3$, what is the perimeter of the room to the nearest tenth of a yard? **7.EE.1, MP 1**

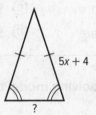

$5x + 4$

?

3 Marcy has the following scores on three rounds of a game: $4x - 3$, $3x + 5$, and $2x + 8$. Jose scores are $3x + 6$, $4x + 9$, and $3x - 14$. If $x = 10$, by how much does Marcy need to increase her score to win? Support your answer. **7.EE.1, MP 2**

_____

_____

_____

_____

4 🔥 **H.O.T. Problem** Susana correctly subtracted the expression on the left. Without actually subtracting, what is the difference of the expression on the right? Explain why. **7.EE.1, MP 7**

$$
\begin{array}{r}
3x + 2 \\
-\ 2x - 8 \\
\hline
x + 10
\end{array}
\qquad
\begin{array}{r}
2x - 8 \\
-\ 3x + 2 \\
\hline
?
\end{array}
$$

_____

_____

_____

Lesson 8 **Multi-Step** Problem Solving

Multi-Step Example

The expressions in the table show Mr. Owusu's and Mr. Carson's monthly income, where x is the number of hours worked. Which expression represents the difference in their monthly income? If $x = 8$, what is the actual difference? **7.EE.1, MP 1**

| Mr. Owusu | $14x - 16$ |
| Mr. Carson | $10x + 8$ |

(A) $4(x - 6)$, $8

(C) $4(x - 8)$, $24

(B) $4(x + 6)$, $38

(D) $4(x + 8)$, $40

Use a problem-solving model to solve this problem.

1 Analyze

Read the problem. Circle **the information you know.**
Underline **what the problem is asking you to find.**

2 Plan

What will you need to do to solve the problem? Write your plan in steps.

Step 1 _____ to find the difference of their income.

Step 2 Factor the difference.

Step 3 Find the actual difference.

Read to Succeed!

The expressions in the answers are in a different form than the ones in the table. You may need to use factoring.

3 Solve

Use your plan to solve the problem. Show your steps.

$(14x - 16) - (10x + 8)$

$14x - 16$

$\underline{(+) -10x - 8}$ The additive inverse of $10x + 8$ is $(-10x - 8)$.

The GCF of 4 and 24 is _____, so $4x - 24 =$ _____ (_____).   Factor the expression.

$4(x - 6) =$ _____   Substitute the value of x.

So, _____ is the correct answer. Fill in that answer choice.

4 Justify and Evaluate

How do you know your solution is accurate?

_____

_____

_____

Lesson 8 (continued)

Use a problem-solving model to solve each problem.

1 A rectangular strip of land is divided into four equal garden plots. One is planted with flowers and the other three with vegetables. If the total area of the garden in square feet is (20x + 300), what are the possible dimensions of the garden? **7.EE.1, (MP) 2**

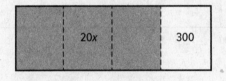

Ⓐ 4 feet by (5x + 72) feet

Ⓑ 5 feet by (4x + 50) feet

Ⓒ 10 feet by (2x + 20) feet

Ⓓ 20 feet by (x + 15) feet

2 Ruben, Theresa, and Arnold raised money for improvements to their local park. Ruben raised d dollars. Theresa raised $75 more than Ruben, and Arnold raised 25% more than Ruben. Write an expression to represent the amount each student earned. If Ruben raised $178, what is the total amount the students raised? Support your answer. **7.EE.1, (MP) 4**

_____

_____

_____

3 A group of eight students went rock climbing. They paid eight admission fees and $10 to park their van. Yolanda paid for herself and her sister with a $20 bill. What was her change in terms of x? **7.EE.2, (MP) 1**

_____

_____

_____

4 ✋**H.O.T. Problem** Two students factor the expression $\frac{3}{8}x + 24$. The table shows their results. **7.EE.1, (MP) 3**

Student 1	$\frac{3}{8}(x + 64)$
Student 2	$\frac{3}{8}\left(x + \frac{1}{64}\right)$

Which student is correct? Justify your answer.

_____

_____

_____

_____

Lesson 1 **Multi-Step** Problem Solving

Multi-Step Example

Devin recorded the weight of his empty backpack and some items he put in it. He found it weighed 15.65 pounds. Janet packed exactly the same items in an identical backpack, but her laptop weighs 1.1 pounds less than Devin's. What is the weight of Janet's laptop? **7.EE.4a,** **MP** **1**

Ⓐ 5.1 lb

Ⓑ 6.2 lb

Ⓒ 7.3 lb

Ⓓ 9.45 lb

Item	Weight (lb)
Empty backpack	1.75
Math book	3.2
Science book	3.5
Water bottle	1.0
Laptop	x

Use a problem-solving model to solve this problem.

Analyze

Read the problem. ⟨Circle⟩ the information you know.
Underline what the problem is asking you to find.

2 Plan

What will you need to do to solve the problem? Write your plan in steps.

Step 1   Determine the value of ___ by writing an equation.

Step 2   Determine the weight of _____.

> **Read to Succeed!** 👀
> The only difference between the weight of the two backpacks and the items in them is the weight of the laptops.

Solve

Use your plan to solve the problem. Show your steps.

$1.75 + 3.2 + 3.5 + 1.0 + x = 15.65$

_____ $+ x = 15.65$, so $x =$ _____   Write and solve an equation.

$6.2 -$ ____ $=$ ____   Find the weight of Janet's laptop.

So, ___ is the correct answer. Fill in that answer choice.

4 Justify and Evaluate

How do you know your solution is accurate?

_____

_____

_____

Lesson 1 *(continued)*

Use a problem-solving model to solve each problem.

1 Devin recorded the percent humidity Monday through Saturday as shown on the graph. The total of the humidity readings for Friday through Sunday is 195. How many percentage points higher was the humidity on Monday than on Sunday? **7.EE.4a, MP 1**

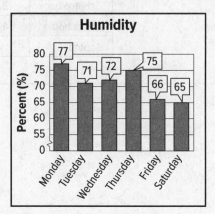

Humidity

(A) 11   (C) 14

(B) 13   (D) 20

2 The table shows how much Prisha read on Saturday and Sunday. If she read at the same rate on Sunday as she did on Saturday, what time did she start reading Sunday night? **7.RP.3, MP 4**

Day	Start Time	End Time	Pages Read
Saturday	12:00 PM	12:30 PM	60
Sunday	?	8:40 PM	40

3 Josiah and Perry were painting their bedroom walls, which have a surface area of 196 square feet. Josiah can paint 16 square feet in 4 minutes, while Perry can paint 7 square feet in 2 minutes. After 10 minutes, how much more total area will Josiah and Perry have left to paint? **7.RP.3, MP 2**

_____

4 👍 **H.O.T. Problem** The maximum speed of the El Toro roller coaster is 70 miles per hour. The difference in speeds of El Toro and the T-Express roller coaster is 5 miles per hour. Using s to represent the speed of T-Express, write and solve two equations that could represent this situation and tell what they mean. What additional information is needed to determine the most appropriate equation for the problem situation? **7.EE.3, MP 6**

_____

_____

_____

_____

_____

_____

Lesson 2 **Multi-Step** Problem Solving

Multi-Step Example

Elisa drove 340 miles to visit her cousins. She drove 65 miles per hour for 4 hours. If she drove 40 miles per hour during the rest of the trip, how long did it take her to drive the 340 miles? **7.EE.4a,** **1**

Ⓐ 5 hours

Ⓑ 6 hours

Ⓒ 7 hours

Ⓓ 8 hours

Use a problem-solving model to solve this problem.

1 Analyze

Read the problem. Circle the information you know.
Underline what the problem is asking you to find.

2 Plan

What will you need to do to solve the problem? Write your plan in steps.

Step 1 Write an equation that sets the following equal to _____ miles:

Distance driven in ___ hours plus distance driven at ____ miles per hour.

Step 2 _____ the numbers of hours driven at each rate.

3 Solve

Use your plan to solve the problem. Show your steps.

65 (__) + ___ (x) = 340   x = (__)   Let x represent the hours
driven at 40 mph.

Add the hours: ___ hours + ___ hours = ___ hours.

So, the correct answer is ___. Fill in that answer choice.

> **Read to Succeed!**
> Elisa drives at two different rates. Add the number of hours that she drove at each rate.

4 Justify and Evaluate

How do you know your solution is accurate?

_____

_____

_____

Lesson 2 (continued)

Use a problem-solving model to solve each problem.

1 Mrs. Watson works as a sales representative and earns a base salary of $300 each week. She also receives a commission, which is a percentage of her total sales. One week she had $5,225 in sales and total pay of $1,083.75. What is her commission rate (R)? **7.EE.4a, MP 1**

   Ⓐ $R = 15\%$

   Ⓑ $R = 20\%$

   Ⓒ $R = 25\%$

   Ⓓ $R = 30\%$

2 Mr. Levy stopped at the grocery store on his way home. He spent $10.50 to buy two loaves of bread, eggs, juice, and milk. Using the information in the table, write and solve an equation that shows how much Mr. Levy spent on each loaf of bread. **7.EE.4, MP 2**

Item	Bread	Eggs	Juice	Milk
Cost ($)		1.25	2.50	3.25

_____

_____

_____

_____

3 Lara's business has orders for a large number of rectangular tabletops from three stores. Each tabletop has an area of 16 square feet. If a bucket of paint will cover 1,000 square feet, how many buckets will Lara need to paint all the tabletops? Write an equation and solve. **7.EE.4a, MP 6**

Store	Tabletops Ordered
New Look	30
Deco Depot	50
Retro Room	90

_____

_____

_____

4 🔥 **H.O.T. Problem** Roberto drove 18 minutes to get to the highway. Once on the highway, he drove the same amount of time but covered twice the distance. Compare the average rate Roberto drove on the highway to the average rate he drove before getting on the highway. Justify your solution. **7.EE.4, MP 4**

_____

_____

_____

_____

Lesson 3   **Multi-Step** Problem Solving

Multi-Step Example

The upper quartile of the data set represented in the box plot at the right is the product of three-fourths and the median. The lower quartile is the quotient of the median and four-sevenths. What is the interquartile range? **7.EE.4a,** **MP** 1

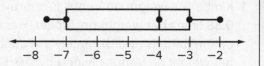

Use a problem-solving model to solve this problem.

1 Analyze

Read the problem. Circle the information you know.
Underline what the problem is asking you to find.

2 Plan

What will you need to do to solve the problem? Write your plan in steps.

Step 1   Use equations to determine the _____ and lower quartile.

Step 2   Subtract the upper quartile from the _____.

3 Solve

Use your plan to solve the problem. Show your steps.

Use equations to determine the median and lower quartile.

$-3 = \frac{3}{4}m$ median = _____

$m \div \frac{4}{7} = q$ lower quartile = _____

Determine the interquartile range.

_____ − _____ = _____   Subtract.

The interquartile range is _____.

> **Read to Succeed!**
>
> Recall that the interquartile range is the distance between the first and third quartiles.

4 Justify and Evaluate

How do you know your solution is accurate?

_____

_____

_____

Lesson 3 *(continued)*

Use a problem-solving model to solve each problem.

1 Kimberly's weight on Venus is approximately 0.38 times her weight on Jupiter. Her weight on the Earth is approximately the quotient of her weight on Venus divided by 0.9. Her weight on the Earth is 100 pounds. What is her weight in pounds on Jupiter, rounded to the nearest whole number? **7.EE.4a,** 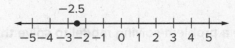 **1**

_____

2 A point on a number line moves to the right $\frac{1}{2}$ unit, to the left $5\frac{1}{2}$ units, and to the right 2 units, landing on the number line as shown. Where does the point start? Express your answer as a decimal. **7.EE.4a,** **MP 2**

−2.5

‹—+—+—+—●—+—+—+—+—+—+—+—›
−5 −4 −3 −2 −1 0 1 2 3 4 5

_____

3 Tevon designates 40% of his income for spending. If he makes $10 per hour, how many hours per week does he have to work to have $100 to spend weekly? **7.EE.4a,** **MP 1**

_____

4 ✋ **H.O.T. Problem** The table below shows the withdrawals and deposits for a checking account. The ending balance is $51.20. Determine the starting balance. Explain. **7.EE.4a,** **MP 4**

Transaction	Amount
Withdrawal	$30
Deposit	$10.20
Deposit	$45.50
Withdrawal	$60

_____

_____

_____

_____

_____

_____

_____

NAME ______________________ DATE ______________ PERIOD ________

Lesson 4 **Multi-Step** Problem Solving

Chapter 6

Multi-Step Example

The graph shows the amount of money customers are charged to rent a moon bounce for an event. Write an equation to represent the total cost. Then use it to determine the cost for renting the moon bounce for 8.5 hours. **7.EE.4a, MP 4**

Ⓐ $200

Ⓑ $220

Ⓒ $230

Ⓓ $240

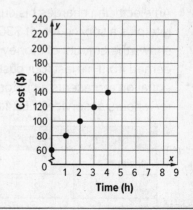

Use a problem-solving model to solve this problem.

1 Analyze

Read the problem. Circle the information you know.
Underline what the problem is asking you to find.

2 Plan

What will you need to do to solve the problem? Write your plan in steps.

Step 1 Determine the cost per ________ to rent the moon bounce.

Step 2 Determine the ____________ for 8.5 hours.

Read to Succeed!

The cost for 0 hours is $60. This must mean there is a rental fee plus an hourly rate to rent the moon bounce.

3 Solve

Use your plan to solve the problem. Show your steps.

There is a ______ rental fee and the rate of change is ______.

$____ h + 60 = t$ Let *h* represent hours and *t* represent total cost.

$____ (8.5) + 60 = t$ Replace *h* with 8.5.

$______ = t$

The cost for renting the moon bounce for 8.5 hours is ______.

The correct answer is ____. Fill in that answer choice.

4 Justify and Evaluate

How do you know your solution is accurate?

____

____

____

Lesson 4 *(continued)*

Use a problem-solving model to solve each problem.

1 An electrician charges his customers an hourly rate plus a service fee of $30. The table shows the amount of money the electrician earned from his last four customers. What equation represents a customer's charge, C, for x hours of service? **7.EE.4a,** Ⓜ **4**

Customer	Hours	Charge ($)
Smith	3	94.50
Jones	2	73.00
Travers	6	159.00
Johnson	7	180.50

Ⓐ $C = 30x + 21.50$

Ⓑ $C = 21.50x + 30$

Ⓒ $C = 25.50x + 30$

Ⓓ $C = 30x + 25.50$

2 Valerie works at a local amusement park. She earns $9.80 per hour. She is also paid $7.00 for meals and $3.00 for transportation each day. Last Friday, Valerie earned $88.40. Write and solve an equation to determine how many hours Valerie worked on Friday. **7.EE.4a,** Ⓜ **2**

_____

_____

3 Write and solve an equation to determine the measures of the angles in the triangle below. **7.EE.4a,** Ⓜ **4**

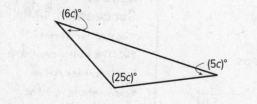

_____

4 🔥**H.O.T. Problem** A seventh grade class is playing a game of *Guess My Rule*. As a student makes a guess, the teacher tells what number the rule gives back. Is it possible for a student to guess 10 with the teacher response being 3? Write a two-step equation that describes the rule to justify your answer. **7.EE.4a,** Ⓜ **3**

Student Guess (x)	Teacher Response (y)
2	−1
5	8
0	−7
6	11

_____

_____

_____

Lesson 5 Multi-Step Problem Solving

Multi-Step Example

Pierre uses two rectangular pieces of paper as bookmarks. The width of the larger bookmark is equal to the length of the smaller bookmark. The length of the larger bookmark is equal to half the perimeter of the smaller bookmark which is 14 inches. What is the perimeter of the larger bookmark? **7.EE.4a,** **MP** 2

Pierre's Bookmarks

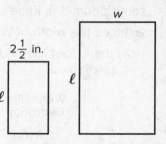

Ⓐ 32 in.   Ⓒ 26 in.

Ⓑ 30 in.   Ⓓ 23 in.

Use a problem-solving model to solve this problem.

1 Analyze

Read the problem. (Circle) the information you know.
Underline what the problem is asking you to find.

2 Plan

What will you need to do to solve the problem? Write your plan in steps.

Step 1   Use the perimeter to determine the _____ of the smaller bookmark.

Step 2   Determine the _____ of the larger bookmark.

3 Solve

Use your plan to solve the problem. Show your steps.

Determine the length of the smaller bookmark.

$$14 = 2\left(2\frac{1}{2}\right) + 2(\ell) \qquad \ell = \underline{\hspace{1.5cm}}$$

Determine the perimeter of the larger bookmark. The length is 7 inches, half of 14 inches.

$$P = 2(\underline{\hspace{0.8cm}}) + 2(7) \qquad P = \underline{\hspace{1.5cm}}$$

The perimeter of the larger bookmark is ____ inches.

So, the correct answer is ____. Fill in that answer choice.

> **Read to Succeed!** 👀
>
> Use the width of the smaller bookmark to solve the equation for the larger bookmark to determine the perimeter.

4 Justify and Evaluate

How do you know your solution is accurate?

_____

_____

_____

Lesson 5 *(continued)*

Use a problem-solving model to solve each problem.

1 Wendell and Katie have bedrooms with the same perimeter. Katie's bedroom has a width $1\frac{1}{3}$ times the width of Wendell's bedroom. How many feet long is Katie's bedroom?
7.EE.4a, MP 2

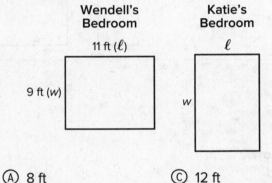

Wendell's Bedroom

11 ft (ℓ)

9 ft (w)

Katie's Bedroom

ℓ

w

Ⓐ 8 ft

Ⓑ 10 ft

Ⓒ 12 ft

Ⓓ 14 ft

2 Diego and two friends are going skating and will choose between two skating rinks. Skate-O-Rama charges $5 admission plus a skate rental fee, which comes to $20.25 for Diego and his friends. Ice Stars charges one dollar less for admission but twice the skate rental fee. If all three friends plan to rent skates, how much more will they spend, in dollars, at Ice Stars than at Skate-O-Rama?
7.EE.4a, MP 1

_____

3 Ella solved the equation $0.5(3 + x) = 2.5$ and then the equation $0.25(4 + y) = x$. If the value of x is the same for both equations, what is the value of y? **7.EE.4, MP 1**

_____

4 ✋ **H.O.T. Problem** Write and solve a real-world problem based on the equation $5(1\frac{3}{8} + x) = 8\frac{3}{4}$. **7.EE.4, MP 4**

_____

_____

_____

_____

Lesson 6   Multi-Step Problem Solving

Multi-Step Example

The maximum weight capacity of the elevator in Maia's apartment building is 900 pounds. One morning she and five other people are on the elevator. Then two more passengers get on the elevator. If Maia weighs 108 pounds, which could be the weights of the two additional passengers without exceeding the maximum weight capacity? **7.EE.4b, MP 4**

Ⓐ 93 lb, 117 lb

Ⓒ 118 lb, 203 lb

Ⓑ 115 lb, 74 lb

Ⓓ 152 lb, 110 lb

Passenger	Weight (lb)
1	126
2	182
3	78
4	135
5	63

Use a problem-solving model to solve this problem.

 Analyze

Read the problem. Circle the information you know.
Underline what the problem is asking you to find.

 Plan

What will you need to do to solve the problem? Write your plan in steps.

Step 1 _____ the weights of the first six passengers.

Step 2 _____ the sum from _____.

Step 3 Compare the difference to the _____ weight in each answer choice.

Read to Succeed!

The phrase "without exceeding" means including but not more than 900 pounds. Use the less than or equal to symbol, ≤.

 Solve

Use your plan to solve the problem. Show your steps.

Write an inequality that sets the sum of the weights as _____ 900.

Use x and y as the unknowns.

$108 + 126 + 182 + 78 + 135 + 63 +$ _____ and _____ ≤ 900.

$692 + x + y \leq 900$

Subtract to find $x + y$. $900 - 692 = 208$

$x + y \leq$ _____

The only answer choice with a sum less than or equal to 208 is $115 + 74 =$ _____,

so the correct answer is _____. Fill in that answer choice.

 Justify and Evaluate

How do you know your solution is accurate?

_____

_____

Lesson 6 (continued)

Use a problem-solving model to solve each problem.

1 Ogima has $12.94 left on a music download gift card. He has the following in his online shopping cart: six $0.99 downloads and three $1.29 downloads. Which additional downloads can Ogima buy using the card? **7.EE.4b, MP 6**

  (A) one $0.99, two $1.29

  (B) two 0.99, one $1.29

  (C) two $1.29

  (D) four $0.99

2 Roland plans to spend no more than $50 at the grocery store and $25 at the hardware store. His shopping lists include the following.

Grocery Store List	Hardware Store List
Milk — $3.50	Duct tape — $3.95
Cereal — $2.95	Hammer — $4.75

What is the difference, in dollars, between the maximum amounts Roland has left to spend at each store? **7.EE.3, MP 1**

_____

3 Blanca solves the inequality $-6 \geq n - 5$ and represents the solution on a number line as shown.

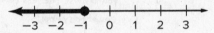

Her friend says the arrow should be pointing the other direction because the solution is $-1 \geq n$. Who is correct? Support your reasoning. **7.EE.4b, MP 3**

_____

_____

_____

4 ✋ **H.O.T. Problem** Write an addition inequality and a subtraction equality that both have the solution $y > 6$. Include a negative integer in both inequalities. **7.EE.4b, MP 4**

_____

_____

_____

Lesson 7 **Multi-Step** Problem Solving

Multi-Step Example

To get the grade she wants in her English class, Elspeth needs an average of 85% from her quiz scores. Each quiz is worth 20 points. The scores of her first four quizzes are shown in the table. There will be one more quiz. What is the minimum score she can receive to earn at least an 85% grade? **7.EE.4b,** **2**

Quiz	Score
1	18
2	16
3	19
4	14

Ⓐ at least 15 points   Ⓒ at least 17 points

Ⓑ at least 16 points   Ⓓ at least 18 points

Use a problem-solving model to solve this problem.

 Analyze

Read the problem. ⟨Circle⟩ the information you know.
Underline what the problem is asking you to find.

 Plan

What will you need to do to solve the problem? Write your plan in steps.

Step 1 Determine the _____ she earned on the first four quizzes.

Step 2 Write an inequality to determine what she must score on the _____.

> **Read to Succeed!**
> To write an inequality, first express the minimum score needed, 85%, as a decimal.

 Solve

Use your plan to solve the problem. Show your steps.

$18 + 16 + 19 + 14 =$ _____   Add the scores for quizzes 1–4.

Write and solve an inequality, where x is the score she needs to earn.

$\dfrac{67 + x}{100} \geq 0.85$ $x \geq$ _____

Elspeth needs to earn at least ____ points on her fifth quiz.

So, the correct answer is ____. Fill in that answer choice.

 Justify and Evaluate

How do you know your solution is accurate?

_____

_____

_____

Lesson 7 (continued)

Use a problem-solving model to solve each problem.

1 Phong and Janice are collecting action cards for a strategy game. They want to collect more than 30 new action cards. Action cards come in packs of 5. What is the least number of packs of action cards they will need to buy to have at least 30 new action cards? **7.EE.4, MP 2**

Ⓐ at least 6

Ⓑ at least 5

Ⓒ at least 4

Ⓓ at least 3

2 Ling earns $9 per hour at the public library. She saves $7 of her earnings from every hour worked for college. How many hours does she have to work each week to save at least $105 for college? Write and solve an inequality to show how many hours she must work each week to save at least $100 for college. **7.EE.4, MP 2**

_____

3 Edwardo is painting the rectangle, which has a rectangular hole in the middle. The rectangular hole in the center is less than 40% of the area of the larger rectangle. What is the greatest possible length of the rectangular hole, to the nearest tenth? **7.EE.4b, MP 2**

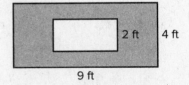

_____

_____

4 ♿ **H.O.T. Problem** Write and solve a real-world problem involving the multiplication inequality below. Then, graph it on a number line. **7.EE.4b, MP 6**

$2m \leq 15$

⟵——————————————⟶

_____

_____

_____

_____

Lesson 8   Multi-Step Problem Solving

Multi-Step Example

Benjamin cannot exceed 10 hours of watching television in a week. He plans to watch a $2\frac{1}{2}$ hour movie on Friday night and not watch any television on Saturday. He writes an inequality to determine how much time he can spend watching television on the other days of the week, if he watches the same amount each day. Which number line represents the solution set of the inequality? **7.EE.4b, MP 4**

Ⓐ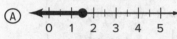

Ⓒ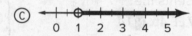

Ⓑ

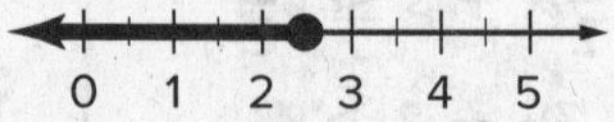

Ⓓ

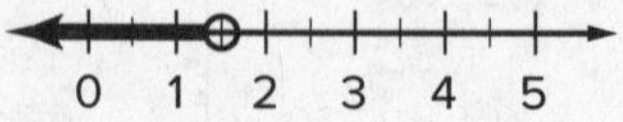

Use a problem-solving model to solve this problem.

 Analyze

Read the problem. ⟨Circle⟩ the information you know.
Underline what the problem is asking you to find.

2 Plan

What will you need to do to solve the problem? Write your plan in steps.

Step 1   Write an _____ to represent the situation.

Step 2   Solve the inequality and compare _____.

Read to Succeed! 👀

Determine the appropriate inequality symbol to use. He cannot exceed 10 hours, which means he can watch less than or equal to 10 hours of television.

3 Solve

Use your plan to solve the problem. Show your steps.

Write an inequality to represent the situation where *x* is the amount of time he can watch television on the other five days in the week.

$2\frac{1}{2} + 5x \le 10$ $x \le$ _____

The graph that represents the solution set for the inequality is ____.

The correct answer is ____. Fill in that answer choice.

 Justify and Evaluate

How do you know your solution is accurate?

_____

_____

_____

Lesson 8   *(continued)*

Use a problem-solving model to solve each problem.

1 Peta has studied $2\frac{1}{2}$ hours for a test and plans to continue studying at the rate of $\frac{3}{4}$ hour per day. She writes an inequality to determine how many more days she needs to study to meet her goal of at least 7 hours total. Which number line represents the solution set of the inequality? **7.EE.4b, MP 4**

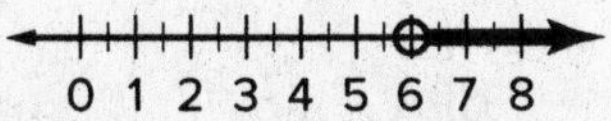

Ⓐ
 0 1 2 3 4 5 6 7 8

Ⓑ
 0 1 2 3 4 5 6 7 8

Ⓒ
 0 1 2 3 4 5 6 7 8

Ⓓ
 0 1 2 3 4 5 6 7 8

2 Jala wrote and correctly solved the two inequalities shown below and then compared their solution sets. What whole number is a solution in both inequalities? **7.EE.4b, MP 6**

Jala's Inequalities

$$\frac{1}{2}a + 5 \le 6\frac{1}{2}$$

$$3b - 2 > 4$$

_____

3 Reggie solved the inequality $1.2x + 4 \le 10$. Faith solved the inequality $5x - 3 \ge 14$. What is the difference between the greatest value of x in Reggie's solution and the least value of x in Faith's solution? **7.EE.4b, MP 6**

_____

4 👍**H.O.T. Problem** Stephanie is solving $-11 < 3x - 3.5$ and $3x - 3.5 \le 14.5$. Help her solve each inequality and graph the solution sets. Then write the complete whole-number solution set. **7.EE.4b, MP 6**

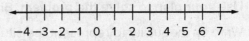
 −4 −3 −2 −1 0 1 2 3 4 5 6 7

_____

Lesson 1 Multi-Step Problem Solving

Chapter 7

Multi-Step Example

The value of the variable in the angle measure in the circle is also equal to the radius r of the circle. If a circle's diameter is twice its radius, what is the diameter of the circle? **7.G.5, MP 4**

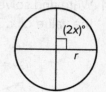

Ⓐ 22.5 units

Ⓑ 45 units

Ⓒ 90 units

Ⓓ 112.5 units

Use a problem-solving model to solve this problem.

 Analyze

Read the problem. Circle the information you know.
Underline what the problem is asking you to find.

 Plan

What will you need to do to solve the problem? Write your plan in steps.

Step 1   Determine the value of ____ by solving an equation.

Step 2   Determine the _____ of the circle.

 Solve

Use your plan to solve the problem. Show your steps.

Write and solve an equation.

$2x = 90$ $\dfrac{2x}{2} = \dfrac{90}{2}$ $x =$ _____

$d = 2r$ $d =$ _____

The diameter of the circle is _____ units.

So, the correct answer is ____. Fill in that answer choice.

> **Read to Succeed!**
>
> The angle symbol in the circle represents a right angle. All right angles measure 90°. Use this to solve the equation.

 Justify and Evaluate

How do you know your solution is accurate?

_____

_____

_____

Lesson 1 (continued)

Use a problem-solving model to solve each problem.

1 Write and solve an equation to determine the value of *x*. **7.G.5, MP 4**

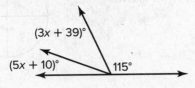

(3x + 39)°
(5x + 10)° 115°

Ⓐ 2

Ⓑ 7

Ⓒ 21

Ⓓ 34

2 The time shown on a clock is 6:00 P.M. The seconds hand is at 11 seconds. The angles formed between the seconds hand and the hour and minute hands are adjacent angles. At what time will those adjacent angles be equal? **7.G.5, MP 1**

_____

_____

3 A class of students was asked for their favorite color. The circle graph shows the results. The sum of the vertical angles for yellow and red in the circle graph is 40° and represents $\frac{1}{9}$ of the students. There are 360° in a circle and 18 students in the class. How many students chose yellow? **7.G.5, MP 2**

Favorite Color

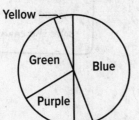

_____

4 ✋ **H.O.T. Problem** An obtuse angle is divided into a right angle and ∠A. If the measures of the angles are whole numbers, what are the possible measures of ∠A? **7.G.5, MP 3**

_____

_____

_____

_____

_____

Lesson 2   **Multi-Step** Problem Solving

Multi-Step Example

The angle shown represents a building support joist. Engineers determined that the measure of angle x needs to be about 7% less to be more supportive. What is the measure of the new angle rounded to the nearest tenth? **7.G.5, MP 1**

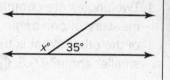

Ⓐ 134.9°   Ⓒ 155.2°

Ⓑ 145°   Ⓓ 165.9°

Use a problem-solving model to solve this problem.

 Analyze

Read the problem. Ⓒircle the information you know.
Underline what the problem is asking you to find.

2 Plan

What will you need to do to solve the problem? Write your plan in steps.

Step 1   Determine the value of ____ by solving an equation.

Step 2   Determine ____ of the measure of angle x.

3 Solve

Use your plan to solve the problem. Show your steps.

Write and solve an equation.

$35 + x = 180$ $x =$ _____

Determine 7% of the measure of angle x.

_____ × 0.07 = _____

_____ − _____ = _____

The measure of the new angle is _____ degrees.

So, the correct answer is ____. Fill in that answer choice.

> **Read to Succeed!** 👀
>
> The angles shown above form a supplementary angle. The sum of their measures is 180°.

 Justify and Evaluate

How do you know your solution is accurate?

_____

_____

_____

Lesson 2 (continued)

Use a problem-solving model to solve each problem.

1 Two angles are complementary. The measure of one angle is 25% the measure of the other. What is the measure of the smaller angle? **7.G.5, MP 2**

- Ⓐ 4.5°
- Ⓑ 18°
- Ⓒ 36°
- Ⓓ 72°

2 The time on a clock is 10:00 A.M. The second hand creates a supplementary angle to the angle formed by the hour and minute hands on a clock. What time, in seconds, does the second hand point to? **7.G.5, MP 1**

_____

3 What is the measure, in degrees, of the angle x that is complementary to the angle with a measure (160y)°? **7.G.5, MP 1**

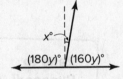

$(180y)°$ $(160y)°$

_____

4 🔥 **H.O.T. Problem** Two lines intersect to form vertical angles that are supplementary. What do you know about the measures of the four angles formed by the lines? **7.G.5, MP 4**

_____

_____

NAME_____ DATE _____ PERIOD _____

Lesson 3   **Multi-Step** Problem Solving

Multi-Step Example

Amie drew an acute triangle as shown. If she moves point C to (0, −3), what are the new measures of angle A and angle C? **7.G.2,** **MP** 4

Ⓐ 25°   Ⓒ 55°

Ⓑ 35°   Ⓓ 90°

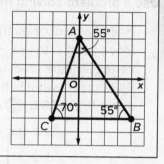

Use a problem-solving model to solve this problem.

1 Analyze

Read the problem. Circle the information you know.
Underline what the problem is asking you to find.

2 Plan

What will you need to do to solve the problem? Write your plan in steps.

Step 1   Determine the _____ of angle C after moving it.

Step 2   Determine the _____ of new angle A.

3 Solve

Use your plan to solve the problem. Show your steps.

If you move point C to _____, it will form a _____ triangle.

The new measure of angle C is _____ because side AC is now

_____ to side CB.

The new measure of angle A is _____ − 90° + _____ = _____

So, the correct answer is ____. Fill in that answer choice.

> **Read to Succeed!**
> Point C is located at (−2, −3). To move it to (0, −3), move two units to the right.

4 Justify and Evaluate

How do you know your solution is accurate?

_____

_____

_____

Copyright © McGraw-Hill Education. Permission is granted to reproduce for classroom use.

Course 2 · Chapter 7 Geometric Figures   **97**

NAME _________________________ DATE _______________ PERIOD _______

Lesson 3 *(continued)*

Use a problem-solving model to solve each problem.

1 Half of an isosceles triangle is shown below. Move point *C* to (−1, −3) and label the new vertex *D*. If the measure of angle *ADB* is 54 degrees, what is the measure of angle *DAB*? **7.G.5, MP 4**

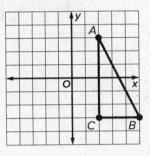

Ⓐ 36°

Ⓑ 54°

Ⓒ 63°

Ⓓ 72°

2 What is the value of *x* in the triangle shown? **7.G.5, MP 2**

____

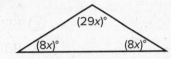

3 What is the measure of the smallest angle in the largest triangle in the figure shown? **7.G.5, MP 2**

____

4 **H.O.T. Problem** What is the measure of ∠*A*? **7.G.5, MP 2**

____

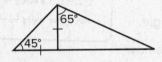

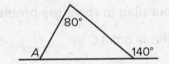

Lesson 4 **Multi-Step** Problem Solving

Multi-Step Example

William is building a storage shed. The blueprint shown uses a scale of 1 inch = 3 feet. How many square feet of storage room will William have? **7.G.1, MP 4**

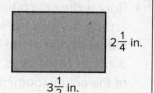

$2\frac{1}{4}$ in.

$3\frac{1}{2}$ in.

Ⓐ $23\frac{5}{8}$ ft²　　　Ⓒ $65\frac{7}{8}$ ft²

Ⓑ $55\frac{1}{8}$ ft²　　　Ⓓ $70\frac{7}{8}$ ft²

Use a problem-solving model to solve this problem.

 Analyze

Read the problem. Circle the information you know.
Underline what the problem is asking you to find.

Plan

What will you need to do to solve the problem? Write your plan in steps.

Step 1　Use the _____ to determine the actual dimensions of the storage shed.

Step 2　Multiply the length by the width to determine the _____.

 Solve

Use your plan to solve the problem. Show your steps.

$\frac{1\text{ in.}}{3\text{ ft}} = \frac{3\frac{1}{2}\text{ in.}}{\ell\text{ ft}}$　$\ell =$ _____　　　$\frac{1\text{ in.}}{3\text{ ft}} = \frac{2\frac{1}{4}\text{ in.}}{w\text{ ft}}$　$w =$ _____

Determine the area.

_____ × _____ = _____

The area of William's storage shed is _____ square feet.

So, the correct answer is ____. Fill in that answer choice.

Read to Succeed!

Make sure you use the scale factor to determine the dimensions of the shed before calculating the area.

 Justify and Evaluate

How do you know your solution is accurate?

_____

_____

_____

Lesson 4   (continued)

Use a problem-solving model to solve each problem.

1 Cory is drawing a housing plan for his architecture class. He is making a scale model of one of the bedrooms. If the scale is 3 inches represents 1 foot, what is the area of the actual room? **7.G.1, MP 4**

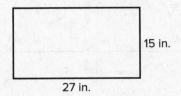

15 in.

27 in.

Ⓐ 45 square feet

Ⓑ 48 square feet

Ⓒ 54 square feet

Ⓓ 63 square feet

2 Shantel wants to know the area of the gymnasium floor at her school. She found a scale drawing that shows the square gym measured $4\frac{1}{2}$ inches long. If the scale is 1 inch = 5 feet, what is the actual area of the gym in square feet? **7.G.1, MP 4**

3 Elisha was born in Aruba but now lives in the U.S. She wants to determine the length of the island of Aruba. Using the scale map below, determine the length of Aruba in yards, from Cudarebe to Ceru Colorado. **7.G.1, MP 4**

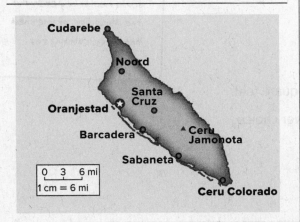

4 🖐 **H.O.T. Problem** Tevon plans to tile a friend's kitchen. On a scale drawing, the rectangular kitchen is 6 inches by 8 inches. The scale shows that 1 inch equal $1\frac{1}{2}$ feet. Use this information to determine how much it would cost to use Travertine, in dollars. **7.G.1, MP 4**

Tile Style	Cost per Square feet ($)
Cermaic	6.50
Marble	8.00
Travertine	9.75

Lesson 5 **Multi-Step** Problem Solving

> **Multi-Step Example**
>
> Armando is making a barbeque using cube-shaped bricks that measure 6 inches per side. The diagram shows top, side, and front views of the bricks he has stacked so far. He needs to save some money to purchase the rest of the bricks. If the bricks cost $2.50 each and Armando needs a total of 40 bricks, how much money does he need to save? *Preparation for* **7.G.3,** **2**
>
>
> Top   Side   Front 
>
> Ⓐ $25   Ⓒ $75
>
> Ⓑ $55   Ⓓ $100

Use a problem-solving model to solve this problem.

 Analyze

**Read the problem. Circle the information you know.
Underline what the problem is asking you to find.**

2 Plan

What will you need to do to solve the problem? Write your plan in steps.

Step 1 Determine the number of bricks Armando has _____ stacked.

Step 2 Determine the number of bricks he _____. Then _____ to find the cost of those bricks.

 Solve

Use your plan to solve the problem. Show your steps.

Use the top, side, and front views to draw a _____ view of the stacked bricks. The top layer has _____ bricks, the middle layer has _____ bricks, and the bottom layer has _____ bricks, so Armando has already stacked _____ bricks.

$40 - 10 =$ _____ bricks needed. $2.5 \times 30 =$ _____

Armando needs to save $75, so, _____ is the correct answer. Fill in that answer choice.

> **Read to Succeed!**
>
>
>
> Sometimes a problem contains extra information. The dimensions of the bricks are not needed to answer the question.

4 Justify and Evaluate

How do you know your solution is accurate?

_____

_____

_____

_____

Lesson 5 (continued)

Use a problem-solving model to solve each problem.

1 Maka has been asked to design a sculpture to be placed in the center of an open courtyard, allowing visitors to walk around all sides of the sculpture. Below is a sketch of the sculpture she will build. On the actual sculpture, if Maka paints every side of one cube, she will use 4.5 pints of paint per cube. However, she plans to paint only the sides that are visible. Which expression, when simplified, will show the amount of paint Maka will use?
Preparation for **7.G.3,** **2**

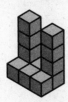

Ⓐ (23)(4.5)   Ⓒ (40)(4.5)

Ⓑ (23)(0.75)   Ⓓ (40)(0.75)

2 The figure below shows a three-dimensional view of a building. Sketch and label front, top, and side views of the building. Then use the appropriate sketch to find the perimeter of the building in feet.
Preparation for **7.G.3,** **2**

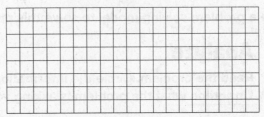

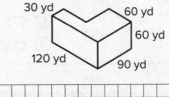

3 Each cube on the figure shown measures 2 centimeters per side. Darnell divides the figure into two congruent parts, as indicated by the arrows. Write and simplify an expression that gives the area of one of the new faces formed when the two congruent parts are separated.
Preparation for **7.G.3,** **4**

4 🔥 **H.O.T. Problem** Kang and Ileana viewed the three drawings shown. Kang says the front, top, and side views are the same. Ileana says that only the top and side views are the same. Are either of them correct? Support your answer.
Preparation for **7.G.3,** **3**

Figure A   Figure B   Figure C

Lesson 6   **Multi-Step** Problem Solving

Multi-Step Example

The figure shown has a rectangular base and top, and the lengths of its sides are congruent. Draw a horizontal cross section on the figure. Describe the shape of the cross section. Then write two inequalities that compare the cross section's perimeter p to the perimeters of the base and the top. **7.G.3, MP 4**

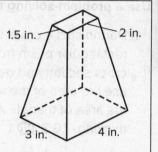

Use a problem-solving model to solve this problem.

1 Analyze

Read the problem. Circle the information you know.
Underline what the problem is asking you to find.

2 Plan

What will you need to do to solve the problem? Write your plan in steps.

Step 1   Draw and name the cross section.

Step 2   Find the _____ of the base and the top of the given figure.

Step 3   Write two _____ statements to compare the perimeters.

> **Read to Succeed!**
> The sides of a horizontal cross section will be parallel to the sides of the base and top.

3 Solve

Use your plan to solve the problem. Show your steps.

The cross section is a(n) _____.

The perimeter of the base is 2(____ + ____) = ____ inches.

The perimeter of the top is 2(____ + ____) = ____ inches.

So, _____

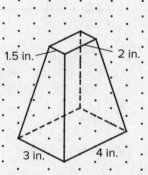

4 Justify and Evaluate

How do you know your solution is accurate?

_____

_____

_____

_____

Lesson 6 *(continued)*

Use a problem-solving model to solve each problem.

1 Dartrin cuts a cross section through the rectangular prism from *AB* to *DC*. Shade the cross section and describe its shape. Then use the area of the resulting shape to find the area of triangle *ADC*. Describe your thinking. **7.G.3, MP 1**

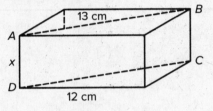

Perimeter of front face = 34 cm

_____

_____

_____

2 Describe the shape resulting from a vertical, horizontal, and angled cross section of a cone. **7.G.3, MP 4**

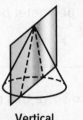

Vertical   Horizontal   Angled

_____

_____

_____

3 The perimeter of a vertical cross section of a box is 20 inches. If the length of the box is 1.5 times its width, what are the dimensions of the cross section? **7.G.3, MP 2**

_____

4 🔥 **H.O.T. Problem** Lorri says that it is not possible to cut an angled slice on this cube that forms an equilateral triangle. Is she correct? If not, provide a counterexample to support your opinion. **7.G.3, MP 3**

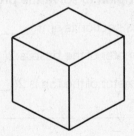

_____

Lesson 1 **Multi-Step** Problem Solving

Multi-Step Example

Kama uses landscape edging to border his circular garden.
The diagram at the right represents Kama's garden. His neighbor
has a garden that has a diameter that is 24 inches larger. How much
landscape edging does his neighbor need to border their garden?
Use 3.14 for π. Round to the nearest tenth. **7.G.4,** **MP** 4

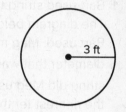

(A) 15.7 feet   (C) 26 feet

(B) 25.1 feet   (D) 31.4 feet

Use a problem-solving model to solve this problem.

1 Analyze

Read the problem. (Circle) the information you know.
Underline what the problem is asking you to find.

2 Plan

What will you need to do to solve the problem? Write your plan in steps.

| Step 1 | Determine the _____ of his neighbor's garden. |
| Step 2 | Determine the _____ of his neighbor's garden. |

3 Solve

Use your plan to solve the problem. Show your steps.

Ramon's garden has a diameter of 6 feet. So, his neighbor's

garden is 24 inches or _____ feet greater.

6 + _____ = _____

Determine the circumference.

3.14 × 8 ≈ _____

Ramon's neighbor will need _____ feet of landscaping border.

So, the correct answer is _____. Fill in that answer choice.

Read to Succeed!

The diameter of his neighbor's garden is 24 inches larger. Make sure you add this distance to Ramon's diameter, not the radius.

4 Justify and Evaluate

How do you know your solution is accurate?

_____

_____

_____

Lesson 1 (continued)

Use a problem-solving model to solve each problem.

1 Bart used string to make this necklace. The diagram below represents the string Bart used. Meg made a necklace with a diameter that was $\frac{1}{2}$ foot longer. How much string did Meg use? Use 3.14 for π. Round to the nearest tenth. **7.G.4, MP 4**

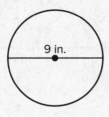

9 in.

Ⓐ 28.3 inches

Ⓑ 29.8 inches

Ⓒ 40.8 inches

Ⓓ 47.1 inches

2 Diego ran around this track one and one-half times. Then he ran 50 more feet. How far did Diego run? Use 3.14 for π. Round to the nearest tenth. **7.G.4, MP 2**

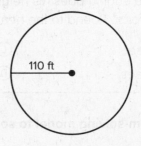

110 ft

_____

3 The radii for a penny and a nickel are shown. What is the difference in circumferences, in millimeters? Use 3.14 for π. Round to the nearest hundredth. **7.G.4, MP 4**

9.525 mm   10.605 mm

_____

4 👍 **H.O.T. Problem** If the radius of a circle is tripled, what would happen to its circumference? Explain and give an example. **7.G.4, MP 6**

_____

_____

_____

_____

_____

_____

Lesson 2   Multi-Step Problem Solving

Multi-Step Example

Julian and Ava are raking the leaves around a tree in their backyard. The tree is 2 feet in diameter and is surrounded by a circle of leaves that is 24 feet in diameter. What is the area in square feet of the ground covered by leaves? Use 3.14 for π. **7.G.4, MP 4**

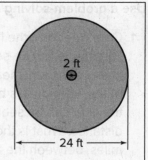

2 ft

24 ft

Use a problem-solving model to solve this problem.

 Analyze

Read the problem. Circle the information you know.
Underline what the problem is asking you to find.

Plan

What will you need to do to solve the problem? Write your plan in steps.

Step 1   Determine the _____ of both circles.

Step 2   Subtract the area of the _____ from
the area of the _____.

Read to Succeed!

Determine the area of the larger circle. Then subtract the area of the trunk of the tree to determine the area where they will rake.

Solve

Use your plan to solve the problem. Show your steps.

Write and solve equations to determine both areas.

$A = \pi r^2$ $\qquad$ $A = \pi(1^2)$ $\qquad$ $A \approx$ _____

$A = \pi r^2$ $\qquad$ $A = \pi(12^2)$ $\qquad$ $A \approx$ _____

_____ − _____ = _____ $\qquad$ Subtract.

The area of the ground covered by leaves is about _____ square feet.

Justify and Evaluate

How do you know your solution is accurate?

_____

_____

_____

Lesson 2 *(continued)*

Use a problem-solving model to solve each problem.

1 On a clear day, the light from a certain lighthouse can be seen from 10 miles away in any direction, measured from the center of the lighthouse's base. On a cloudy day, the light can be seen from only half the distance. What is the difference, in square miles, between the area that the light is visible on a clear day and on a cloudy day? Use 3.14 for π. **7.G.4, MP 2**

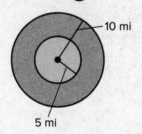

2 Two semicircles are drawn in a rectangle as shown.

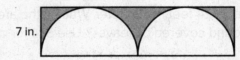

Determine the area of the shaded region in the figure shown. Use $\frac{22}{7}$ for π. **7.G.4, MP 1**

_____

3 Carter has 88 feet of fencing to make a dog pen in his yard. He is trying to decide whether to make the pen circular or square. Assuming he uses all of the fencing, what is the difference between the area of the circular pen and the square pen? Use $\frac{22}{7}$ for π. **7.G.4, MP 1**

_____

4 🔥 **H.O.T. Problem** Brian is performing in a play at the community theater. The theater is round with a seating area around a circular stage as shown below. One quarter of the seating area is taken up by the orchestra and the rest is for audience seating. What is the area of the audience seating? Use 3.14 for π. Explain your method. **7.G.4, MP 1**

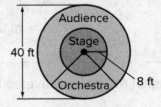

_____

_____

_____

_____

_____

Lesson 3 **Multi-Step** Problem Solving

Multi-Step Example

Erin is putting wallpaper on her bedroom wall shown at the right. Determine the area of wallpaper needed for the wall shown. **7.G.6, MP 1**

Ⓐ 63 square feet   Ⓒ 84 square feet

Ⓑ 75 square feet   Ⓓ 96 square feet

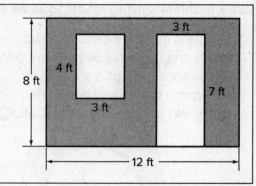

Use a problem-solving model to solve this problem.

Analyze

**Read the problem. Circle the information you know.
Underline what the problem is asking you to find.**

Plan

What will you need to do to solve the problem? Write your plan in steps.

Step 1 | Determine the _____ of the entire larger rectangle.

Step 2 | Subtract _____ of the two smaller rectangles.

Solve

Use your plan to solve the problem. Show your steps.

The area of the entire wall is 12 × 8 or ____ square feet.

The area of the window is 3 × 4 or ____ square feet.

The area of the door is 3 × 7 or ____ square feet.

Subtract the window and door area from the wall area.

____ − ____ − ____ = ____

The area of the wall that will need wallpaper is ____ square feet.

So, the correct answer is ____. Fill in that answer choice.

> **Read to Succeed!**
>
> Erin will not put wallpaper over the window or doorway. You will need to subtract those areas from the area of the wall.

4 Justify and Evaluate

How do you know your solution is accurate?

_____

_____

_____

Lesson 3 (continued)

Use a problem-solving model to solve each problem.

1 Juliana is making a cartoon about space travel, and drew this design for the Moon and sky as seen through a spaceship's window. Determine the area of the shaded region of her design. Use 3.14 for π. **7.G.6,** **MP** **4**

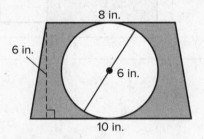

8 in.

6 in.

6 in.

10 in.

Ⓐ 39.87 square inches

Ⓑ 31.74 square inches

Ⓒ 28.26 square inches

Ⓓ 25.74 square inches

2 The figure shows the dimensions of a home plate for baseball, rounded to the nearest half-inch. If the plate is cut from a two-foot square piece of plastic, what is the area of the unused plastic? **7.G.6,** **MP** **1**

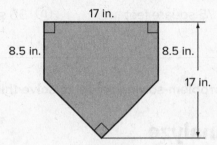

17 in.

8.5 in.   8.5 in.

17 in.

3 Felipe's backyard has a two-foot walkway with outside dimensions of 64 feet long and 36 feet wide. He wants to seed a lawn inside the area enclosed by the walkway. There is a pool, with dimensions shown, at one end of the yard. What is the total area in square feet of the lawn Felipe will plant? Use 3.14 for π. **7.G.6,** **MP** **1**

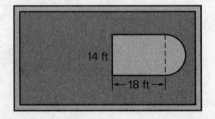

14 ft

18 ft

4 🔥 **H.O.T. Problem** The floor plan shows Carmen's studio apartment. She is installing new carpeting, which will cover the entire area except a triangular entertainment center, a closet, and a 10-foot wall with kitchen appliances as shown in the sketch. How many square feet of carpet will Carmen need? Show your calculations. **7.G.6,** **MP** **2**

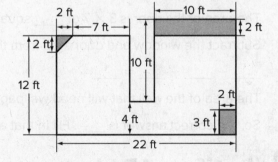

2 ft

7 ft   10 ft

2 ft

2 ft

10 ft

12 ft

2 ft

4 ft   3 ft

22 ft

Lesson 4   Multi-Step Problem Solving

Multi-Step Example

A drink cooler is in the shape of a rectangular prism. How many liters of lemonade will it hold if half of the volume is taken up by ice? (*Hint*: 1 L = 1,000 cm³) **7.G.6, MP 2**

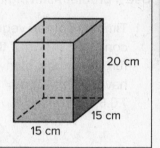

20 cm
15 cm
15 cm

Ⓐ 1.65 L   Ⓒ 4.5 L

Ⓑ 2.25 L   Ⓓ 9 L

Use a problem-solving model to solve this problem.

 Analyze

Read the problem. Circle the information you know.
Underline what the problem is asking you to find.

 Plan

What will you need to do to solve the problem? Write your plan in steps.

Step 1   Determine the _____ of the rectangular prism.

Step 2   Determine half of the volume, then _____ to liters.

Solve

Use your plan to solve the problem. Show your steps.

The volume of the cooler is 15 × 15 × 20 or

_____ cubic centimeters.

Half of the volume is _____ ÷ 2, or _____ cubic centimeters.

Convert cubic centimeters to liters.

_____ ÷ 1,000 = _____

The cooler will hold _____ liters of lemonade.

So, the correct answer is _____. Fill in that answer choice.

> **Read to Succeed!**
> To convert cubic centimeters to liters, you will need to divide the volume in cubic centimeters by 1,000.

 Justify and Evaluate

How do you know your solution is accurate?

_____

_____

_____

Lesson 4 *(continued)*

Use a problem-solving model to solve each problem.

1 Timothy poured vegetable broth into the container shown. If the container is now 75% full, about how many cups of broth did he have? (*Hint*: 1 cup ≈ 14.4 cubic inches) **7.G.6, MP 1**

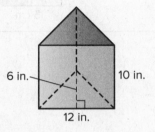

6 in.   10 in.

12 in.

Ⓐ 12.5 cups

Ⓑ 15.25 cups

Ⓒ 18.75 cups

Ⓓ 25 cups

2 Thema has a raised garden bed in her backyard that is a rectangular prism with dimensions 6 feet by 3 feet by $\frac{2}{3}$ feet. How many bags of soil should Thema buy to fill the bed if each bag holds 960 cubic inches of soil? **7.G.6, MP 2**

_____

3 The base of a triangular prism has dimensions with a base of 3 meters and a height of 2.5 meters. If the volume of the triangular prism is 5.625 cubic meters, what is the height of the triangular prism? **7.G.6, MP 1**

_____

4 🖐 **H.O.T. Problem** Compare the volume of the two triangular prisms shown. What do you notice? Explain. **7.G.6, MP 6**

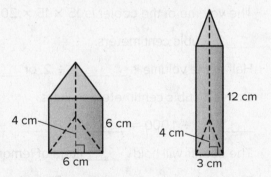

4 cm   6 cm

6 cm

12 cm

4 cm

3 cm

_____

_____

_____

_____

_____

Lesson 5 **Multi-Step** Problem Solving

Multi-Step Example

Yukiko has 10,000 cubic centimeters of sand. She pours it into the pyramid shown. What fraction of the pyramid can she fill with sand?

7.G.6, 4

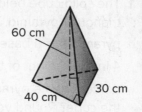

60 cm
30 cm
40 cm

Ⓐ $\frac{1}{2}$

Ⓒ $\frac{3}{4}$

Ⓑ $\frac{5}{9}$

Ⓓ $\frac{5}{6}$

Use a problem-solving model to solve this problem.

⓵ Analyze

Read the problem. Ⓒircle the information you know.
Underline what the problem is asking you to find.

② Plan

What will you need to do to solve the problem? Write your plan in steps.

Step 1 Determine the _____ of the triangular pyramid.

Step 2 Determine the _____ of the pyramid that is filled.

Read to Succeed!

The pyramid shown is a triangular pyramid. Use the formula for the triangle with determining the base B.

③ Solve

Use your plan to solve the problem. Show your steps.

Determine the volume.

$V = \frac{1}{3}Bh$ $V = \frac{1}{3}\left(\frac{1}{2} \cdot 40 \cdot 30\right) \cdot 60$ $V = _____$ cm³

Write the volume of sand Yukiko has over the volume of the pyramid.

_____ or _____

The pyramid will be _____ full.

So, the correct answer is __. Fill in that answer choice.

④ Justify and Evaluate

How do you know your solution is accurate?

_____

_____

Lesson 5 *(continued)*

Use a problem-solving model to solve each problem.

1 The solid cube below fits inside a hollow triangular pyramid. The triangular base of the pyramid has a base of $7\frac{1}{2}$ in. and a height of 4 in. The height of the pyramid is 5 in. What percent of the pyramid's volume is filled by the cube? Round your answer to the nearest thousandth, if necessary. **7.G.6, MP 2**

2 in.

Ⓐ 5%

Ⓑ 16.7%

Ⓒ 25%

Ⓓ 32%

2 A square pyramid trophy is being shipped in a rectangular prism shaped package. The square pyramid has a base edge of 6 inches and height of 8 inches. What is the minimum volume that the package must be in order for the trophy to fit inside? **7.G.6, MP 1**

_____

3 The rectangular pyramid block shown was cut in half. What is the volume of each half of the pyramid block? **7.G.6, MP 4**

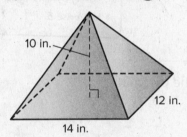

10 in.

12 in.

14 in.

_____

4 ✋ **H.O.T. Problem** A triangular pyramid is placed on top of a triangular prism with a congruent base. If the volumes are equal, and the height of the prism is 1 unit, what is the total height of the both figures? Explain. **7.G.6, MP 6**

_____

_____

_____

_____

_____

_____

Lesson 6 **Multi-Step** Problem Solving

Multi-Step Example

The drawings show two views of a house a builder is covering with vinyl siding. The builder will subtract 160 square feet for windows and doors and then cover the remaining parts of the walls with vinyl siding that costs $200 per square. What is the minimum amount the builder can spend on siding?
(*Hint*: 1 square = 100 ft^2). **7.G.6,** 1

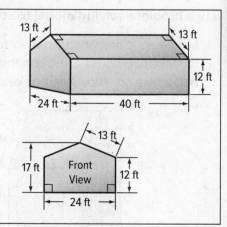

- Ⓐ $3,632
- Ⓒ $3,072
- Ⓑ $3,312
- Ⓓ $3,000

Use a problem-solving model to solve this problem.

Analyze

Read the problem. Circle **the information you know.**
Underline **what the problem is asking you to find.**

2 Plan

What will you need to do to solve the problem? Write your plan in steps.

Step 1   Determine the _____ of the house to be covered.

Step 2   Determine the _____ of _____ needed.

Read to Succeed!
Don't forget to subtract the area of the windows and doors when calculating the area of the walls to be covered by siding.

3 Solve

Use your plan to solve the problem. Show your steps.

The area of the house consists of four _____ and two _____,

less ____ square feet for windows and doors.

The area is _____ + _____ − _____ or _____ square feet.

Each square of siding covers _____ square feet. The builder needs to order

_____ squares. The cost of the siding will be _____(_____) or _____.

So, the correct answer is ____.

4 Justify and Evaluate

How do you know your solution is accurate?

_____

_____

Lesson 6 *(continued)*

Use a problem-solving model to solve each problem.

1 Mrs. Reno is preparing a project for 22 students to make bird houses. The dimensions of the bird house are shown in the sketch.

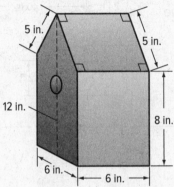

If wood costs $1 for 3 square feet, what is the cost of the wood needed for the project? **7.G.6, MP 2**

Ⓐ $16   Ⓒ $104

Ⓑ $48   Ⓓ $191

2 Refer to the problem on the previous page. The builder will cover the roof with shingles that cost $30 per bundle. Three bundles of shingles cover 100 square feet. How much will the builder spend on shingles? **7.G.6, MP 1**

_____

_____

_____

3 Kareem plans to make a tent in the shape of a triangular prism, as shown. He will use nylon fabric for the walls and floor of the tent. When ordering the fabric, Kareem ordered an extra 10%. If the fabric costs $0.50 per square foot, how much will the fabric cost to the nearest dollar? **7.G.6, MP 2**

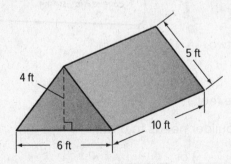

_____

4 🔥 **H.O.T. Problem** Sarah is a packaging technology student at a community college. Her teacher writes the following assignment on the board:

> Assignment: Design a rectangular box with all whole number dimensions that has a volume of 60 cubic inches and has the least possible surface area.

What is the surface area of the box that meets the requirements? Explain. **7.G.6, MP 6**

_____

_____

_____

_____

_____

_____

_____

Lesson 7 **Multi-Step** Problem Solving

Multi-Step Example

A team of students will make a square pyramid, for the set for the school play. They will paint every surface, and then paste glitter on the lateral surfaces. One gallon of paint costs $62 and will cover about 75 square feet. A $\frac{1}{4}$ –pound bag of glitter costs $5 and will cover about 38 square feet. About how much will it cost to paint and glitter the pyramid? **7.G.6,** 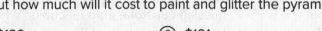 **4**

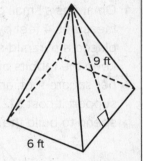
9 ft
6 ft

Ⓐ $139

Ⓒ $191

Ⓑ $144

Ⓓ $195

Use a problem-solving model to solve this problem.

1 Analyze

Read the problem. Ⓒircle the information you know.
Underline what the problem is asking you to find.

2 Plan

What will you need to do to solve the problem? Write your plan in steps.

Step 1   Find the surface area that will be _____ and its cost.

Step 2   Find the surface area that will be _____ and its cost.

Step 3   Find the total cost.

3 Solve

Use your plan to solve the problem. Show your steps.

Glittered area: *L.A.* = $\frac{1}{2}P\ell$ = $\frac{1}{2}$(____)(____) = ____ ft^2

108 ft^2 ÷ ____ ft^2 per bag ≈ ____ bags

(____)($____) = ($____) cost of glitter

Painted area: *L.A.* + *B* = 108 + ____ = ____ ft^2

144 ft^2 ÷ ____ ft^2 per can ≈ ____ cans   (____)($____) = $____ cost of paint

Total cost: $____, so, ____ is the correct answer. Fill in that answer choice.

> **Read to Succeed!**
> They will paint the entire pyramid but will put glitter on the sides only. Use different areas to find the cost of the paint and the glitter.

4 Justify and Evaluate

How do you know your solution is accurate?

_____

_____

Lesson 7   *(continued)*

Use a problem-solving model to solve each problem.

1 Omar has a small garden for lettuce that measures 4 feet by 4 feet, as shown. He placed a pyramid-shaped net tent over it to keep the rabbits out. The netting cost $1.40 per square foot, and the framework to support it cost $12. How much did Omar spend to build the net tent? **7.G.6, MP 4**

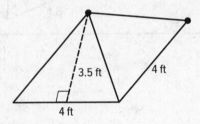

3.5 ft   4 ft

4 ft

Ⓐ $32.80

Ⓑ $39.20

Ⓒ $51.20

Ⓓ $73.60

2 The Great Pyramid in Egypt was built using a measure called a *royal cubit*, which is about 1.7 feet. Its apex, or capstone, is missing so it does not come to a point. The diagram shows some suggested dimensions of the missing capstone in royal cubits. What is the lateral surface area of the missing capstone in square feet? Round to the nearest tenth. **7.G.6, MP 1**

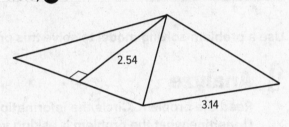

2.54

3.14

_____

3 A garden ornament is shaped like a rectangular pyramid with a base that measures 17.9 centimeters by 16.2 centimeters. Its slant height is 15 centimeters. Ama orders 24 of the ornaments and plans to completely cover $\frac{2}{3}$ of them with a waterproof covering. She should buy enough spray to cover how many square meters? Round to the nearest tenth. **7.G.6, MP 4**

_____

_____

4 ✋**H.O.T. Problem** Suppose you have a regular triangular pyramid with base sides of 2 units and a slant height of 1.5 units. Without using the formula $L.A. = \frac{1}{2}P\ell$, describe another way to find the lateral surface area of the pyramid. Support your method by using the given dimensions, then check using the standard formula. **7.G.6, MP 3**

_____

_____

_____

_____

Lesson 8   Multi-Step Problem Solving

Multi-Step Example

The Garcia's built the garden shed shown. The frame and walls cost $368. Now they will paint it and shingle the roof. Mr. Garcia estimates that it will cost about $0.10 per square foot for the paint. A bundle of shingles costs $20 and covers about 32 square feet. What is the approximate total cost of the project? Round to the nearest ten dollars. **7.G.6,** 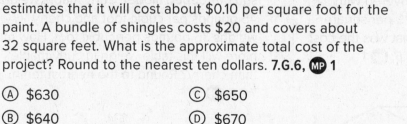 **1**

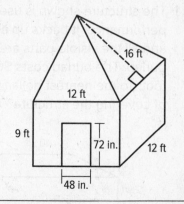

Ⓐ $630   Ⓒ $650

Ⓑ $640   Ⓓ $670

Use a problem-solving model to solve this problem.

Analyze

Read the problem. (Circle) the information you know. Underline what the problem is asking you to find.

Read to Succeed! 👀
Think of the shed as a composite figure. The top is a square pyramid and the bottom is a square prism.

2 Plan

What will you need to do to solve the problem? Write your plan in steps.

Step 1   Determine the total surface area of the _____ that will

be painted and the total surface area of the _____.

Step 2   Determine the total cost of the _____ and _____.

Solve

Use your plan to solve the problem. Show your steps.

The surface area of the sides is 4 × ____ square feet − ____ square feet = ____ square feet. The area of the roof is $\frac{1}{2}P\ell = \frac{1}{2} \times 48 \times 16 =$ ____ square feet.

The cost of the paint will be about $_____. He will need ____ bundles of shingles.

The total cost of the shed is $40.80 + $240 + $____ = $_____. So, ____ is the correct answer. Fill in that answer choice.

Justify and Evaluate

How do you know your solution is reasonable?

_____

_____

_____

Lesson 8 *(continued)*

Use a problem-solving model to solve each problem.

1 The structure shown is used in a performance. It backs up against a solid wall, and all the visible parts are covered with burlap. The burlap costs $0.29 per square foot. To the nearest dollar, what was the cost of covering the structure? **7.G.6, MP 1**

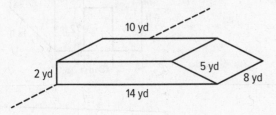

- Ⓐ $125
- Ⓑ $128
- Ⓒ $376
- Ⓓ $438

2 Pam makes tables from several types of wood. The diagram shows the design for a square-topped model. Curly maple weighs 45 pounds per cubic foot and cherry weighs 36 pounds per cubic foot. How much more will this table weigh in curly maple than cherry? Round to the nearest tenth. **7.G.6, MP 2**

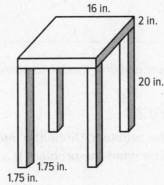

3 Steps are made up of a *tread* that you step on, and a *rise*, which is the height. On the steps shown, the depth of the tread is 14 inches and the rise is 5.5 inches. If the concrete used to make the steps cost $2.78 per cubic foot, what was the cost of the concrete for these steps to the nearest dollar? **7.G.6, MP 7**

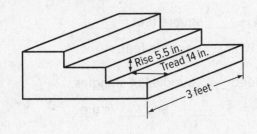

_____

4 🖐 **H.O.T. Problem** The diagram shows a composite solid figure. If each length is multiplied by 2, the volume of the figure is multiplied by what scale factor? Support your answer. **7.G.6, MP 5**

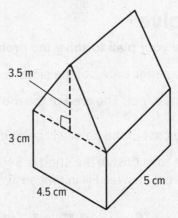

_____

_____

Lesson 1   **Multi-Step** Problem Solving

Multi-Step Example

The table shows Bobby's number of hits for his entire baseball season. How much greater is the probability that Bobby hit a single or double compared to a triple or homerun? **7.SP.7, MP 1**

Ⓐ $\frac{9}{25}$ Ⓒ $\frac{11}{25}$

Ⓑ $\frac{2}{5}$ Ⓓ $\frac{18}{25}$

Result	Number of Times
Singles	41
Doubles	13
Triples	14
Homeruns	7

Use a problem-solving model to solve this problem.

 Analyze

Read the problem. (Circle) the information you know.
Underline what the problem is asking you to find.

2 Plan

What will you need to do to solve the problem? Write your plan in steps.

Step 1   Determine the _____ of each event.

Step 2   Combine the probabilities, then determine the _____ .

3 Solve

Use your plan to solve the problem. Show your steps.

P(single or double) = _____ P(triple or homerun) = _____

Determine the difference between the probabilities.

____ − ____ = ____

The probability of Bobby hitting a single or double is ____ greater than hitting a triple or homerun.

So, the correct answer is ____. Fill in that answer choice.

Read to Succeed!

Add the number of favorable outcomes for each type of hit before expressing it as a fraction and determining the probability.

 Justify and Evaluate

How do you know your solution is accurate?

_____

_____

_____

Lesson 1 (continued)

Use a problem-solving model to solve each problem.

1 Suppose you spin the spinner one time. How much greater is the probability that the spinner will land on A compared to C or D? **7.SP.7, MP 1**

ⓐ 12.5%

ⓑ 25%

ⓒ 37.5%

ⓓ 50%

2 These six numbered squares are placed in a bag. If you randomly select one square from the bag, how much greater is the probability that you select an even number than an odd number? Express your answer as a fraction, percent, and decimal. **7.SP.7a, MP 2**

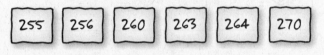

3 The bar graph shows the number of colored candies in a bag. Blaze's favorite colored candy is blue. If he chooses one candy from the bag without looking, how much greater is the probability that he will choose a green, yellow, or orange candy compared to a red or blue candy? Express your answer as a fraction, percent, and decimal. **7.SP.5, MP 2**

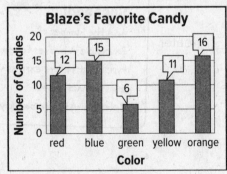

4 👍 **H.O.T. Problem** What is the probability that a randomly chosen number from 1 to 100 is *not a* multiple of 5? Express your answer as a fraction, percent, and decimal. **7.SP.5, MP 2**

_____

Lesson 2 **Multi-Step** Problem Solving

Multi-Step Example

Jarvis is playing a board game with his brother. The table shows the results of his number cube rolls throughout the game. If his next roll is an odd number, he will win the game. How much greater is the probability that he will win? **7.SP.7a, MP 2**

Number	Number of Occurrences
1	4
2	5
3	7
4	5
5	3
6	1

Ⓐ $\frac{11}{25}$ Ⓒ $\frac{1}{5}$

Ⓑ $\frac{2}{5}$ Ⓓ $\frac{3}{25}$

Use a problem-solving model to solve this problem.

Analyze

Read the problem. Circle the information you know.
Underline what the problem is asking you to find.

Plan

What will you need to do to solve the problem? Write your plan in steps.

Step 1   Determine the _____ of each event.

Step 2   Determine the _____ of the probabilities.

Solve

Use your plan to solve the problem. Show your steps.

$P(\text{odd}) =$ _____ $P(\text{even}) =$ _____

Determine the difference between the probabilities.

_____ – _____ = _____

The probability of Jarvis winning is _____ times greater than losing.

So, the correct answer is _____. Fill in that answer choice.

Read to Succeed!

You can use a tree diagram, list, or table to help determine the outcomes for this problem.

Justify and Evaluate

How do you know your solution is accurate?

_____

_____

_____

Lesson 2 *(continued)*

Use a problem-solving model to solve each problem.

1 Mary performed an experiment where she flipped three coins 20 times. The table shows her results. How much greater is the probability that the result will be at least two tails compared to at least two heads?
7.SP.7a, MP 2

Result	Number of Occurrences
3 heads	2
2 heads, 1 tail	6
1 head, 2 tails	11
3 tails	1

Ⓐ $\frac{4}{5}$ Ⓑ $\frac{7}{10}$ Ⓒ $\frac{2}{5}$ Ⓓ $\frac{1}{5}$

2 Yesterday, 75 orchard customers bought apples and 15 of those customers bought gala apples. If 300 customers buy apples tomorrow, predict the number of customers you would expect to buy gala apples.
7.SP.7, MP 7

_____

3 High school students were asked to report their favorite lunch combo option. The chart shows the survey results. Predict the number of students who will have to purchase a lunch combo for the school to sell 140 bowls of soup? **7.SP.7b, MP 2**

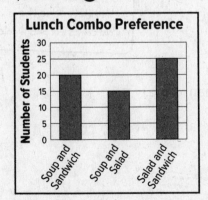

_____

4 🔥 **H.O.T. Problem** The probability of spinning red on a spinner is $\frac{1}{8}$, the probability of blue is $\frac{1}{2}$, and the probability of yellow is $\frac{1}{4}$. There are 3 sections that are green. What is the minimum number of total sections on the spinner? Explain.
7.SP.7b, MP 7

_____

_____

Lesson 3 Multi-Step Problem Solving

Multi-Step Example

Morgan rolls a number cube, twice. If the number 1 shows up at least once, Morgan wins. Otherwise, Jaclyn wins. How much greater is the probability that Morgan will win compared to Jaclyn winning? **7.SP.8b, MP 1**

(A) $\frac{1}{3}$ (B) $\frac{7}{18}$ (C) $\frac{4}{9}$ (D) $\frac{2}{3}$

Use a problem-solving model to solve this problem.

1 Analyze

Read the problem. Circle the information you know.
Underline what the problem is asking you to find.

2 Plan

What will you need to do to solve the problem? Write your plan in steps.

Step 1 Make a list to determine the _____.

Step 2 Determine the _____ for Morgan and Jaclyn. Then _____.

3 Solve

Use your plan to solve the problem. Show your steps.

Use a list.

_____

_____

Determine the probabilities and then subtract.

P(Morgan wins) = _____ P(Jaclyn wins) = _____

____ ____ _____

The probability of Jaclyn winning is _____ times greater than Morgan winning.

So, the correct answer is _____. Fill in that answer choice.

> **Read to Succeed!**
>
> A number cube has six sides that are numbered 1 through 6. Use this information to help make a list.

4 Justify and Evaluate

How do you know your solution is accurate?

_____

_____

_____

Lesson 3 (continued)

Use a problem-solving model to solve each problem.

1 Nicolás tosses a coin three times. If heads appears at least once, he wins. Otherwise, Manny wins. How much greater is the probability that Nicolás will win compared to Manny winning? **7.SP.8a,** **MP** **1**

Ⓐ $\frac{1}{8}$

Ⓑ $\frac{1}{2}$

Ⓒ $\frac{3}{4}$

Ⓓ $\frac{7}{8}$

2 The table shows the colors of socks, shoes, and belts that Landon owns. If he randomly selects a pair of socks, a pair of shoes, and a belt, what is the probability that the colors will all match? Write the probability as a decimal rounded to the nearest hundredth. **7.SP.8,** **MP** **2**

Socks	Shoes	Belt
Navy	Brown	Brown
Brown stripes	Black	Black leather
Black		Black nylon
Brown dots		
Tan		

_____

3 Jarek randomly selects a card from a pile of 3 unique cards, replaces it, and randomly selects again. What is the probability of selecting any card three times in a row? Write the probability as a percent, rounded to the nearest tenth. **7.SP.8a,** **MP** **1**

_____

4 🔥 **H.O.T. Problem** Dakotah was randomly assigned a computer password, where each number can be any digit 0 through 9, but digits will not repeat. The first three digits are shown. If he randomly guesses the last two digits, what is the probability he will guess correctly? Explain. **7.SP.8a,** **MP** **2**

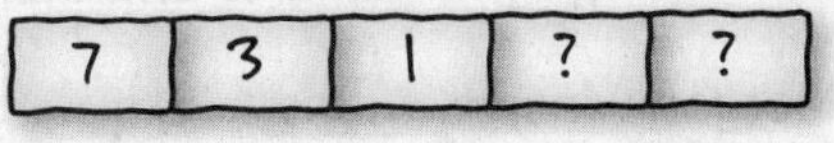

7	3	1	?	?

_____

_____

_____

_____

_____

_____

Lesson 4   **Multi-Step** Problem Solving

Multi-Step Example

Rico conducts a simulation. He spun a spinner with four equal sections labeled A, B, C, and D, twice. The letter D showed up five times, each resulted in a win for Rico. Natasha won all the other games. Based on the simulation, what percent more did Natasha win compared to Rico winning? Write your answer as a percent. 7.SP.8, **MP** 1

Use a problem-solving model to solve this problem.

1 Analyze

Read the problem. Circle the information you know.
Underline what the problem is asking you to find.

2 Plan

What will you need to do to solve the problem? Write your plan in steps.

Step 1   Determine the _____.

Step 2   Determine the _____ for

Rico and Natasha. Then _____.

Read to Succeed!

Use a list or tree diagram to help determine the total number of outcomes for the simulation.

3 Solve

Use your plan to solve the problem. Show your steps.

There are a total of _____ outcomes.

Determine the probabilities and then subtract.

P(Rico won) = _____ P(Natasha won) = _____

_____ _ _____ _____ which is equal to _____

Natasha won _____ more than Rico.

4 Justify and Evaluate

How do you know your solution is accurate?

_____

_____

_____

Lesson 4   (continued)

Use a problem-solving model to solve each problem.

1 Marlene conducts a simulation. She rolled a number cube, twice. The sum of 8 or greater showed up 21 times, each resulted in a win for her. Ashton won all the other games. Based on the simulation, what percent more did Marlene win compared to Ashton winning? Write your answer as a percent rounded to the nearest tenth. **7.SP.8, MP 1**

_____

2 There is a 25% chance of rain every day this week. Sandra set up a spinner to simulate the probability of rain. She spun the spinner below 7 times and her experimental probability was $\frac{2}{7}$. How much greater was the experimental probability compared to the theoretical probability? **7.SP.8, MP 2**

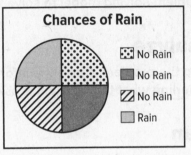

Chances of Rain

☷ No Rain
▨ No Rain
▧ No Rain
▥ Rain

_____

3 Rebecca received a $50 check from her grandmother for her birthday. She used the money to buy some new clothes. If she spent $49.75, how many ways could she receive change if no pennies are used? **7.SP.8, MP 4**

_____

4 ✋ **H.O.T. Problem** Juan is playing basketball. During a game, he is fouled 8 times. Each time, he goes to the free-throw line to shoot two shots. A simulation was conducted to determine the experimental probability of making a free-throw shot. Compare the experimental probability, $\frac{3}{8}$, to the theoretical probability, 50%. **7.SP.8, MP 2**

_____

_____

_____

Lesson 5   Multi-Step Problem Solving

Multi-Step Example

Zaku is going to buy a fresh fruit smoothie and a personal pizza for lunch. For the smoothie, he can choose one of five different fruits, one of six different types of juice, and either milk or ice cream. For Zaku's pizza, he can choose one of three crusts and one of four toppings. How many different pizza and smoothie choices does Zaku have for his lunch? **7.SP.8, MP 2**

Ⓐ 12   Ⓑ 60   Ⓒ 72   Ⓓ 720

Use a problem-solving model to solve this problem.

 Analyze

Read the problem. Circle the information you know.
Underline what the problem is asking you to find.

> **Read to Succeed!** 👀
>
> When reading the problem, identify different categories and how many choices are in each category.

2 Plan

What will you need to do to solve the problem? Write your plan in steps.

Step 1   Identify how many possible options there are for each category.

Step 2   Calculate the total number of _____.

Step 3   _____ the total number of pizza and smoothie combinations.

3 Solve

Use your plan to solve the problem. Show your steps.

Possible smoothie outcomes: _____

Possible pizza outcomes: _____

Multiply the options together to find the amount of different

meal options for Zaku for a total of _____.

The correct answer is _____. Fill in that answer choice.

 Justify and Evaluate

How do you know your solution is accurate?

_____

_____

_____

Lesson 5 *(continued)*

Use a problem-solving model to solve each problem.

1 Alana goes to a school that requires her to wear a uniform. Girls are allowed to wear a polo style shirt in one of four colors; khaki pants, blue pants, or a khaki skirt; and either tennis shoes or dress shoes. From how many different types of outfits can girls choose? 7.SP.8, **MP** 2

Ⓐ 3

Ⓑ 9

Ⓒ 24

Ⓓ 54

2 Kitan would like to order from the children's menu at Jonny John's Burger Haven. The kid's menu allows her to choose from five different types of burgers, eight different drinks, seven different sides, and either a girl's toy or a boy's toy. How many unique types of children's meals does Jonny John's offer? 7.SP.8, **MP** 1

_____

3 The menu for Sam's Scoops lists the following different cones and toppings.

Cones	Toppings
Cake	None
Sugar	Chocolate sprinkles
Waffle	Nuts
Chocolate waffle cone	Multi-colored sprinkles
	Sugar sprinkles
	Caramel sauce
	Chocolate sauce
	Cookie crumbles
	Chocolate chips

If Sam's Scoops claims they can make 828 different ice cream cones with up to one topping, how many different ice cream flavors do they offer? 7.SP.8b, **MP** 2

_____

4 ✋ **H.O.T. Problem** Determine the number of possible outcomes for rolling one number cube, two number cubes, three number cubes, and four number cubes. Write a rule for rolling *n* number cubes if each number cube has six different numbers. Explain how you determined your rule. 7.SP.8a, **MP** 4

_____

_____

_____

_____

_____

Lesson 6 **Multi-Step** Problem Solving

Multi-Step Example

Jimena, Jade, and Jaqui all raced in the 100-yard dash. How many different ways could they place first, second, and third? **7.SP.8, 2**

Ⓐ 3 Ⓑ 6 Ⓒ 12 Ⓓ 16

Use a problem-solving model to solve this problem.

Analyze

Read the problem. (Circle) the information you know.
Underline what the problem is asking you to find.

2 Plan

What will you need to do to solve the problem? Write your plan in steps.

Step 1 Identify that the problem is interested in the different ways

something can be _____.

Step 2 Identify _____ items are being ordered.

Step 3 Find the _____ of the number of items.

> **Read to Succeed!**
>
> When determining the total combinations of different items, it is important to determine if order matters.

3 Solve

Use your plan to solve the problem. Show your steps.

The problem is interested in how many different orders the girls could finish the race.

There are _____ different girls who raced and _____ ways they can finish.

The total number of different ways the girls could place in the race

is _____. The correct answer is _____. Fill in that answer choice.

Justify and Evaluate

How do you know your solution is reasonable?

_____

_____

_____

Lesson 6 (continued)

Use a problem-solving model to solve each problem.

1 The five starting players for the school basketball team line up to shake hands with their opponents. In how many ways can the five players line up? **7.SP.8, MP 2**

- Ⓐ 5
- Ⓑ 15
- Ⓒ 25
- Ⓓ 120

2 Five talented boys are auditioning for the lead role in the school play. One boy will be selected as the lead actor and one will be selected as the understudy, or replacement in case of illness. Find the probability that Sanjay gets the lead and Eli is the understudy. **7.SP.8a, MP 2**

_____

3 The Mount Clair School Fair currently offers vanilla, chocolate, and strawberry ice cream. If the school adds one more flavor of ice cream, how many more ways could the ice cream be arranged in the display case if order is important? **7.SP.8a, MP 7**

_____

4 🔥 **H.O.T. Problem** The new state license plates will each have six characters. The first three characters on the plates must be letters and the second three must be numbers 0–9, with no repeat of any letter or number. Will the department of motor vehicles be able to make enough unique license plates for a population that registers 14 million vehicles? Explain your answer. **7.SP.8, MP 8**

_____

_____

_____

_____

Lesson 7   Multi-Step Problem Solving

Multi-Step Example

Wesley exercises about 3% of the number of hours in a week. Suppose he is tracking the hours he exercises in a year or 52 weeks. Which prediction could represent the number of hours you would expect Wesley to exercise rounded to the nearest tenth? **7.SP.8a, MP 1**

Ⓐ 52.1 hours

Ⓒ 252 hours

Ⓑ 162.1 hours

Ⓓ 262.1 hours

Use a problem-solving model to solve this problem.

1 Analyze

Read the problem. Circle the information you know. Underline what the problem is asking you to find.

Read to Succeed!

You can express 3% as a decimal or a fraction in order to solve this problem.

2 Plan

What will you need to do to solve the problem? Write your plan in steps.

Step 1   Determine the number of _____ he works out each week.

Step 2   _____ the hours he exercises each week by ____ weeks.

3 Solve

Use your plan to solve the problem. Show your steps.

There are 24 hours in a day. Multiply that by 7 to determine the hours in a week.

24 × 7 = _____

Wesley exercises 3% or _____ of a week. Multiply by the hours in a week.

_____ × _____ = _____

Multiply by the number of weeks in a year, 52.   _____ × 52 = _____

Wesley would exercise about _____ hours in a year.

So, the correct answer is ____. Fill in that answer choice.

4 Justify and Evaluate

How do you know your solution is accurate?

_____

_____

_____

Lesson 7 *(continued)*

Use a problem-solving model to solve each problem.

1 One letter tile is selected and the spinner is spun. What is the probability that the tile will be a vowel and the spinner will land on a consonant? **7.SP.8,**  **1**

- (A) $\frac{1}{4}$
- (B) $\frac{1}{3}$
- (C) $\frac{1}{6}$
- (D) $\frac{1}{12}$

2 Sonya has a bag with 4 green, 7 orange, and 9 blue marbles. She randomly selects one marble and then another. What is the probability that Sonya picks two blue marbles? Express your answer as a percent, rounded to the nearest tenth. **7.SP.8a,** **2**

3 Deepak wants a new video game but is not sure which one to buy. His choices are 5 sports games, 3 role-playing games, and 8 action games. He writes the game titles on pieces of paper and puts them all in a bag. He randomly selects one piece of paper from the bag, does not replace it, and selects another piece of paper. What is the probability that Deepak selects two sports games? Express your answer as a percent, rounded to the nearest hundredth. **7.SP.8,** **2**

4 ✋ **H.O.T. Problem** Tyrell is rolling two number cubes. He rolls them both at the same time. What is the probability that the sum of the two outcomes will be an even number? **7.SP.8,** **2**

Lesson 1 **Multi-Step** Problem Solving

Multi-Step Example

Adrian's class surveyed 150 students to determine their favorite ice cream flavors. The results are shown in the circle graph at the right. How many more students favored vanilla than mint chocolate chip? 7.SP.1, **MP** 2

Favorite Ice Cream

20% Cookie Dough
26% Chocolate
18% Mint Chocolate Chip
24% Vanilla
12% Strawberry

Use a problem-solving model to solve this problem.

1 Analyze

Read the problem. Circle the information you know.
Underline what the problem is asking you to find.

2 Plan

What will you need to do to solve the problem? Write your plan in steps.

Step 1 Determine _____ of 150 and _____ of 150.

Step 2 Then subtract the _____.

> **Read to Succeed!**
> You can use another method by subtracting the percents first before multiplying by 150.

3 Solve

Use your plan to solve the problem. Show your steps.

Determine 24% of 150.   Determine 18% of 150.

0.24 × 150 = ____   0.18 × 150 = ____

____ − ____ = ____   Subtract.

There are ____ more students who favor vanilla than mint chocolate chip.

4 Justify and Evaluate

How do you know your solution is accurate?

_____

_____

_____

Lesson 1 *(continued)*

Use a problem-solving model to solve each problem.

1 All the seventh graders in Carla's school voted on where to go for their class trip. There are a total of 350 students in the seventh grade. How many fewer students voted for the two least popular choices than for the two most popular choices? 7.SP.1, **MP** 2

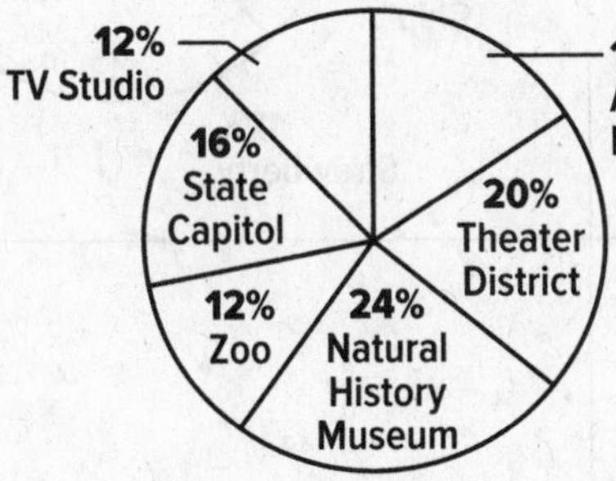

Field Trip Votes

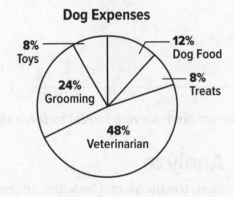

2 Billy spent $500 on his dog last year, and he made a circle graph to show how he spent the money. This year, he spent $100 less on the veterinarian but the same amount on every other category. This year, what percent of dog expenses was spent on the veterinarian? 7.SP.1, **MP** 2

Dog Expenses

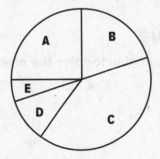

3 Kya and Nicholas each kept a list of trees that their class saw during a nature project. To show their results, Kya made a circle graph and Nicholas made a table. If Kya's circle graph represents 27 beech trees, how many more total trees are represented on her graph than on Nicholas's table? 7.SP.1, **MP** 2

Trees Counted

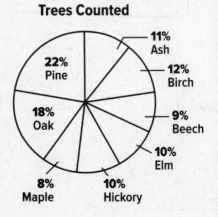

Trees Counted	
Tree	Number
Ash	33
Birch	29
Beech	27
Elm	30
Hickory	30
Maple	20
Oak	52
Pine	22

4 ✋ **H.O.T. Problem** Look at the divisions on the circle graph. Assign approximate percents to each section. Then, write a real-world problem about the graph. 7.SP.2, **MP** 6

Lesson 2 **Multi-Step** Problem Solving

Multi-Step Example

The table shows the results of a survey of students in Janette's class about their favorite pencil-and-paper puzzles. If there are 360 students in Janette's grade, predict how many more favor word searches compared to word scrambles. **7.SP.1, MP 2**

Kind of Puzzle	Students
Crossword	6
Sudoku	8
Word Search	14
Word Scramble	7

Ⓐ 36

Ⓒ 144

Ⓑ 72

Ⓓ 216

Use a problem-solving model to solve this problem.

 Analyze

Read the problem. Circle the information you know.
Underline what the problem is asking you to find.

 Plan

What will you need to do to solve the problem? Write your plan in steps.

Step 1 Determine how many more students favor _____

compared to _____ written as a fraction.

Step 2 Determine the _____ out of 360 students.

 Solve

Use your plan to solve the problem. Show your steps.

There were 35 students surveyed. Write the number of students that prefer each puzzle over 35. Then subtract.

$\dfrac{14}{35} - \dfrac{7}{35} =$ _____ or _____   Subtract.

_____ _____ × 360 = _____   Multiply.

There would be _____ students more that favor word searches.

So, the correct answer is _____. Fill in that answer choice.

 Read to Succeed!

You can also express the difference as a decimal before multiplying. One-fifth is equal to 0.2 or 20%.

 Justify and Evaluate

How do you know your solution is accurate?

_____

_____

Lesson 2 *(continued)*

Use a problem-solving model to solve each problem.

1 The table shows the results of a student survey at a shopping mall in which they asked people what store they were visiting first. During the survey, the students observed 30 shoppers entering the mall. If 390 people were surveyed, predict how many more would have said they were visiting the electronics store or clothing store compared to the bookstore. 7.SP.1, **MP** 2

Store	Shoppers
Bookstore	8
Electronics	11
Clothing	7
Sporting Goods	4

Ⓐ 234   Ⓒ 130

Ⓑ 195   Ⓓ 104

2 Jack surveyed two classes in his school to determine how many students had savings accounts. The circle graphs show his results. If there are 250 total seventh-graders and 220 eighth-graders in Jack's school, predict the difference in the number of students who have savings accounts between the two grades. 7.SP.1, **MP** 2

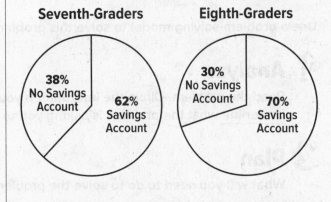

Seventh-Graders — 38% No Savings Account, 62% Savings Account

Eighth-Graders — 30% No Savings Account, 70% Savings Account

3 Kristen at the Yummy Lunch restaurant kept track of how many people ordered different dishes in one day. She used the results to predict how many orders the restaurant would receive during the following week. If 750 people visited Yummy Lunch that week, predict how many more people ordered salad than soup. 7.SP.2, **MP** 2

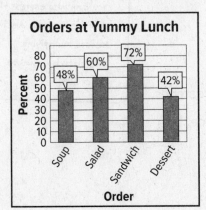

Orders at Yummy Lunch
Soup 48%, Salad 60%, Sandwich 72%, Dessert 42%

4 🔥**H.O.T. Problem** The graph shows the results of a survey of families in the town of Jefferson about their household's newspaper subscriptions. If there are a total of 4,300 households in Jefferson, predict how many more families subscribe to State Telegram or Jefferson Gazette compared to County Journal or The City Sentinel. 7.SP.1, **MP** 2

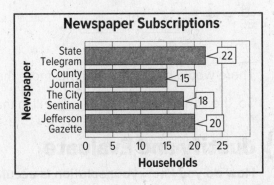

Newspaper Subscriptions
State Telegram 22, County Journal 15, The City Sentinel 18, Jefferson Gazette 20

Lesson 3 Multi-Step Problem Solving

Multi-Step Example

A furniture store sells wood, metal, and wicker chairs. The store workers survey 80 customers at random about their favorite type of chair. The table shows the results of this survey. If 200 chairs are ordered, about how many more should be wood than metal?
Extension of 7.SP.1, 1

Chair Type	Number
Wood	45
Metal	27
Wicker	8

Ⓐ 18   Ⓒ 68

Ⓑ 45   Ⓓ 113

Use a problem-solving model to solve this problem.

1 Analyze

Read the problem. Ⓒircle the information you know.
Underline what the problem is asking you to find.

2 Plan

What will you need to do to solve the problem? Write your plan in steps.

Step 1 Determine how many more people favor _____ compared

to _____ written as a fraction.

Step 2 Determine the _____ out of 200 chairs.

3 Solve

Use your plan to solve the problem. Show your steps.

There were 80 people surveyed. Write the number of people that prefer each chair type over 80. Then subtract.

$\frac{45}{80} - \frac{27}{80} =$ ____ or ____ ____   Subtract.

____ × 200 = ____   Multiply.

The store would expect about ____ more wood chair orders than metal.

So, the correct answer is ____. Fill in that answer choice.

> **Read to Succeed!**
> You can also express the difference as a decimal before multiplying. It can be expressed as 0.225 or 22.5%.

4 Justify and Evaluate

How do you know your solution is accurate?

_____

_____

_____

Lesson 3 *(continued)*

Use a problem-solving model to solve each problem.

1 A toy store sells three different versions of a popular game as a board game, electronic, or a travel-size version. The store workers survey 120 customers at random about their favorite version of the game. The table shows the results of this survey. If 420 games are ordered, about how many more should be electronic than travel-size?
Extension of 7.SP.1, **MP** 1

Game Type	Number
Board	42
Electronic	50
Travel-Size	28

ⓐ 273   ⓒ 98

ⓑ 175   ⓓ 77

2 A sporting goods store sells three different versions of athletic shoes. The store workers surveyed 200 customers at random. The results are shown in the table. The store ordered 500 shoes. Out of the shoes they ordered, 220 were cross trainers. Based on the survey, make an inference about how many cross trainers they will still need.
Extension of 7.SP.1, **MP** 2

Shoe Type	Number in Survey
Cross Trainer	100
High Top	24
Tennis Shoes	76

_____

3 Two pharmacies on opposite sides of town each surveyed a random sample of customers in their store about what type of cold medicine they prefer. If store A and store B each order 150 units of cold medicine, make an inference to determine how many more should be in the pill form for store A compared to store B.
Extension of 7.SP.1, **MP** 2

Medicine Form	Store A	Store B
Pill	33	38
Syrup	10	15
Spray	2	4

_____

4 👍 **H.O.T. Problem** A jewelry store wanted to survey customers to determine if they preferred silver, gold, or platinum chain. The store surveyed 67 customers who made a purchase and 23 customers who did not make a purchase. Explain why neither of the data collection methods is valid, and what would be a better way to collect the data.
Extension of 7.SP.1, **MP** 4

_____

_____

_____

_____

_____

_____

_____

_____

Lesson 4 Multi-Step Problem Solving

Multi-Step Example

Four models of televisions are on sale this week at the local electronic store. In their advertisement, the store claims that their average price for a television is $2,106.25. The sale prices of the televisions are shown in the graph. By how much should they increase this amount to give a more accurate representation of the average price, in dollars, of the televisions on sale? 7.SP.4, **MP** 2

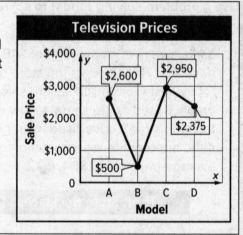

Television Prices

Ⓐ $381.25

Ⓒ $535.42

Ⓑ $450.50

Ⓓ $575.00

Use a problem-solving model to solve this problem.

1 Analyze

Read the problem. Circle the information you know.
Underline what the problem is asking you to find.

2 Plan

What will you need to do to solve the problem? Write your plan in steps.

Step 1   Determine the more appropriate _____ to describe to data.

Step 2   Determine the _____ between the mean and median.

3 Solve

Use your plan to solve the problem. Show your steps.

The median is the more appropriate measure. Determine the median.

$2,375 + $2,600 = _____   _____ ÷ 2 = _____

_____ − $2,106.25 = _____   Subtract.

The more accurate price would be the median that is _____ greater than the mean.

So, the correct answer is _____. Fill in that answer choice.

Read to Succeed!

There is no mode for the data. You should only compare the mean and median to determine which is more appropriate for the data.

4 Justify and Evaluate

How do you know your solution is accurate?

_____

_____

_____

Lesson 4 (continued)

Use a problem-solving model to solve each problem.

1 A certain thrift store claims they will buy used jewelry at an average of $48 per necklace. The amounts the store has paid for the last four necklaces are shown in the graph. Based on these data, how much less than the store's advertised average is the more appropriate representation of the average payment? **7.SP.4, MP 2**

Thrift Store Necklaces

Ⓐ $13.50   Ⓒ $34.50

Ⓑ $25.75   Ⓓ $61.50

2 The table shows the times, in minutes, of the jogs that Fernando and Nakita ran last week. What is the difference, in minutes, between the measures that best describe Fernando's running times and Nakita's running times? **7.SP.4, MP 1**

Running Times (in min)	
Fernando	Nakita
16	5
20	20
12	23

3 ✋**H.O.T. Problem** A ski resort claims they have an average of 190,000 visitors per year. The circle graph shows the number of visitors to the resort during each of the four seasons. Explain why 190,000 is a misleading descriptor of the average number of visitors. What would be a better way to convey the appropriate information? **7.SP.4, MP 6**

Ski Resort Visitors by Season

_____

_____

_____

_____

_____

Lesson 5   **Multi-Step** Problem Solving

Multi-Step Example

The double box plot shows the test scores for two different math classes. Use the information to determine which of the following inferences is *not* true. *Extension of* **7.SP.1,** **MP** 2

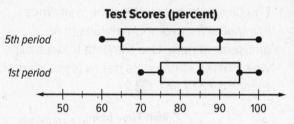

Ⓐ Only one of the data sets is symmetric.

Ⓑ The median test score in 1st period is greater than 5th period.

Ⓒ The highest test score is the same in both periods.

Ⓓ The interquartile range of 1st period is larger than 5th period.

Use a problem-solving model to solve this problem.

1 Analyze

Read the problem. Circle the information you know.
Underline what the problem is asking you to find.

2 Plan

What will you need to do to solve the problem? Write your plan in steps.

[**Step 1**]   Determine the _____ of the two scores.

[**Step 2**]   Determine which inference is _____.

3 Solve

Use your plan to solve the problem. Show your steps.

The 1st period is _____, but the 5th period is _____.

The median for 1st period is _____. The median for 5th period is _____.

Both periods have a high test score of _____.

The interquartile range for 1st period is _____, and it is _____ for 5th period.

So, the correct answer is _____. Fill in that answer choice.

> **Read to Succeed!**
> Recall that box plots separate data into four parts. Each part contains 25% of the data.

4 Justify and Evaluate

How do you know your solution is accurate?

_____

_____

_____

Lesson 5 *(continued)*

Use a problem-solving model to solve each problem.

1 The box plots below show the wait times in minutes for two popular rides at an amusement park. Use the data to determine which of the statements below is *not* correct. *Extension of* 7.SP.1, **MP** 2

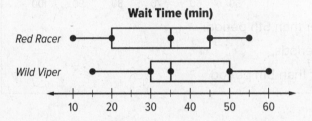

Wait Time (min)

Ⓐ The median wait time for both rides is 35 minutes.

Ⓑ The Red Racer has a shorter maximum wait time than the Wild Viper.

Ⓒ The Wild Viper has a larger range of wait times than the Red Racer.

Ⓓ The Red Racer has a larger interquartile range than the Time Warp.

2 The double dot plot below shows the number of hours Kayla and Carmen studied during a two week period in college. Determine the most appropriate measure of variation for each data set. What is the difference between the centers? *Extension of* 7.SP.1, **MP** 2

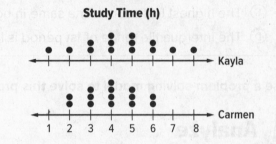

Study Time (h)

_____

_____

3 🔥**H.O.T. Problem** Juan works for an agricultural company and is studying the growth of two different types of corn. The table below shows the growth of each type of corn in inches for each month. Compare the shapes, centers, and spreads for both types of corn. Make an inference based on your findings. *Extension of* 7.SP.1, **MP** 6

	Corn A	Corn B
1st month	20	28
2nd month	20	19
3rd month	26	15
4th month	18	7
5th month	13	26

_____

_____

_____

_____

_____

NAME _____ DATE _____ PERIOD _____

Lesson 1 Multi-Step Problem Solving

Chapter 1

Multi-Step Example

Makayla and her friends earn money by babysitting after school. At the end of one week, they deposit their weekly earnings at the bank. Which friend earns the most money per hour babysitting? 7.RP.2b, MP 2

Name	Hours Worked	Deposit Amount ($)
Makayla	15	138.75
Gael	13	136.50
Jason	16	168.00
Cecilia	9	101.25

Ⓐ Makayla   Ⓒ Jason
Ⓑ Gael   Ⓓ Cecilia

Use a problem-solving model to solve this problem.

1 Analyze

Read the problem. (Circle) the information you know. Underline what the problem is asking you to find.

2 Plan

What will you need to do to solve the problem? Write your plan in steps.

Step 1 Calculate the **unit rate** for each person.

Step 2 Compare the unit rates to determine **which friend** earns the most.

3 Solve

Use your plan to solve the problem. Show your steps.

Makayla: $138.75 ÷ 15 = __$9.25__ per hour

Gael: $136.50 ÷ 13 = __$10.50__ per hour

Jason: $168 ÷ 16 = __$10.50__ per hour

Cecilia: $101.25 ÷ 9 = __$11.25__ per hour

Cecilia earns __$11.25__ per hour, which is the greatest unit rate.

So, the correct answer is __D__ . Fill in that answer choice.

Read to Succeed!

Be sure to calculate each unit rate. Do not assume that a lower deposit amount will result in a lower unit rate.

4 Justify and Evaluate

How do you know your solution is accurate?

Sample answer: I know can check each unit rate by multiplying the hours worked by the amount earned per hour to check my answer. $11.25 × 9 = $101.25

So, my solution is accurate.

Course 2 • Chapter 1 Ratios and Proportional Reasoning   1

NAME _____ DATE _____ PERIOD _____

Lesson 1 *(continued)*

Use a problem-solving model to solve each problem.

1 An automobile magazine compared the gas mileage for new cars. The distance traveled and amount of gasoline used for each car is shown in the table. Which car had the greatest gas mileage(miles per gallon)? 7.RP.2b, MP 2

Car	Distance (mi)	Gasoline (gal)
Car A	650	20
Car B	426	12
Car C	515	15
Car D	280	8

Ⓐ Car A
Ⓑ Car B
Ⓒ Car C
Ⓓ Car D

2 The graph shows the amount of electricity used by one household over six months. If the cost per kilowatt hour usage is $0.12, approximately how much would it cost per day for the month of April? (*Hint:* There are 30 billable days in the month of April.) 7.RP.2b, MP 1

Electricity Use by Month

Month	Kilowatts
June	1,700
May	1,100
April	1,200
March	1,700
Feb	1,300
Jan	1,500

Kilowatts: 0 500 1,000 1,500 2,000

__$4.80__

3 The graph shows the first 45 minutes of Darlene's bike trip. If she continues at a constant rate, how far will she travel in two hours? 7.RP.2, MP 7

Distance (mi) vs. Time (min)

__24 miles__

4 🧠 **H.O.T. Problem** Kai can run 100 meters in 12.5 seconds and Josalin can run 150 meters in 20 seconds. If they both ran a 400-meter race at this rate, how many meters ahead would Kai cross the finish line before Josalin? 7.RP.2, MP 4

__25 meters__

Course 2 • Chapter 1 Ratios and Proportional Reasoning   2

Answers

NAME _____ DATE _____ PERIOD _____

Lesson 2 (continued)

Use a problem-solving model to solve each problem.

1 Emma has been training for a bike race. She recorded her training times in the table below. Emma believes that if her average speed is above 15 miles per hour, then she has a good chance of winning the race. On which day(s) was Emma's average speed over 15 miles per hour? **7.RP.1, MP 2**

Day	Time (hr)	Distance (mi)
Monday	$1\frac{1}{2}$	27
Wednesday	$3\frac{1}{3}$	$63\frac{1}{3}$
Saturday	$2\frac{1}{2}$	35
Sunday	$\frac{3}{4}$	9

Ⓐ Monday only
Ⓑ Saturday only
Ⓒ Monday and Wednesday
Ⓓ All four days

3 A cheetah is one of the fastest land running animals. A cheetah can run $17\frac{1}{2}$ miles in $\frac{1}{4}$ hour. If a cheetah ran at this rate, how far would it travel in $1\frac{1}{2}$ hours? **7.NS.3, MP 2**

105 miles

2 The table shows the percent commission that a sales person earns based on monthly sales. Last month, Elijah's sales totaled $8,924. Including commission, how much did he earn last month? **7.RP.3, MP 1**

Sales	Commission
under $5,000	5%
$5,000 – $7,499	$9\frac{1}{2}$%
$7,500 – $9,999	$12\frac{1}{2}$%
$10,000 and higher	15%

$10,039.50

4 ⌨ **H.O.T. Problem** The distance between the two islands shown on the map is 210 miles. A ruler measures this distance on the map as $3\frac{1}{2}$ inches. How many miles would be represented by $1\frac{3}{4}$ inches on the map? **7.RP.1, MP 8**

105 miles

4

NAME _____ DATE _____ PERIOD _____

Chapter 1

Lesson 2 Multi-Step Problem Solving

Multi-Step Example

Carolina and her friends went kayaking over the weekend. The distance and time traveled is shown in the table. Which person kayaked at the greatest speed, in miles per hour? **7.RP.1, MP 1**

Person	Distance (mi)	Time (h)
Carolina	$3\frac{1}{2}$	$\frac{1}{2}$
Leslie	$5\frac{1}{4}$	$\frac{3}{4}$
Bryan	$4\frac{1}{2}$	$\frac{3}{4}$
Javier	$2\frac{1}{2}$	$\frac{1}{3}$

Ⓐ Carolina
Ⓑ Leslie
Ⓒ Bryan
Ⓓ Javier

Use a problem-solving model to solve this problem.

1 Analyze
Read the problem. Circle the information you know. Underline what the problem is asking you to find.

2 Plan
What will you need to do to solve the problem? Write your plan in steps.

Step 1 Calculate the __unit rate__ for each person.

Step 2 Compare the unit rates to determine __which person__ kayaks at the fastest rate, in miles per hour.

3 Solve
Use your plan to solve the problem. Show your steps.

Calculate each unit rate.

Carolina: $3\frac{1}{2} \div \frac{1}{2} = $ __7__ mi/h   Leslie: $5\frac{1}{4} \div \frac{3}{4} = \frac{7}{1} = $ __7__ mi/h

Bryan: $4\frac{1}{2} \div \frac{3}{4} = $ __6__ mi/h   Javier: $2\frac{1}{2} \div \frac{1}{3} = \frac{7}{1} = $ __$7\frac{1}{2}$__ mi/h

Compare the unit rates to determine which person kayaked at the fastest rate.

Javier kayaked at a rate of __$7\frac{1}{2}$__ miles per hour, which is the fastest unit rate.

So, the correct answer is __D__ . Fill in that answer choice.

4 Justify and Evaluate
How do you know your solution is accurate?

Sample answer: I can check each unit rate by multiplying the time kayaking by the rate at with each person kayaked to check the distance. My solution is accurate because $\frac{1}{3} \times 7\frac{1}{2} = 2\frac{1}{2}$.

Read to Succeed!
Use the formula $v = d \div t$ to help you calculate the unit rate for each person.

3

NAME _____ DATE _____ PERIOD _____

Lesson 3 Multi-Step Problem Solving

Multi-Step Example

The table shows the price of almonds at three different grocery stores. What is the cost, in dollars per pound, for the cheapest almonds? 7.RP.2b, MP 1

Store	Weight (oz)	Price ($)
A	64	19.96
B	80	21.75
C	112	33.95

Use a problem-solving model to solve this problem.

1 Analyze

Read the problem. Circle the information you know. Underline what the problem is asking you to find.

2 Plan

What will you need to do to solve the problem? Write your plan in steps.

Step 1 Calculate each **unit rate** and convert to an equivalent rate.

Step 2 Compare the unit rates to determine **the cheapest** per pound.

Read to Succeed!
When you are converting a smaller unit to a larger unit, you need to multiply.

3 Solve

Use your plan to solve the problem. Show your steps.

Store A: $\frac{\$19.96}{64\ oz} \cdot \frac{16\ oz}{1\ lb} = \frac{\$319.36}{64\ lb} = \frac{\$4.99}{1\ lb}$

Store B: $\frac{\$21.75}{80\ oz} \cdot \frac{16\ oz}{1\ lb} = \frac{\$348}{80\ lb} = \frac{\$4.35}{1\ lb}$

Store C: $\frac{\$33.95}{112\ oz} \cdot \frac{16\ oz}{1\ lb} = \frac{\$543.20}{112\ lb} = \frac{\$4.85}{1\ lb}$

Compare the unit rates. $4.35 < 4.85 < 4.99$

Store B sells the cheapest almonds for $4.35 per pound.

4 Justify and Evaluate

How do you know your solution is accurate?

Sample answer: Check each unit rate by dividing by 16 to determine the price per ounce. Then multiply the quotient by the number of ounces shown in the table. So, $4.35 ÷ 16 = $0.271875 and $0.271875 × 80 = $21.75.

NAME _____ DATE _____ PERIOD _____

Lesson 3 (continued)

Use a problem-solving model to solve each problem.

1 The table shows the speeds of several runners on a track team. What is the speed, in feet per minute, of the fastest runner? 7.RP.3, MP 1

Runner	Distance (yd)	Time (s)
Imani	12	3
Jada	9	2
Tenesha	34	8

810

2 Lian used her garden hose to fill her 15,000-gallon swimming pool in 5 hours. She plans to graph the fill rate on a coordinate grid, showing the amount of water, in pints, on the y-axis and time, in minutes on the x-axis. What will be the y-value on the coordinate grid at 1 minute? (Hint: There are 8 pints in one gallon.) 7.RP.2, MP 8

400

3 Adam painted the rectangular wall shown below in 1 hour. On average, how many square feet did he paint per minute? 7.RP.3, MP 2

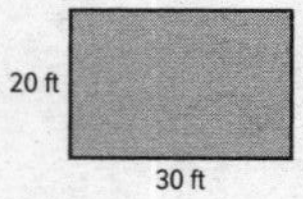

20 ft   30 ft

10 square feet per minute

4 H.O.T. Problem Use dimensional analysis to determine whether the rate 3,000 grams per week is 1,000 times faster than 3 kilograms per week. Explain. 7.RP.3, MP 3

no; Sample answer: The rates are equivalent. If you use dimensional analysis to convert 3,000 grams per week to kilograms per week, you will determine they are equal rates.

Answers

NAME _____ DATE _____ PERIOD _____

Lesson 4 (continued)

Use a problem-solving model to solve each problem.

1 Laurita is writing a research paper. If the relationship remains proportional, how many pages will she complete in 7 hours? 7.RP.2b, MP 2

Time (hr)	Pages Completed
2	3
3	4.5

10.5

2 The table shows three membership options at a fitness center. Logan chooses the membership that represents a proportional relationship between the number of classes and the monthly cost. How much will he spend, in dollars, if he takes 12 classes in a month? 7.RP.2, MP 2

Membership	Cost
Basic	$20 per class
Fit Plus	$60 per month plus $10 per class
Fit Extreme	$75 per month plus $30 enrollment fee

240

3 Carla donates 3% of her salary to charity each year. She makes $35,000 each year. If the relationship remains proportional, how much money will she have donated after 8 years? 7.RP.3 MP 1

$8,400

4 ✎ **H.O.T. Problem** The graph shows the distance of a race car over time. Is this relationship between distance and time proportional? Justify your answers. 7.RP.2a, MP 7

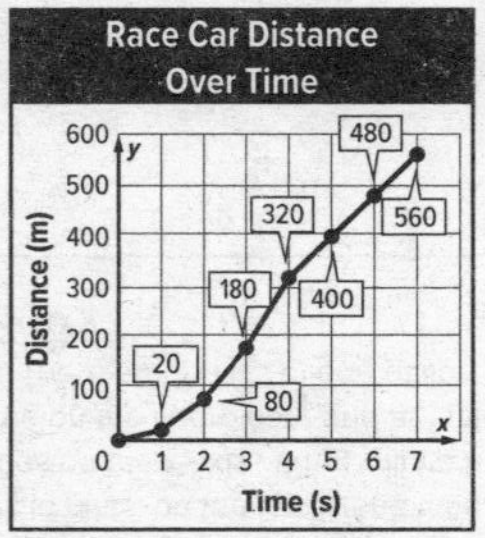

Race Car Distance Over Time

no; The ratio of distance and time is not constant. At 1 second, it is $\frac{20}{1} = 20$ meters per second. At 2 seconds, it is $\frac{80}{2} = 40$ meters per second.

Course 2 • Chapter 1 Ratios and Proportional Reasoning

NAME _____ DATE _____ PERIOD _____

Lesson 4 **Multi-Step** Problem Solving

Chapter 1

Multi-Step Example

Federico pays sales tax equal to $\frac{3}{50}$ of the retail price of his purchases. If the sales tax rate remains proportional, what is the total cost, in dollars, for a purchase amount of $84? 7.RP.2b, MP 2

Purchase Amount ($)	Sales Tax Amount ($)	Total Amount ($)
12	0.72	12.72
24	1.44	25.44
36	2.16	38.16
48	2.88	50.88

Read to Succeed!

To determine the sales tax amount, multiply the purchase amount by the fractional tax amount.

Use a problem-solving model to solve this problem.

1 Analyze

Read the problem. Circle the information you know. Underline what the problem is asking you to find.

2 Plan

What will you need to do to solve the problem? Write your plan in steps.

Step 1   Determine the _sales tax_ for his purchase of $84.

Step 2   Add the purchase amount and sales tax to determine the _total cost_.

3 Solve

Use your plan to solve the problem. Show your steps.

Determine the sales tax.

$\frac{3}{50} \times \$84 = 5\frac{1}{25}$ or 5.04

$\$84 + \$5.04 = \$89.04$ Add.

The total amount Federico will pay for a purchase of $84 is _$89.04_.

4 Justify and Evaluate

How do you know your solution is accurate?

Sample answer: Since the relationship is proportional, the purchase amount increases by $12 and the sales tax increases by $0.72. I know that $84 is 7 times $12, so $0.72 times 7 is equal to $5.04. Add this to the purchase amount of $84. $84 + $5.04 = $89.04, so my solution is accurate.

Course 2 • Chapter 1 Ratios and Proportional Reasoning   **7**

NAME _____ DATE _____ PERIOD _____

Lesson 5 Multi-Step Problem Solving

Chapter 1

Multi-Step Example

The amount of time it takes a car to travel a certain distance is shown in the table. Choose the statement below that best describes the appearance of the graph of the relationship between time traveled and distance traveled. 7.RP.2, MP 4

Time (min)	Distance (mi)
10	10
20	18
35	30
45	38

(A) a straight line that passes through the origin
(B) a curved line that passes through the origin
(C) a curved line that does not pass through the origin
(D) a straight line that does not pass through the origin

Read to Succeed!
Be sure to graph the ordered pairs on a coordinate plane to determine if the graph is a straight line.

Use a problem-solving model to solve this problem.

1 Analyze

Read the problem. **Circle** the information you know. **Underline** what the problem is asking you to find.

2 Plan

What will you need to do to solve the problem? Write your plan in steps.

Step 1 Graph _____ ordered pairs on a coordinate plane.

Step 2 Analyze the ____ line ____ to describe the relationship shown.

3 Solve

Use your plan to solve the problem. Show your steps.

Graph the ordered pairs (time, distance) on the coordinate plane. Then connect the ordered pairs with a line.

[Graph: Distance Traveled]

The line is **straight** and **does not** pass through the origin.

So, the correct answer is **D**. Fill in that answer choice.

4 Justify and Evaluate

How do you know your solution is accurate?

Sample answer: I can write and compare ratios to determine if the relationship is proportional; $\frac{10}{10} \neq \frac{20}{18} \neq \frac{35}{30} \neq \frac{45}{38}$. The ratios are not constant, so the relationship is not proportional. That means the line does not pass through the origin.

9

NAME _____ DATE _____ PERIOD _____

Lesson 5 (continued)

Use a problem-solving model to solve each problem.

1 Raisins are sometimes sold by the pound. The table below shows the cost for different weights of raisins. Choose the statement below that best describes the appearance of the graph of the relationship between weight and cost of raisins sold. 7.RP.2, MP 4

Weight of Raisins (lb)	Cost ($)
1	4.60
2	9.20
4	18.40
5.5	25.30

(A) a straight line that passes through the origin
(B) a curved line that passes through the origin
(C) a curved line that does not pass through the origin
(D) a straight line that does not pass through the origin

2 Line A shows the distance traveled for five minutes by a giant tortoise. Line B shows the distance traveled for five minutes by a three-toed sloth. If each animal kept traveling at its same rate for one hour, how much farther would the sloth have traveled than the tortoise? 7.RP.2a, MP 4

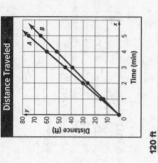

[Graph: Distance Traveled]

120 ft

3 The relationship between the side length s of a square and the perimeter P of the square is a proportional relationship. Given that the side length of the smaller square is $\frac{4}{5}$ the side length of the larger square, determine the perimeter, in centimeters, of the smaller square. 7.RP.2a, MP 2

s = 5 cm

P = 20 cm

16 cm

4 H.O.T. Problem Jarrod is comparing gym memberships. Gym A charges $38 per month for membership, with no annual fees. Gym B charges an annual fee of $15 and a monthly membership cost of $35. Which gym charges more for a yearly membership? By how much more? Justify your response. 7.RP.2a, MP 2

Gym A; $21; Sample answer: Gym A charges $38 per month, so a yearly membership would cost $456. Gym B has an annual fee of $15, plus $35 per month, so a yearly membership would cost $435. So, Gym A costs $21 more per year.

10

Chapter 1 Lesson 6 Answer Keys

Lesson 6 (continued)

Use a problem-solving model to solve each problem.

1 On average, Rai correctly answers 12 out of 18 questions in a trivia game. Assuming the situation is proportional, how many more questions is she likely to correctly answer if there are 36 questions in all? 7.RP.2, MP 2

Correct answers	Total questions
12	18
?	36

A 12 questions
B 18 questions
C 20 questions
D 24 questions

2 Kareem needs a new car and is making a decision between the three cars listed below based on fuel efficiency. Determine which car has the best fuel efficiency in kilometers per gallon. (*Hint:* 1 km ≈ 0.62 mile) 7.RP.2c, MP 4

Car	Miles	Gallons
Car A	248	10
Car B	210	10
Car C	225	12

Car A: 40 km/gal

3 Aaron bought $\frac{1}{2}$ pound of cheese for $6. Assuming the situation is proportional, write and solve an equation to determine how many dollars d Aaron will pay for $3\frac{1}{2}$ pounds of cheese c. 7.RP.2, MP 4

$d = 12c$; $42

4 H.O.T. Problem Taylor bought 12 more pencils this month than last month. Taylor paid $2.88 last month and $7.20 this month for the pencils. Assuming the situation is proportional, how many pencils did she buy this month? 7.RP.3, MP 2

20 pencils

Course 2 • Chapter 1 Ratios and Proportional Reasoning

Lesson 6 Multi-Step Problem Solving

Multi-Step Example

Hugo can run 4 miles in 25 minutes. How many more miles can Hugo run in 90 minutes than in 25 minutes? Assume the situation is proportional and he always runs at the same rate. 7.RP.2, MP 1

Distance (mi)	Time (min)
4	25
m	90

A 10.2 miles
C 14.4 miles
B 10.4 miles
D 18.4 miles

Use a problem-solving model to solve this problem.

1 Analyze

Read the problem. Circle the information you know. Underline what the problem is asking you to find.

2 Plan

What will you need to do to solve the problem? Write your plan in steps.

Step 1 Calculate the **unit rate** for Hugo's running rate. Then multiply the rate by 90 minutes to determine his distance.

Step 2 **Subtract** the distances to determine how much **more** he runs in 90 minutes compared to 25 minutes.

3 Solve

Use your plan to solve the problem. Show your steps.
Calculate the unit rate.

$4 \div 25 =$ **0.16** mile per minute
Determine how many miles he runs in 90 minutes.

$90 \times$ **0.16** = **14.4**
Subtract to determine how much more he runs in 90 minutes.

14.4 − 4 = **10.4**

So, Hugo runs **10.4** miles more in 90 minutes. The correct answer is **B**. Fill in that answer choice.

Read to Succeed!
Don't forget to subtract! The problem asks for how much more, which tells you to subtract the distances.

4 Justify and Evaluate

How do you know your solution is accurate?
Sample answer: I can determine his time, in minutes, per mile, 25 ÷ 4 = 6.25.
Then divide 90 minutes by 6.25 to determine the distance traveled,
14.4 miles. Subtract to determine how much more, 14.4 − 4, or 10.4 miles.

Course 2 • Chapter 1 Ratios and Proportional Reasoning

150 Course 2 • Chapter 1 Ratios and Proportional Reasoning

NAME _____ DATE _____ PERIOD _____

Lesson 7 (continued)

Use a problem-solving model to solve each problem.

1 The table compares number of apples purchased and the total cost. Choose which set of values would give a constant rate of change with a cost of $0.75 per apple. 7.RP.2b, MP 2

Number of Apples	Cost ($)
4	a
6	b
10	c

Ⓐ a = $3.00, b = $6.00, c = $7.50

Ⓑ a = $3.00, b = $3.75, c = $4.50

Ⓒ a = $3.00, b = $3.75, c = $5.25

Ⓓ a = $3.00, b = $4.50, c = $7.50

2 Noah has been growing at a constant rate as shown in the graph below. What is his average rate of change in inches per month? 7.RP.2b, MP 7

Noah's Growth

(graph with points; 48.4 and 47.0 labeled)

Height (in.) vs Month

0.28 inch

3 The table gives the distance traveled over a certain amount of time. What is the value of a that will result in a constant rate of change? 7.RP.2, MP 2

Time (hr)	Distance (mi)
3	213
5	a
8	568

355

4 H.O.T. Problem The table below shows ordered pairs on a graph. Determine the missing value that will guarantee a constant rate of change. 7.RP.2d, MP 8

x	y
a	30
a + 2	42
a + 3	?

48

14

NAME _____ DATE _____ PERIOD _____

Lesson 7 Multi-Step Problem Solving

Chapter 1

Multi-Step Example

The table shows the number of feet walked, given a certain amount of footsteps. Choose the set of values that would yield a constant rate of change. 7.RP.2b, MP 2

Number of Footsteps	Distance Walked (ft)
5	a
10	b
15	c
25	d

Ⓐ a = 12, b = 24, c = 36, d = 48

Ⓑ a = 12, b = 24, c = 36, d = 60

Ⓒ a = 12, b = 24, c = 48, d = 96

Ⓓ a = 12, b = 24, c = 46, d = 68

Use a problem-solving model to solve this problem.

1 Analyze

Read the problem. Circle the information you know. Underline what the problem is asking you to find.

2 Plan

What will you need to do to solve the problem? Write your plan in steps.

Step 1 Calculate the **unit rate** using the values in the answer choices.

Step 2 Compare the **unit rates** to determine a constant rate of change.

Read to Succeed! Make sure you calculate the unit rate between each set of numbers.

3 Solve

Use your plan to solve the problem. Show your steps.

A: $\frac{12}{5} = $ **2.4** $\frac{24}{10} = $ **2.4** $\frac{36}{15} = $ **2.4** $\frac{48}{25} = $ **1.92**

B: $\frac{12}{5} = $ **2.4** $\frac{24}{10} = $ **2.4** $\frac{36}{15} = $ **2.4** $\frac{60}{25} = $ **2.4**

C: $\frac{12}{5} = $ **2.4** $\frac{24}{10} = $ **2.4** $\frac{48}{15} = $ **3.2** $\frac{96}{25} = $ **3.84**

D: $\frac{12}{5} = $ **2.4** $\frac{24}{10} = $ **2.4** $\frac{46}{15} = $ **3.0$\overline{6}$** $\frac{68}{25} = $ **2.72**

Answer choice **B** is the only answer choice that has a constant rate of change.

So, the correct answer is **B**. Fill in that answer choice.

4 Justify and Evaluate

How do you know your solution is accurate?

Sample answer: I can use the unit rate to check my answer. I know that B is correct because 2.4 × 5 = 12, 2.4 × 10 = 24, 2.4 × 15 = 36, and 2.4 × 25 = 60.

13

Answers

NAME _____ DATE _____ PERIOD _____

Lesson 8 Multi-Step Problem Solving

Multi-Step Example

The table represents the rates at Jin's Internet Café for last year. This year, his rates will be $1\frac{1}{4}$ times greater to help pay his increase of rent costs. How much more will a customer pay to use the Internet for 6 hours? 7.RP.2b, MP 2

Time (h) (x)	1	2	3	4
Cost ($) (y)	7	14	21	28

Ⓐ $1.75   Ⓒ $10.50
Ⓑ $7.00   Ⓓ $15.75

Use a problem-solving model to solve this problem.

1 Analyze
Read the problem. Circle the information you know. Underline what the problem is asking you to find.

2 Plan
What will you need to do to solve the problem? Write your plan in steps.

Step 1 Determine the __cost__ for 6 hours of Internet usage.

Step 2 Multiply the cost by __$1\frac{1}{4}$__ and subtract the two costs.

3 Solve
Use your plan to solve the problem. Show your steps.

Determine the cost for 6 hours.

$7(6) = $ __42__

Determine the increased cost for 6 hours. Then subtract.

$42 \cdot \left(1\frac{1}{4}\right) = $ __52.5__

$52.50 - 42 = $ __10.5__   Subtract.

The cost will be __$10.50__ greater.

So, the correct answer is __C__. Fill in that answer choice.

4 Justify and Evaluate
How do you know your solution is accurate?

Sample answer: You can also determine $1\frac{1}{4}$ times the current cost, or $8.75 per hour. Then multiply the increased cost by 6 hours, 8.75×6, or $52.50. Then subtract $42 from this amount. The difference is $10.50.

Read to Succeed!
Interpret the slope in the table as the cost per hour for Internet usage. The slope shown in the table is $7 per hour.

Course 2 · Chapter 1 Ratios and Proportional Reasoning   15

NAME _____ DATE _____ PERIOD _____

Lesson 8 (continued)

Use a problem-solving model to solve each problem.

1 The table represents the number of push-ups completed by Diego over the past 5 days. The next 5 days, he will increase the number of push-ups to be $2\frac{1}{2}$ times greater. How many more push-ups will he complete on day 5 after the increase compared to the number he completed on day 5 in the table below? 7.RP.2b, MP 2

Day	1	2	3	4	5
Push-ups	10	20	30	40	50

Ⓐ 50 push-ups
Ⓑ 75 push-ups
Ⓒ 100 push-ups
Ⓓ 125 push-ups

2 Mrs. Timken took her students on a hiking trip. She wants to avoid steep trails. On the steepest part of Evergreen Path, the path rises 12 feet over a horizontal distance of 60 feet. On Shady Glen Path, the path rises 18 feet over a horizontal distance of 45 feet. How much greater is the slope of the steeper path? Explain. 7.RP.2, MP 1

0.2 foot rise over a horizontal distance of 1 foot; $\frac{2}{5} - \frac{1}{5} = \frac{1}{5}$ or $\frac{0.2 \text{ ft}}{1 \text{ ft}}$

3 The tables compare the number of bowling games and costs at two different bowling alleys. What is the difference in slopes? 7.RP.2, MP 2

Number of Games	2	3	4
Cost ($)	9	10.50	12

Number of Games	2	3	5
Cost ($)	9	11	15

$0.50

4 🤚 **H.O.T. Problem** The slope of a line is -0.5. Two points on the line are (2, -1) and (6, a). What is the value of a? Use the graph to help you solve. 7.RP.2d, MP 4

-3

Course 2 · Chapter 1 Ratios and Proportional Reasoning   16

Chapter 1 Lesson 9 Answer Keys

NAME _____ DATE _____ PERIOD _____

Lesson 9 Multi-Step Problem Solving

Multi-Step Example

The graph shows the distance a car travels over a certain amount of time. What is the ratio of kilometers traveled to the time in hours? (*Hint:* 1 mi ≈ 1.61 km) **7.RP.2b, MP 1**

Ⓐ 40 kilometers per hour
Ⓑ **64.4** kilometers per hour
Ⓒ 80 kilometers per hour
Ⓓ 128.80 kilometers per hour

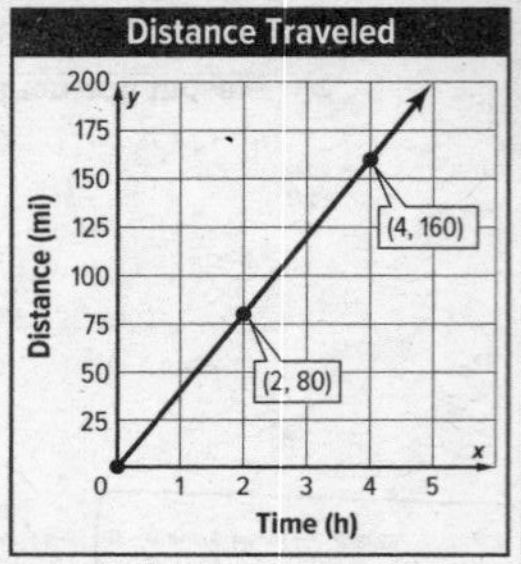

Distance Traveled

(graph — y-axis: Distance (mi) 25 to 200; x-axis: Time (h) 0 to 5; points (2, 80) and (4, 160))

Read to Succeed!
Use the symbols $y = kx$ to help you determine the ratios from the graph.

Use a problem-solving model to solve this problem.

1 Analyze

Read the problem. Circle the information you know. Underline what the problem is asking you to find.

2 Plan

What will you need to do to solve the problem? Write your plan in steps.

Step 1 Use the graph to determine the constant of **proportionality**.

Step 2 Convert miles to **kilometers**.

3 Solve

Use your plan to solve the problem. Show your steps.

$\frac{80}{2} = $ **40** $\frac{160}{4} = $ **40**   The rate of change is **40** miles per hour.

Convert miles to kilometers.

$\frac{40 \text{ mi}}{1 \text{ h}} \times \frac{1.61 \text{ km}}{1 \text{ h}} \approx$ **64.4**

The car traveled about **64.4** kilometers per hour.

So, the correct answer is **B**. Fill in that answer choice.

4 Justify and Evaluate

How do you know your solution is accurate?

Sample answer: I can check my solution by converting it back to miles per hour by dividing by 1.61. 64.4 ÷ 1.61 is equal to 40. Since that is the unit rate shown in the graph, my solution is accurate.

Course 2 • Chapter 1 Ratios and Proportional Reasoning

17

NAME _____ DATE _____ PERIOD _____

Lesson 9 (continued)

Use a problem-solving model to solve each problem.

1 Dante is shoveling dirt in his backyard to make a level area for a swing set. He keeps track of the number of pounds of dirt he shovels over time. What is the ratio of kilograms shoveled to the time in minutes? Round to the nearest tenth. (*Hint:* 1 lb ≈ 0.4536 kg) **7.RP.2b, MP 1**

Time (min)	Dirt Shoveled (lb)
20	100
45	225

Ⓐ 2.3 kilograms per minute
Ⓑ 4.5 kilograms per minute
Ⓒ 5 kilograms per minute
Ⓓ 11.0 kilograms per minute

2 The table shows the wages Ramona earned for the number of hours she spent babysitting. If her wage is a direct variation of hours babysitting, how many hours does she need to babysit to earn $60? **7.RP.2, MP 2**

Hours Babysitting	Wage ($)
2	15
3	22.50
5	37.50

8 hours

3 Reynaldo needs to purchase cupcakes for the after-school picnic. The table shows the price of different numbers of cupcakes. How many cupcakes can Reynaldo purchase with $45? **7.RP.2, MP 1**

Number of Cupcakes	Price ($)
3	6.75
6	13.50
12	27.00

20 cupcakes

4 **H.O.T. Problem** Change one *y*-value in the table below so that it represents a direct variation. Explain your reasoning, and identify the constant of proportionality. **7.RP.2a, MP 3**

x	11	25	41	58
y	27.5	62.5	100	145

For a set of values to represent a direct variation, the ratio $\frac{y}{x}$ should be equal for each pair of *x-y* values. When x = 11, 25, and 58, the ratio $\frac{y}{x}$ = 2.5, so this is the constant of proportionality, *k*. For all four values to represent a direct variation, an *x*-value of 41 needs to correspond to a *y*-value 41 × 2.5 = 102.5 (not 100).

Course 2 • Chapter 1 Ratios and Proportional Reasoning

18

Answers

Chapter 2 Lesson 1 Answer Keys

Lesson 1 Multi-Step Problem Solving

Multi-Step Example

The table shows how much Alfonso earns per week at his summer job. He wants to put 30% of his earnings into a savings account. How much should he deposit into a savings account? 7.RP.3, MP 1

Week	Money Earned ($)
1	100
2	150
3	250
4	75
5	175
6	125
7	115
8	210

Ⓐ $360
Ⓑ $400
Ⓒ $1,200
Ⓓ $3,600

Use a problem-solving model to solve this problem.

1 Analyze

Read the problem. Circle the information you know. Underline what the problem is asking you to find.

2 Plan

What will you need to do to solve the problem? Write your plan in steps.

Step 1 __Add__ the money Alfonso makes for all 8 weeks.

Step 2 Determine __30%__ of his earnings.

Read to Succeed!

Alfonso wants to save a percentage of his earnings. You can eliminate answer choice D, since the amount is more than he earns.

3 Solve

Use your plan to solve the problem. Show your steps.

100 + 150 + 250 + 75 + 175 + 125 + 115 + 210 = __1,200__   Add.

Determine 30% of __1,200__.   0.3 × __1,200__ = __360__

Alfonso will need to put __$360__ into his savings account.

So, the correct answer is __A__. Fill in that answer choice.

4 Justify and Evaluate

How do you know your solution is accurate?

Sample answer: Determine 30% of each week's earnings, then add those amounts. Those amounts would be 30 + 45 + 75 + 22.5 + 52.5 + 37.5 + 34.5 + 63 or 360. So, my solution is accurate.

19

Lesson 1 *(continued)*

Use a problem-solving model to solve each problem.

1 Ella and her family normally pay $165 per month for electricity. The utility company is adding a 5% tax to help fund research for eco-friendly energy sources. How much tax will Ella's family pay for the entire year? 7.RP.3, MP 1

Ⓐ $990.00
Ⓑ $99.00
Ⓒ $66.00
Ⓓ $8.25

2 The local newspaper asked people to vote for their favorite candidate for mayor. The results are shown. If 2,500 people voted, how many more people voted for Candidate B than Candidate C? 7.EE.3, MP 1

Candidate	Percent of Vote
A	20
B	56
C	24

__800 people__

3 Mr. Jenkins buys a hat for $18 and a coat for $63. He has a coupon that allows him to get 15% off the total cost. He pays with four $20 bills. How much change should he receive, in dollars? 7.RP.3, MP 2

__$11.15__

4 H.O.T. Problem Rodrigo is at the mall shopping for new shoes. Two stores are offering a special deal on the pair of shoes he wants. How much is each store charging, and which is a better deal? 7.RP.3, MP 7

Store	Original Cost	Percent Discount
A	$70	15
B	$85.50	40

A = $59.50, B = $51.30; Store B is a better deal.

20

NAME _____ DATE _____ PERIOD _____

Lesson 2 (continued)

Use a problem-solving model to solve each problem.

1 Elena works on a farm that has three types of animals. There are a total of 47 animals. About how many more cows are there than chickens? 7.RP.3, MP 2

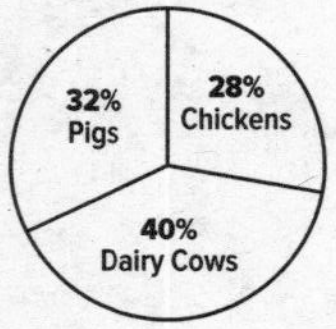

28% Chickens
32% Pigs
40% Dairy Cows

Ⓐ 2 cows
Ⓑ 5 cows
Ⓒ 12 cows
Ⓓ 564 cows

2 Brad borrowed money from his sister to buy a new video game that costs $62. He has paid back 78% of the cost of the game. About how much money does he still owe his sister, in dollars? 7.RP.3, MP 2

Sample answer: $14

3 Dana buys the camping supplies shown below. About how many dollars does she spend if sales tax is 6%? 7.RP.3, MP 1

Item	Cost ($)
Sleeping bag	29
Tent	52
Flashlight	18

Sample answer: $110

4 🖐 **H.O.T. Problem** The table shows the number of shots taken and the percent made by the top female basketball players. Estimate who made the most shots and about how many more shots were made than the next best player. 7.RP.3, MP 7

Player	Shots Taken	Percent Made
Rosa	301	43
Domenica	384	52
Melinda	501	50

Sample answer: Melinda made the most shots by about 50 shots.

Course 2 • Chapter 2 Percents

21

22

Answers

NAME _____ DATE _____ PERIOD _____

Chapter 2

Lesson 2 Multi-Step Problem Solving

Multi-Step Example

The students at Elgin Middle School voted on a new mascot. The principal found that 19% of each grade chose a tiger for a new mascot. About how many more 7th graders voted for a tiger than 8th graders? 7.RP.3, MP 2

Grade	Number of Students
6	149
7	168
8	123

Ⓐ 4 students
Ⓑ 10 students
Ⓒ 34 students
Ⓓ 44 students

Use a problem-solving model to solve this problem.

1 Analyze
Read the problem. Circle the information you know. Underline what the problem is asking you to find.

2 Plan
What will you need to do to solve the problem? Write your plan in steps.
Step 1 Estimate **19%** of 170 and 120.
Step 2 **Subtract** to determine the difference.

3 Solve
Use your plan to solve the problem. Show your steps.

Estimate of 7th graders.   Estimate of 8th graders.
19% of $168 \approx 0.2 \times 170$ 19% of $123 \approx 0.2 \times 120$
≈ 34 ≈ 24

$34 - 24 = 10$ Subtract.

About **10** more 7th graders voted for a tiger than 8th graders.

So, the correct answer is **B**. Fill in that answer choice.

Read to Succeed!
You can also estimate using an equivalent fraction to determine the number of students.

4 Justify and Evaluate
How do you know your solution is accurate?
Sample answer: I can determine $\frac{1}{5}$ of 170 and 120 to get 34 and 24.
The difference between 34 and 24 is 10. So, my solution is accurate.

Course 2 • Chapter 2 Percents

NAME _____ DATE _____ PERIOD _____

Lesson 3 (continued)

Use a problem-solving model to solve each problem.

1 Carlos is saving up to buy two new books. He has saved 60% of the cost of one book that costs $18, and 30% of the cost of another book that costs $21. How much more does he need to save? **7.RP.3, MP 2**

Ⓐ $17.10
Ⓑ $18.20
Ⓒ $21.30
Ⓓ $21.90

2 Hasina entered a raffle 5 times and there are 125 entries. She decided to buy 15 more raffle tickets. By what percent does her chance of winning increase? Round to the nearest percent. **7.RP.3, MP 1**

10%

3 Rudy took a test and earned a 92%. Camilo earned an 88% on the same test. If Rudy answered 46 questions correctly, how many more questions did he answer correctly than Camilo? **7.RP.3, MP 7**

2 questions

4 ✎ **H.O.T. Problem** Alma bought a rocking chair for $266. She used a coupon to save some money. If she paid $226.10 for the chair, what percent discount did Alma get on the chair? **7.RP.3, MP 2**

15

24 Course 2 • Chapter 2 Percents

NAME _____ DATE _____ PERIOD _____

Lesson 3 Multi-Step Problem Solving

Chapter 2

Multi-Step Example

The recommended caloric intake for boys ages 9–13 is 1,800 Calories per day. The table shows what percent of the Calories should be divided into different nutrients. How many daily Calories should *not* come from protein? **7.RP.3, MP 2**

Nutrient	Percent of Daily Calories
Carbohydrates	45
Fat	20
Protein	35

Ⓐ 810 Ⓒ 1,170
Ⓑ 990 Ⓓ 1,440

Use a problem-solving model to solve this problem.

1 Analyze
Read the problem. Circle the information you know. Underline what the problem is asking you to find.

2 Plan
What will you need to do to solve the problem? Write your plan in steps.

Step 1 Determine the percent of daily Calories that *do not come from* **protein** .

Step 2 Write a **proportion** to determine the number of Calories.

3 Solve
Use your plan to solve the problem. Show your steps.

$100\% - 35\% =$ **65%**   Subtract.

$\dfrac{p}{1,800} = \dfrac{65}{100}$ Write the proportion.

$p =$ **1,170**

The daily Calories that should *not* come from protein is **1,170** .

So, the correct answer is **C** . Fill in that answer choice.

4 Justify and Evaluate
How do you know your solution is accurate?

Sample answer: I know that 45% and 20% or 65% of the daily Calories come from Carbohydrates and fat. This is the percent of Calories that is NOT from protein. I can determine 65% of 1,800, which is 1,170. My solution is accurate.

Course 2 • Chapter 2 Percents **23**

Read to Succeed!
You can add the percent of daily Calories that come from Carbohydrates and fat to determine the percent that does not come from protein.

NAME _____ DATE _____ PERIOD _____

Lesson 4 Multi-Step Problem Solving

Multi-Step Example

Three friends work on a sales team. The table shows their sales for the month of January. What percent of the team's total sales was sold by Inali and Nigel? Express your answer as a decimal. 7.RP.2, MP 1

Employee	January Sales ($)
Inali	28,000
Nigel	32,000
Sydney	20,000

Use a problem-solving model to solve this problem.

1 Analyze

Read the problem. Circle the information you know. Underline what the problem is asking you to find.

2 Plan

What will you need to do to solve the problem? Write your plan in steps.

Step 1 Determine the **total sales** and sales from Inali and Nigel.

Step 2 Determine the **percent** of the total sales that was from Inali and Nigel.

3 Solve

Use your plan to solve the problem. Show your steps.

Total sales: 28,000 + 32,000 + 20,000 = **80,000**   Add.

Inali and Nigel: 28,000 + 32,000 = **60,000**   Add.

Use the percent equation to determine the percent.

$$60,000 = n \cdot 80,000$$

$$n = \underline{0.75}$$

Inali and Nigel sold **0.75** of the team's total sales.

Read to Succeed!
Inali and Nigel's sales are part of the total sales. Make sure you use the percent equation appropriately.

4 Justify and Evaluate

How do you know your solution is accurate?

Sample answer: I can check my solution by calculating 25% of the total sales. 80,000 · 0.25 = 20,000, which represents Sydney's sales. If you add Sydney's sales with Inali's and Nigel's, 20,000 + 60,000, you get 80,000.

Course 2 · Chapter 2 Percents   25

NAME _____ DATE _____ PERIOD _____

Lesson 4 (continued)

Use a problem-solving model to solve each problem.

1 The table shows the distribution of entries for a science fair. The middle school consists of grades 6 through 8, and the high school consists of grades 9 through 12. What percent more of science projects are completed by middle school students than high school students? Express your answer as a decimal. 7.EE.3, MP 1

Grade Level	Number of Science Projects
6	6
7	8
8	11
9	7
10	3
11	3
12	2

0.25

2 The circle graph shows the types of movies Abul watched last year. If he saw a total of 40 movies, how many more independent movies did he see than drama and action movies combined? 7.RP.3, MP 2

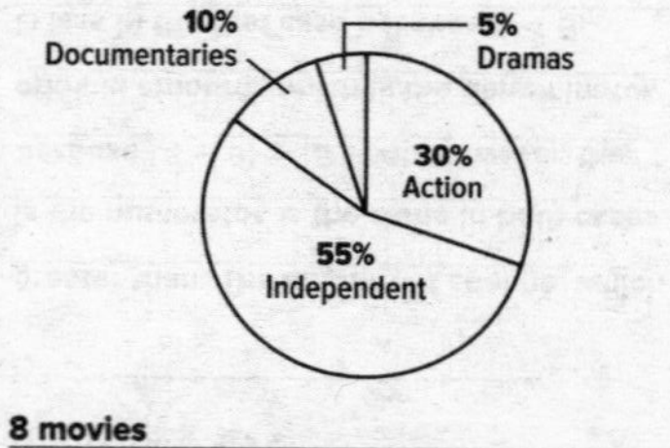

55% Independent
30% Action
5% Dramas
10% Documentaries

8 movies

3 The low-fuel light in Sophia's car comes on when her fuel tank is 10% full. If she has used 18.2 gallons when the light comes on, how many gallons does her fuel tank hold? Round to the nearest tenth. 7.RP.3, MP 2

20.2 gallons

4 H.O.T. Problem An art dealer sells art for two galleries. He makes 25% commission on sales at Gallery A and 35% commission on sales at Gallery B. Will the higher commission rate always result in a higher monthly commission income? Justify your reasoning. 7.RP.3, MP 6

No; Sample answer: If he sells more at Gallery A, he may make more. For example, if he sells $10,000 at Gallery A, he will make $2,500. If he sells $6,000 at Gallery B, he will make $2,100, which is less than the Gallery A commission.

26   Course 2 · Chapter 2 Percents

Answers

Chapter 2 Lesson 5 Answer Keys

NAME _____ DATE _____ PERIOD _____

Lesson 5 Multi-Step Problem Solving

Multi-Step Example

The track and field coach records Ian's 400-meter race times during several practices. How much greater was the percent of change from practice 1 to practice 2 than from practice 2 to practice 3? Round to the nearest tenth. 7.EE.3, MP 1

Practice	Time (s)
1	63
2	60
3	58

Ⓐ 1.5% Ⓒ 4.8%
Ⓑ 3.3% Ⓓ 7.9%

Use a problem-solving model to solve this problem.

1 Analyze
Read the problem. (Circle) the information you know. Underline what the problem is asking you to find.

2 Plan
What will you need to do to solve the problem? Write your plan in steps.

Step 1 Determine the **percent of change** between each practice.

Step 2 **Subtract** to determine how much greater the percent of change was between each practices.

3 Solve
Use your plan to solve the problem. Show your steps.

practice 1 to practice 2   practice 2 to practice 3

$\dfrac{63-60}{63} = \dfrac{3}{63}$ or 0.048 $\dfrac{60-58}{60} = \dfrac{2}{60}$ or $0.0\overline{3}$

Write each as a percent, then subtract.

4.8% − 3.3% = **1.5%**

Ian's percent of decrease was **1.5%** greater between practice 1 and 2.

So, the correct answer is **A**. Fill in that answer choice.

4 Justify and Evaluate
How do you know your solution is accurate?

Sample answer: I can check my answer by checking each percent of decrease. 4.7% of 63 is about 3 and 3.3% of 60 is about 2. This is close to the time difference in the table, so my solution is accurate.

Read to Succeed!
Since his time is decreases, this situation represents a percent of decrease. Subtract to calculate the percent of decrease.

NAME _____ DATE _____ PERIOD _____

Lesson 5 (continued)

Use a problem-solving model to solve each problem.

1 The table shows Dashawna's science grade during four grading periods. How much greater was the percent of change in her grade from grading period 1 to 2, than from grading period 2 to 3? Round to the nearest tenth. 7.EE.3, MP 1

Grading Period	Grade
1	92%
2	96%
3	99%
4	96%

Ⓐ 1.0%
Ⓑ 1.2%
Ⓒ 3.1%
Ⓓ 4.3%

2 Earth follows an elliptical orbit around the Sun. At its nearest point on the orbit, it is about 147 million kilometers from the Sun. At its farthest point, it is about 152 million kilometers away. What is the percent change, rounded to the nearest tenth, from its nearest point to its farthest? 7.RP.3, MP 1

3.4%

3 The graph below shows Alexa's bank account balance over the past four months. Between which months is the percent of increase the greatest? 7.EE.3, MP 2

Bank Account Balance

Balance ($): 280, 260, 240, 220, 200
January 230.59   February 263.16   March 243.24   April 275.89
Month

February and March

4 **H.O.T. Problem** Is the percent increase from A to B greater than or less than the percent decrease from B to A? Explain your answer. 7.RP.3, MP 6

[number line: 0   A   B]

greater than; The amount of change, which is the numerator, is the same in both cases because $|A − B| = |B − A|$. However, the original amount, which is the denominator, is less in the first case because $A < B$. Because a lesser denominator results in a greater quotient, the percent change from A to B is greater.

NAME _____ DATE _____ PERIOD _____

Lesson 6 Multi-Step Problem Solving

Multi-Step Example

Takara orders the rib basket meal at a barbecue restaurant. She wants to leave an 18% tip. Sales tax is 6.5% at the restaurant. She also buys one bottle of barbecue sauce, plus tax. How much does Takara spend, in dollars? 7.RP.3, MP 6

Purchase	Price ($)
Rib basket	21
Barbecue sauce	15

Use a problem-solving model to solve this problem.

1 Analyze

Read the problem. (Circle) the information you know.
Underline what the problem is asking you to find.

2 Plan

What will you need to do to solve the problem? Write your plan in steps.

Step 1 Determine the **tip** for just the meal.

Step 2 Determine the **sales tax**. Then add the tip, sales tax, and total bill.

Read to Succeed!

Takara only wants to leave a tip for the meal and not the bottle of sauce. Be sure to only determine the tip for the meal.

3 Solve

Use your plan to solve the problem. Show your steps.

Tip: $21 × 0.18 = **$3.78**

Total Bill: $21 + $15 = **$36**

Sales Tax: $36 × 0.065 = **$2.34**

Add the tip, sales tax, and total bill.

$3.78 + $2.34 + $36 = **$42.12**

Takara spends **$42.12** at the restaurant.

4 Justify and Evaluate

How do you know your solution is accurate?

Sample answer: I can add the percent of sales tax to 100% to solve a different way. $36 × 1.065 = $38.34. Then add the tip, $38.34 + $3.78, to get a total bill of $42.12. So, my solution is accurate.

NAME _____ DATE _____ PERIOD _____

Lesson 6 (continued)

Use a problem-solving model to solve each problem.

1 Brian has $24 worth of pizzas delivered to his house for a $3 delivery fee. He pays 7% sales tax and a 15% tip, which are both calculated on the total price before the delivery fee. How much change does he receive, in dollars, if he pays with two $20 bills? 7.RP.3, MP 6

7.72

2 Yoselin bought a broken antique table at a garage sale for $30. She plans to repair and paint it before reselling it. Her supplies will cost $45 plus 6% sales tax. She takes the amount that she spent on the table and increases the price by 100%. How much does she charge for the table, in dollars? Round to the nearest cent, if necessary. 7.EE.2, MP 2

$155.40

3 Two customers buy the same couch, but live in different states. The table shows the couch pricing information. What is the difference, in percent, between the sales tax in New Jersey and the sales tax in New York? 7.EE.3, MP 2

Location	Price before tax	Price after tax
New York	$2,500	$2,600
New Jersey	$2,000	$2,140

3%

4 H.O.T. Problem Umar sells personalized sports T-shirts at the City Sports Festival. Each shirt costs him $15 to make. The bar graph shows the number of shirts he sold last weekend. He charged a 50% markup on Friday and Saturday, and then lowered it to 30% on Sunday to increase sales. On which day did he make the most money? Justify your answers. 7.RP.3, MP 1

T-Shirts Sold

(bar graph: Number of T-shirts vs. Friday, Saturday, Sunday; Friday 6, Saturday 15, Sunday 22)

He made $7.50 × 6, or $45 on Friday, $7.50 × 15, or $112.50 on Saturday, and $4.50 × 22, or $99 on Sunday. Umar will make the most money on Saturday.

NAME _____ DATE _____ PERIOD _____

Lesson 7 Multi-Step Problem Solving

Multi-Step Example

At the end of the summer season, a garden store discounts all of its summer merchandise. The table shows the discounts for beach umbrellas. Which umbrella would be the least expensive to purchase after the discount and a 6% tax? **7.RP.3, MP 2**

Umbrella	Original Price ($)	Percent Discount
A	75	30
B	68	20
C	85	40
D	80	35

Ⓐ Umbrella A   Ⓒ Umbrella C
Ⓑ Umbrella B   Ⓓ Umbrella D

Use a problem-solving model to solve this problem.

1 Analyze

Read the problem. Circle the information you know. Underline what the problem is asking you to find.

2 Plan

What will you need to do to solve the problem? Write your plan in steps.

Step 1 Determine the amount of __discount__ for each umbrella.

Step 2 Apply the __tax__ after the discount is applied.

Read to Succeed!
Calculate the amount of discount before applying the tax to determine the final price.

3 Solve

Use your plan to solve the problem. Show your steps.

Discount: A: $75 × 0.7 = **$52.50**   B: $68 × 0.8 = **$54.40**

C: $85 × 0.6 = **$51.00**   D: $80 × 0.65 = **$52.00**

Tax: A: $52.50 × 1.06 = **$55.65**   B: $54.40 × 1.06 = **$57.66**

C: $51.00 × 1.06 = **$54.06**   D: $52.00 × 1.06 = **$55.12**

The least expensive umbrella is **umbrella C**.

So, the correct answer is **C**. Fill in that answer choice.

4 Justify and Evaluate

How do you know your solution is accurate?

Sample answer: The discount for umbrella C would be $85 × 0.4 or $34.

Subtract, $85 − $34, which equals $51. Then apply the tax, $51 × 0.06 = $3.06.

Add the tax, $51 + $3.06 = $54.06. So, my solution is accurate.

NAME _____ DATE _____ PERIOD _____

Lesson 7 *(continued)*

Use a problem-solving model to solve each problem.

1 The table shows the percent discount that a customer will save based on the original cost of an item. If Jeremy buys a $35 item and an $80 item, how much will he spend after the discount is applied to each item? **7.RP.3, MP 2**

Original Cost	Percent Discount
Under $50	10
$50–$100	20
over $100	25

Ⓐ $95.50
Ⓑ $86.25
Ⓒ $19.50
Ⓓ $28.75

2 A pair of jeans that regularly cost $75 is on sale for 30% off. Javier has a coupon for an additional 15% off, which is calculated after the initial discount. How much will Javier pay for the jeans, in dollars? Round to the nearest cent. **7.RP.3, MP 6**

$44.63

3 Christian was excited when he saw an ad for a local electronics store in the newspaper that was going out of business. Everything in the store was 40% off. He would like to purchase a new television that originally costs $1,250. How many months would it take him to pay for the television if he paid $75 each month? **7.EE.3, MP 2**

10 months

4 🖐 **H.O.T. Problem** Maria purchased a new jacket for $78.12. The original price of the jacket was discounted 20%, and Maria had to pay a 5% sales tax. What was the original price of the jacket? **7.RP.3, MP 1**

$93

NAME _____ DATE _____ PERIOD _____

Lesson 8 Multi-Step Problem Solving

Chapter 2

Multi-Step Example

Donte is buying a car that costs $8,000. He is deciding between a 3-year loan and a 4-year loan. Use the rates in the table to determine how much money he will save if he chooses the 3-year loan instead of the 4-year loan. 7.RP.3, MP 1

Ⓐ $20 Ⓒ $100
Ⓑ $60 Ⓓ $260

Time (y)	Simple Interest (%)
3	2.25
4	2.5
5	3

Use a problem-solving model to solve this problem.

1 Analyze

Read the problem. Circle the information you know. Underline what the problem is asking you to find.

2 Plan

What will you need to do to solve the problem? Write your plan in steps.

Step 1 Determine the _interest_ for each loan.

Step 2 Subtract to determine how much _money_ he will save.

3 Solve

Use your plan to solve the problem. Show your steps.

Use the simple interest formula.

3 year loan: $I = 8{,}000 \cdot 0.0225 \cdot 3 = $ **540**

4 year loan: $I = 8{,}000 \cdot 0.025 \cdot 4 = $ **800**   Subtract.

$800 - $540 = **$260**

Donte would save **$260** if he chooses a 3-year loan.

So, the correct answer is __D__. Fill in that answer choice.

4 Justify and Evaluate

How do you know your solution is accurate?

Sample answer: I can determine the total amount Donte would owe in each situation. In 3 years he would owe $8,540 and in 4 years, $8,800. The difference is $8,800 − $8,540, or $260.

33

NAME _____ DATE _____ PERIOD _____

Lesson 8 (continued)

Use a problem-solving model to solve each problem.

1 Evan has $4,000 that he wants to put into a savings account until he leaves for college, which will be 6 years from now. How much more money will he have in his savings account if he chooses Bank B instead of Bank A? 7.RP.3, MP 1

Bank	Interest Rate
Bank A	4.5%
Bank B	4.9%

Ⓐ $16
Ⓑ $96
Ⓒ $1,176
Ⓓ $1,080

2 Isabel has $1,500 to deposit into a savings account with a 3.2% interest rate. She wants to wait until she earns $240 in interest before withdrawing the money. How many years will she have to wait before she can withdraw the money? 7.EE.3, MP 8

5 years

3 A higher interest rate and a longer loan term lead to a higher amount of interest. Given the information in the table, what percent interest rate for Bank B would make the amount of interest from each bank the same? 7.EE.3, MP 2

	Bank A	Bank B
Interest rate	4.2%	▓
Term	4 year	5 year
Principal	$4,000	$4,000

3.36%

4 ✎ **H.O.T. Problem** Alex is buying a car that costs $18,000. He will make a down payment of $2,000, and the tax rate is 7%. He is considering a 5-year loan with an interest rate of 6.2%. What is the total cost of the car including tax and interest over the life of the loan? 7.RP.3, MP 6

$24,610.60

34

Read to Succeed!

Remember to change each percent to a decimal before calculating the simple interest.

Answers

NAME _____ DATE _____ PERIOD _____

Lesson 1 Multi-Step Problem Solving

Multi-Step Example

Doug is playing a game and has a score of 6. He draws a card that reads, "Lose 10 points." What is his score now? *Preparation for 7.NS.3.* MP4

Ⓐ −10
Ⓑ −4
Ⓒ 4
Ⓓ 10

(number line: −7 −6 −5 −4 −3 −2 −1 0 1 2 3 4 5 6 7)

Use a problem-solving model to solve this problem.

1 Analyze
Read the problem. Circle the information you know. Underline what the problem is asking you to find.

2 Plan
What will you need to do to solve the problem? Write your plan in steps.

Step 1 Identify the integer that represents Doug's score before he draws the "Lose 10 points" card.

Step 2 Represent "Lose 10 points" as a negative integer.

Step 3 Use |−10| to find Doug's new score.

3 Solve
Use your plan to solve the problem. Show your steps.

The integer **6** represents Doug's score. The integer **−10** represents the points he loses. |−10| = **10**

Since this is a loss, count 10 spaces to the **left** of 6.

So, the integer **−4** represents Doug's new score.

The correct answer is **B**. Fill in that answer choice.

4 Justify and Evaluate
How do you know your solution is accurate?

Sample answer: I can use positive and negative counters and make zero pairs. Six positive counters and 10 negative counters gives 6 zero pairs and 4 leftover negative counters.

Read to Succeed!
A number's absolute value is its distance from zero on the number line. Read |n| as "the absolute value of n."

Course 2 · Chapter 3 Integers

35

NAME _____ DATE _____ PERIOD _____

Lesson 1 *(continued)*

Use a problem-solving model to solve each problem.

1 A group of hikers start their hike on a trail 200 feet above the rim of a canyon. They walk 320 feet down the trail into the canyon. Which integer represents the hikers' elevation (in feet) below the rim of the canyon? *Preparation for 7.NS.3.* MP4

(number line: Canyon Rim / Hikers −200 −100 0 100 200)

Ⓐ 520
Ⓑ 180
Ⓒ −120
Ⓓ −320

2 Rebecca recorded the temperature every 3 hours from 6:00 A.M. to 6 P.M. The table shows her results. Between which two consecutive time periods can the temperature change be represented as a negative integer? Explain your answer in terms of comparing integers. *Preparation for 7.NS.3.* MP6

Time	Temperature (°F)
6:00 A.M.	−10
9:00 A.M.	−3
12:00 P.M.	7
3:00 P.M.	12
6:00 P.M.	8

3:00 P.M. to 6:00 P.M.; Sample answer: When the temperature change is a negative integer, it means that the temperature has decreased. Since −3 > −10, 7 > −3, and 12 > 7, these are not decreases. But 8 < 12, so this is a decrease and would be represented by a negative integer.

3 The number line shows the position of a diver below the surface of the water. The diver descends another 8 feet. Write an absolute value expression that shows the total number of feet the diver descended. How many feet did the diver descend below the surface of the water? *Preparation for 7.NS.3.* MP4

(number line: Diver / Sea level −30 −20 −10 0 10)

Sample answer: |−17| + |−8|;
|−17| + |−8| = 17 + |−8| = 17 + 8 or 25
So, the diver descended a total of 25 feet below the surface of the water.

4 🔷 **H.O.T. Problem** If |x| = 15 and |y| = 15, do x and y have the same value? Support your reasoning. *Preparation for 7.NS.3.* MP3
They may or may not have the same value. Sample answer: The integer 15 is the absolute values of the integers 15 and −15. So, the value of x and y could be both be 15, they could both be −15, or one could be 15 and the other −15. The problem does not give enough information to determine their actual values.

36

Course 2 · Chapter 3 Integers

NAME _____ DATE _____ PERIOD _____

Lesson 2 Multi-Step Problem Solving

Multi-Step Example

Carlos is swimming at the beach. The number line shows his vertical movement in feet. Which expression is represented on the number line model? Describe his vertical movement in relation to the surface of the water. **7.NS.1b, MP 4**

-8 -7 -6 -5 -4 -3 -2 -1 0 1 2 3 4 5 6 7

(A) (-6) + (-4); He swam 6 feet down and then 4 feet down. He is 10 feet below the surface.

(B) 0 + (-6); He swam 6 feet down and is 6 feet below the surface of the water.

(C) (-4) + (-2); He swam 4 feet down and then 2 feet down. He is 6 feet below the surface.

(D) (-6) + 2; He swam 6 feet down and then 2 feet up. He is 4 feet below the surface.

Use a problem-solving model to solve this problem.

1 Analyze

Read the problem. Circle the information you know.
Underline what the problem is asking you to find.

2 Plan

What will you need to do to solve the problem? Write your plan in steps.

Step 1 Determine the direction and length of the red arrow.

Step 2 Determine the direction and length of the blue arrow.

3 Solve

Use your plan to solve the problem. Show your steps.

One arrow starts at 0 and goes to the left to __-6__ . Then, the other arrow goes to the right 2 units and ends at __-4__ .

So, Carlos swims 6 feet down to -6, then 2 feet up to -4.

He is __4__ feet __below__ the surface. Choice __D__ is correct.

4 Justify and Evaluate

How do you know your solution is accurate?
Sample answer: Draw the number line vertically and recheck the amounts.

Read to Succeed!

When an arrow goes to the right, it means adding or a positive number. When it goes to the left, then it means subtraction or a negative number.

NAME _____ DATE _____ PERIOD _____

Lesson 2 (continued)

Use a problem-solving model to solve each problem.

1 The table describes the change in temperature from the previous day over three consecutive days. Which expression shows the overall temperature change between Sunday and Wednesday? Express the temperature change as an integer. **7.NS.1b, MP 1**

Day	Change in Temperature (°F)
Monday	dropped 2°
Tuesday	dropped 5°
Wednesday	rose 3°

(A) (5) + (-2); 3°F

(B) (-2) + (-3) + 5, 0°F

(C) (-2) + (-5) + 3; -4°F

(D) (-2) + (-5) + (-3); -10°F

2 In golf, a score of 0 is called *par*. A score *over par* is represented with a positive integer, and a score *under par* is represented with a negative integer. The goal is to get the lowest score possible. Justin and Omar played three rounds of golf, with their scores for each round as shown in the table. What is the winning final score? Who wins the three rounds? **7.NS.1b, MP 1**

	Round 1	Round 2	Round 3
Justin	-2	0	3
Omar	2	-3	1

0; Omar

3 The table shows the transactions of Sierra's checking account during one week. What is her account balance at the end of the week? **7.NS.1b, MP 1**

Transaction	Amount
Beginning balance	$124
ATM withdrawal	$20
Deposit	$35
Bank card purchase	$12

$127

4 H.O.T. Problem In a convenience store, a tray by the register contains leftover change. Customers can use this change for their purchases, or place their change in the tray for other customers to use. At the beginning of the day, there is 27¢ in the tray. At end of the day, there is 15¢ left in the tray. Only two customers used the change tray, and one of these customers added 6¢. How did the other customer use the tray? Justify your response. **7.NS.3, MP 2**

The other customer used 18¢ from the tray; Sample answer. After the first customer added 6¢, there would be a total of 33¢ in the tray. So, 18¢ must have been used by the other customer to end up with

15¢ left. 27 + 6 + (-18) = 15

Chapter 3 Lesson 3 Answer Keys

NAME _____ DATE _____ PERIOD _____

Lesson 3 Multi-Step Problem Solving

Multi-Step Example

On the first play of a football game, the quarterback ran with the football and gained 4 yards. On the next play, he lost 7 yards. The two plays are illustrated on the number line. Write a subtraction equation that represents the two consecutive plays and the net yardage. **7.NS.1, MP 4**

(A) $-4 - 7 = -3$ yards

(B) $4 - 7 = -3$ yards

(C) $7 - 3 = 4$ yards

(D) $3 - 7 = -4$ yards

Use a problem-solving model to solve this problem.

1 Analyze

Read the problem. Circle the information you know. Underline what the problem is asking you to find.

2 Plan

What will you need to do to solve the problem? Write your plan in steps.

Step 1 Determine the integer that represents the yards after the first play.

Step 2 Determine the integer that represents the yards after the second play.

Read to Suceed!
When a value is gained, it represents a positive integer. A loss represents a negative integer.

3 Solve

Use your plan to solve the problem. Show your steps.

The quarterback gained 4 yards, so the first arrow ends at 4. He then lost 7 yards, so the second arrow goes to the left 7 units. The arrow ends at −3.

So, the subtraction equation is $4 - 7 = -3$. Choice **B** is correct.

4 Justify and Evaluate

How do you know your solution is accurate?

Sample answer: You can check your answer using counters. Starting with 4 positive counters, you would need to add 3 zero pairs in order to take away 7 positive counters. There are 3 negative counters remaining.

NAME _____ DATE _____ PERIOD _____

Lesson 3 (continued)

Use a problem-solving model to solve each problem.

1 The highest elevation in a city is 25 feet. The lowest elevation is 8 feet below sea level. Express the range of elevation of the city as a subtraction expression and an addition expression. **7.NS.1c, MP 4**

(A) $25 - 8$; $25 + (-8)$

(B) $8 - 25$; $-25 + 8$

(C) $-8 - (-25)$; $-8 + 25$

(D) $25 - (-8)$; $25 + 8$

2 Eratosthenes and Ptolemy were both mathematicians that made significant contributions in the areas of mathematics, as well as astronomy and geography. The time line below shows the estimated times they lived. Find the difference between the number of years they lived. **7.NS.1, MP 1**

Eratosthenes 276 BCE 195 BCE   Ptolemy 90 CE 168 CE

300 BCE   200 BCE   100 BCE   0   100 CE   200 CE

3 years

3 Kai is working on her budget. The table below is her budget for a month. Find the amount of money Kai has left over at the end of the month. Make three suggestions that change Kai's budget and allow her to save more money each month **7.NS.1d, MP 3**

According to her budget, Kai has −$69 at the end of the month. Sample suggestions for saving money:

- **Stop using credit card and try to pay it off.**
- **Cancel cable TV or get a cheaper package.**
- **Cancel gym membership or get a cheaper membership.**
- **Cut down on cell phone use or get a cheaper plan.**
- **Look into working overtime or get a part-time job.**

Description	Amount ($)
Net pay	2,000
Cable TV	220
Car insurance	74
Cell phone	175
Credit card payment	125
Electric	135
Food	400
Gym membership	90
Rent	800
Savings	50

NAME _____ DATE _____ PERIOD _____

Lesson 4 Multi-Step Problem Solving

Multi-Step Example

Each time Min uses an ATM that belongs to a bank other than the one he has a checking account with, he is charged a fee. The number line shows his ATM fees for one month. Write a numerical expression that represents his ATM fees and explain the meaning. 7.NS.2, MP 4

A (−3)4; Min uses an ATM 4 times and is charged $3 for each use.

B (−12)1; Min is charged $12 for 1 ATM use.

C (−4)3; Min uses an ATM 3 times and is charged $4 for each use.

D (−4)12; Min uses the ATM 12 times and is charged $4 for each use.

Use a problem-solving model to solve this problem.

1 Analyze

Read the problem. Circle the information you know. Underline what the problem is asking you to find.

2 Plan

What will you need to do to solve the problem? Write your plan in steps.

Step 1 Determine the direction of the arrows.

Step 2 Determine the integer for each arrow.

3 Solve

Use your plan to solve the problem. Show your steps.

Since the arrows are going to the __left__ the integers represented are __negative__. There are three arrows that each represent __−4__.

$(-4) \cdot 3 = \underline{-12}$

So, Min used the ATM 3 times and was charged $4 each time.

The correct answer is __C__. Fill in that answer choice.

Read to Succeed!

There are three groups of equal arrows. These three groups represent the three fees.

4 Justify and Evaluate

How do you know your solution is accurate?

Sample answer: Use counters to check. Place three groups of four negative counters. There are a total of 12 negative counters.

41

NAME _____ DATE _____ PERIOD _____

Lesson 4 (continued)

Use a problem-solving model to solve each problem.

1 The table below shows the descent of an airplane. Use the data in the table to find the rate of descent in feet per minute. Assume the plane continues to descend at a constant rate. Write a multiplication expression that represents how far the plane has descended in 7 minutes and find the product. 7.NS.2, MP 7

Distance (ft)	Minutes
−1,200	1
−2,400	2
−3,600	3
−4,800	4

A (−1,200)7; −8,400 feet

B (−2,400)7; −16,800 feet

C (−1,400)7; −9,800 feet

D (−1,371)7; −9,600 feet

2 Olivia is playing a trivia game where you gain points for each right answer and lose points for each wrong answer. Some questions are worth 3 points and some questions are worth 5 points. Olivia gets four 3-point questions right and three 3-point questions wrong. She gets three 5-point questions right and two 5-point questions wrong. How many points does she have? 7.EE.3, MP 2

8 points

3 Jose drives a limousine and he wants to calculate his profit at the end of the day. He spent money on gasoline but made money on trips. He bought 14 gallons worth of gasoline at $4 per gallon. He drove customers 75 miles and charged them a rate of $5 per mile. How much profit did he make, in dollars, at the end of the day? 7.EE.3, MP 4

$319

4 H.O.T. Problem Tom multiplies 5 negative integers. Is the product positive, negative, or zero? Explain and include an example. Then write a general rule about the product of negative numbers. 7.NS.2a, MP 8.

negative; Sample answer: $(-3)^5 =$
$(-3)(-3)(-3)(-3)(-3)$. **Multiplying an odd amount of negative integers will always result in a negative product.**

42

Answers

NAME _____ DATE _____ PERIOD _____

Lesson 5 *(continued)*

Use a problem-solving model to solve each problem.

1 Dakota earns the money shown in the table. After buying 4 chairs, she has $30 left. How much did Dakota pay for each chair? **7.NS.2b,** MP **1**

Job	Amount Earned
Babysitting	$120
Pet sitting	$65
Dog walking	$45

Ⓐ $22.50
Ⓑ $50 *(circled)*
Ⓒ $47.50
Ⓓ $200

2 The table below shows the temperature for a town over 5 consecutive days. Use the data to find the average temperature. Then convert the average to degrees Fahrenheit using the formula below. **7.NS.3,** MP **4**

$$F = \frac{9C + 160}{5}$$

Day	Temperature (C)
1	−19°C
2	−18°C
3	−15°C
4	−15°C
5	−18°C

−17°C; 1.4°F

3 Basir played a game, starting with a certain number of points. He lost 6 points each of the first three rounds. He gained 3 points and then gained 7 points the next two rounds. Then he lost 8 points each of two rounds. His final score is −9. How many points did he have in the beginning of the game? **7.NS.3,** MP **2**

15

4 ✎ **H.O.T. Problem** Susan divides two negative integers. She divides the quotient by a positive integer and multiplies the quotient by a negative integer. Is the result positive or negative? Explain. **7.NS.2,** MP **8**

negative; Sample answer: The quotient of two negative integers is positive. The quotient of two positive integers is positive. The product of a positive and negative is negative. So the final result is negative.

44   Course 2 • Chapter 3 Integers

NAME _____ DATE _____ PERIOD _____

Lesson 5 **Multi-Step** Problem Solving

Multi-Step Example

The table shows the distance and time for each phase of a submersible's trial run. Which expression represents the average speed throughout the trial run? **7.NS.2b,** MP **1**

Distance (m)	Time (sec)
−15	5
−30	6
+5	5
−50	10

Ⓐ 3 m/s
Ⓑ −3 m/s *(circled)*
Ⓒ −3.5 m/s
Ⓓ 3.5 m/s

Use a problem-solving model to solve this problem.

1 Analyze

Read the problem. Circle the information you know. Underline what the problem is asking you to find.

2 Plan

What will you need to do to solve the problem? Write your plan in steps.

Step 1 Determine the speed for each phase of the trial run.

Step 2 Add the speeds and divide to find the average speed.

Read to Succeed!
To find the average, add the values and divide by the number of values.

3 Solve

Use your plan to solve the problem. Show your steps.

Phase 1: −15 ÷ 5 = −3   Phase 2: −30 ÷ 6 = −5
Phase 3: 5 ÷ 5 = 1   Phase 4: −50 ÷ 10 = −5

The average speed is $\dfrac{(-3) + (-5) + (1) + (-5)}{4}$ or −3.

So, the average speed of the submersible is **−3** meters per second.

The correct answer is **B** . Fill in that answer choice.

4 Justify and Evaluate

How do you know your solution is accurate?

Sample answer: Use the inverse operation of multiplication to determine distance based on the time and speed.

Course 2 • Chapter 3 Integers   43

NAME _____ DATE _____ PERIOD _____

Lesson 1 Multi-Step Problem Solving

Multi-Step Example

Thirty-six 7th graders were asked to choose their favorite color. The table shows the fraction of students that chose each color. What decimal shows the difference between the most and least popular colors? 7.NS.2d, MP 8

Ⓐ $0.1\overline{6}$ Ⓒ $0.\overline{3}$

Ⓑ $0.\overline{1}$ Ⓓ 0.5

Color	Fraction
Red	$\frac{5}{18}$
Yellow	$\frac{1}{6}$
Blue	$\frac{4}{9}$
Green	$\frac{1}{9}$

Use a problem-solving model to solve this problem.

1 Analyze

Read the problem. Circle the information you know. Underline what the problem is asking you to find.

2 Plan

What will you need to do to solve the problem? Write your plan in steps.

Step 1 Express each fraction as a __decimal__ .

Step 2 Determine which decimal is the __greatest__ and which is the __least__ . Then subtract.

Read to Succeed!
Read the question carefully. Since it asks for the difference, you will need to subtract.

3 Solve

Use your plan to solve the problem. Show your steps.

Express each fraction as a decimal. Subtract the least from the greatest.

$\frac{5}{18} = $ __0.27__ $\frac{1}{6} = $ __0.16__ $\frac{4}{9} = $ __0.4__ $\frac{1}{9} = $ __0.1__

__0.4__ – __0.1__ or __0.3__ Subtract.

There were __0.3__ more of the students chose __blue__ as their favorite color over __green__ . So, the correct answer is __C__ . Fill in that answer choice.

4 Justify and Evaluate

How do you know your solution is accurate?

Sample answer: I know my solution is accurate because I can add my answer to the least decimal, $0.\overline{3} + 0.\overline{1}$, which is equal to $0.\overline{4}$. This is the greatest decimal and most popular color. My solution is accurate.

NAME _____ DATE _____ PERIOD _____

Lesson 1 (continued)

Use a problem-solving model to solve each problem.

1 The table shows the lengths of the straws, in centimeters, that Jessica has available for an art project.

Straw	Length (cm)
Striped	12.5
White	10.75
Clear	13.35
Blue	11.3

She cut the white straw into two equal-size pieces. What mixed number represents the length of each piece of white straw after cutting? 7.NS.3, MP 6

Ⓐ $6\frac{1}{4}$

Ⓑ $5\frac{13}{20}$

Ⓒ $5\frac{3}{8}$

Ⓓ $5\frac{1}{8}$

3 Destiny read $\frac{1}{4}$ of a book on the day she received it. The next day, she read $\frac{5}{8}$ of the book. On the third day, she finished reading the book. What decimal represents the fraction of the book Destiny read on the third day? 7.NS.3, MP 2

0.125

2 Roger made a square sign to place on his bedroom door shown below in the sketch. What is the decimal equivalent of the perimeter, in inches, of his sign? 7.NS.3, MP 1

Roger's Room

$8\frac{7}{8}$ in.

35.5 inches

4 🖐 H.O.T. Problem Graph and label the fractions $-\frac{2}{3}$, $\frac{3}{5}$, and $-\frac{5}{8}$ on the number line shown using their equivalent decimal value. Explain how you determined where to place each fraction. 7.NS.2d, MP 2

Sample answer: I expressed each fraction as a decimal first. Then I used the number line to place a dot to represent each decimal number.

-0.7 -0.6 -0.65 -0.625 -0.6 -0.6

NAME _____ DATE _____ PERIOD _____

Lesson 2 *(continued)*

Use a problem-solving model to solve each problem.

1 In Mr. Nguyen's class, 24 out of 30 students have a pet. In Ms. Young's class, 55% of students have a pet. Which statement below correctly compares the fraction of students who have a pet in Mr. Nguyen's class to the fraction of students who have a pet in Ms. Young's class? **7.EE.3, MP 6**

Ⓐ $\frac{4}{5} = \frac{11}{20}$

Ⓑ $\frac{4}{5} < \frac{11}{30}$

Ⓒ $\frac{4}{5} > \frac{4}{55}$

Ⓓ $\frac{4}{5} > \frac{11}{20}$

2 The circle graph below shows the favorite subjects of seventh-grade students in a gym class. There are 32 students in the class. How many more students chose Math than Social Studies and Language Arts? **7.EE.3, MP 2**

Favorite Subject

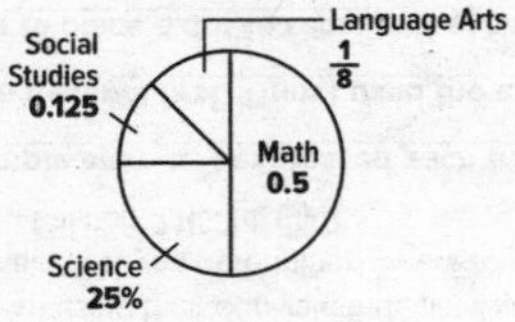

Language Arts $\frac{1}{8}$

Math 0.5

Social Studies 0.125

Science 25%

8 students

3 The table shows the amount of time Pablo practiced his saxophone over three days. Pablo realized he made an error by writing the reciprocal for the time spent on Monday. Once he corrects the error, what is the decimal equivalent of the number that would come first if the times were ordered from greatest to least? **7.EE.3, MP 1**

Day	Time (hr)
Monday	$\frac{4}{3}$
Tuesday	$\frac{7}{8}$
Wednesday	$\frac{5}{6}$

0.875

4 ✎ **H.O.T. Problem** Which of the following numbers is closest to 88% on the number line? **7.NS.2d, MP 4**

$\frac{4}{5}$ $\frac{8}{9}$ $\frac{21}{25}$

Write both the decimal and fraction form of the number. **7.NS.2d, MP 4**

$\frac{8}{9}$, $0.\overline{8}$

48

NAME _____ DATE _____ PERIOD _____

Lesson 2 **Multi-Step** Problem Solving

Chapter 4

Multi-Step Example

The table shows the change in value for four stocks over one day. What is the difference between the greatest value change and the least value change expressed as a decimal? **7.EE.3, MP 6**

Stock	Value
MCD	+1.75%
THC	+0.65
BIG	$+\frac{7}{8}$
GES	$+1\frac{1}{4}$

Ⓐ 1.25   Ⓒ 1.1

Ⓑ 1.2325   Ⓓ 0.6

Use a problem-solving model to solve this problem.

1 Analyze

Read the problem. (Circle) the information you know. Underline what the problem is asking you to find.

2 Plan

What will you need to do to solve the problem? Write your plan in steps.

Step 1 Express each number as a __decimal__. Then compare.

Step 2 Determine which decimal is the __greatest__ and which is the __least__. Then subtract.

Read to Succeed!

Remember to move the decimal point two places to the left when changing the percent 1.75% to a decimal.

3 Solve

Use your plan to solve the problem. Show your steps.

Write each percent or fraction as a decimal. Then subtract.

1.75% = __0.0175__ 0.65 = __0.65__ $\frac{7}{8}$ = __0.875__ $1\frac{1}{4}$ = __1.25__

1.25 − 0.0175 = __1.2325__   Subtract.

The difference between the greatest value change and least value change is __1.2325__.

The correct answer is __B__. Fill in that answer choice.

4 Justify and Evaluate

How do you know your solution is accurate?

Sample answer: I can check my solution by adding my solution and the least value change, which should result in the greatest value change.

1.2325 + 0.0175 = 1.25 So, my answer is accurate.

47

NAME _____ DATE _____ PERIOD _____

Chapter 4

Lesson 3 Multi-Step Problem Solving

Multi-Step Example

Rosa asked her classmates where they would like to take a vacation. The bar graph shows the fraction of the class that chose each option. What fraction more of the class prefer the beach than the other three vacations combined? 7.NS.3, MP 1

Vacation Preference

(bar graph showing: Amusement Park $\frac{1}{16}$, Beach $\frac{11}{16}$, Road Trip $\frac{1}{16}$, Skiing $\frac{3}{16}$)

Ⓐ $\frac{3}{8}$ Ⓒ $\frac{5}{8}$

Ⓑ $\frac{9}{16}$ Ⓓ $\frac{5}{16}$

Use a problem-solving model to solve this problem.

1 Analyze

Read the problem. Circle the information you know. Underline what the problem is asking you to find.

2 Plan

What will you need to do to solve the problem? Write your plan in steps.

Step 1 Add _____ the fractions for amusement park, road trip, and skiing.

Step 2 Subtract _____ the sum from the classmates that prefer the beach.

3 Solve

Use your plan to solve the problem. Show your steps.

$\frac{1}{16} + \frac{1}{16} + \frac{3}{16} = \frac{5}{16}$ Determine the sum.

$\frac{11}{16} - \frac{5}{16} = \frac{6}{16}$ or $\frac{3}{8}$ Subtract to determine the difference.

There are $\frac{3}{8}$ more of the class that prefer a beach vacation.

The correct answer is __A__. Fill in that answer choice.

4 Justify and Evaluate

How do you know your solution is accurate?

Sample answer: I can add my answer to the sum of the fractions that do not prefer beach vacations. $\frac{3}{8} + \frac{5}{16} = \frac{11}{16}$ **So, my solution is accurate.**

Read to Succeed!

Is your answer simplified? Check to see if the fraction is in simplest form. If not, be sure to write it in simplest form.

NAME _____ DATE _____ PERIOD _____

Lesson 3 (continued)

Use a problem-solving model to solve each problem.

1 The table below shows how Mason spends his monthly income. If he starts saving the money that he originally spent on video games and dining out, how much greater is the fraction that he spends than saves? 7.NS.3, MP 1

Category	Fraction of Income
Clothing	$\frac{7}{15}$
Music	$\frac{2}{15}$
Video Games	$\frac{4}{15}$
Dining Out	$\frac{2}{15}$

Ⓐ $\frac{1}{5}$ Ⓑ $\frac{3}{2}$ Ⓒ $\frac{3}{5}$ Ⓓ $\frac{2}{5}$

2 The table shows two types of music notes and how many beats they represent. How many total beats are represented by an augmented eighth followed by two sixteenth notes and another augmented eighth note? 7.NS.3, MP 2

Note	Symbol	Beats
Sixteenth Note	♬	$\frac{1}{4}$
Augmented Eighth Note	♪.	$\frac{3}{4}$

2 beats

3 The table shows the time Jira spends as she gets ready for school. The tasks are listed in order of when she completes them. How many minutes does she spend getting ready before she brushes her teeth? 7.EE.3, MP 1

Task	Time Spent (hours)
Shower	$\frac{2}{12}$
Get dressed	$\frac{1}{12}$
Eat breakfast	$\frac{3}{12}$
Brush teeth	$\frac{1}{12}$
Fix hair	$\frac{5}{12}$

30 minutes

4 H.O.T. Problem The table shows two data sets. Which set has a greater average? By how much greater? 7.NS.3, MP 6

Data Set 1	$\frac{10}{11}$	$\frac{2}{11}$	$\frac{7}{11}$	$\frac{5}{11}$
Data Set 2	$\frac{9}{31}$	$\frac{1}{31}$	$\frac{3}{31}$	$\frac{1}{31}$

Data Set 1; $\frac{3}{62}$

Answers

NAME _____ DATE _____ PERIOD _____

Lesson 4 Multi-Step Problem Solving

Chapter 4

Multi-Step Example

Hakeem has a reading assignment to complete this week. He completes some of the assignment each day. By Wednesday night, he has completed two-thirds of his assignment. What fraction more of his assignment does Hakeem complete on Wednesday than on Tuesday?
7.EE.3, MP 2

Day	Total Fraction Completed
Monday	$\frac{1}{6}$
Tuesday	$\frac{1}{4}$
Wednesday	$\frac{2}{3}$

- Ⓐ $\frac{5}{12}$
- Ⓒ $\frac{1}{3}$
- Ⓑ $\frac{1}{12}$
- Ⓓ $\frac{1}{4}$

Use a problem-solving model to solve this problem.

1 Analyze

Read the problem. (Circle) the information you know.
Underline what the problem is asking you to find.

2 Plan

What will you need to do to solve the problem? Write your plan in steps.

Step 1   Determine the **fraction** completed on Wednesday and Tuesday.

Step 2   Determine how much more he completed **Wednesday**

3 Solve

Use your plan to solve the problem. Show your steps.

$$\frac{2}{3} - \frac{1}{4} = \frac{5}{12}$$

Determine how much more was completed on Wednesday.

$$\frac{5}{12} - \frac{1}{12} = \frac{4}{12} = \frac{1}{3} \text{ or } \frac{2}{3}$$ Subtract.

He completed **$\frac{1}{3}$** more of the assignment on Wednesday.

The correct answer is **C** . Fill in that answer choice.

4 Justify and Evaluate

How do you know your solution is accurate?
Sample answer: The "fraction more" completed is the *difference* between
the fraction completed on Wednesday and the fraction completed on Tuesday.
I can use the inverse to confirm my solution: $\frac{1}{3} + \frac{1}{12} = \frac{5}{12}$.

Read to Succeed!
The fractions in the table are cumulative, meaning they are the total fraction he has completed. It is not the fraction he completes each day.

NAME _____ DATE _____ PERIOD _____

Lesson 4 *(continued)*

Use a problem-solving model to solve each problem.

1 Over three days, a veterinarian measures the difference between a cat's weight and the weight on its first visit. What is the net weight change of the cat's weight, in pounds, from the second visit to the fourth?
7.EE.3, MP 2

Visit	Difference from Original Weight (lb)
Second	$-\frac{1}{2}$
Third	$-\frac{1}{5}$
Fourth	$-\frac{3}{10}$

- Ⓐ $\frac{1}{5}$
- Ⓑ $\frac{1}{10}$
- Ⓒ $\frac{1}{5}$
- Ⓓ $\frac{1}{10}$

2 How many units greater is the perimeter of Triangle *B* than the perimeter of Triangle *A*?
7.NS.3, MP 1

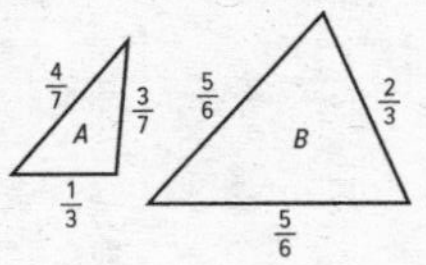

Triangle *A*: $\frac{4}{7}$, $\frac{3}{7}$, $\frac{1}{3}$ Triangle *B*: $\frac{5}{6}$, $\frac{2}{3}$, $\frac{5}{6}$

1 unit

3 The table shows the fraction of each soccer game that Zoe spent playing goalie. On average, how much of one game did Zoe spend playing goalie? Express your answer as a decimal. **7.NS.1d, MP 1**

Game	Fraction of Game as Goalie
1	$\frac{1}{4}$
2	$\frac{5}{8}$
3	$\frac{1}{2}$
4	$\frac{5}{8}$

0.5

4 **H.O.T. Problem** The circle graph shows how Elena handles her monthly income. What fraction more does she spend or give to charity than she saves? **7.NS.3, MP 1**

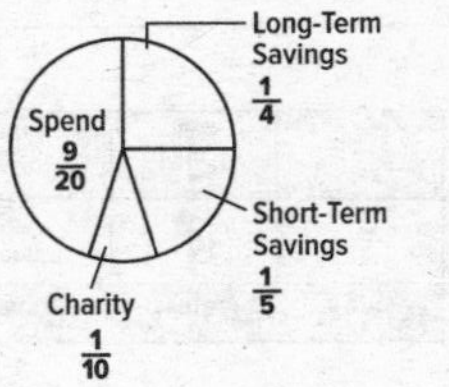

Circle graph: Spend $\frac{9}{20}$, Long-Term Savings $\frac{1}{4}$, Short-Term Savings $\frac{1}{5}$, Charity $\frac{1}{10}$

$\frac{1}{10}$

NAME _____ DATE _____ PERIOD _____

Lesson 5 (continued)

Use a problem-solving model to solve each problem.

1. The table shows Lily's length from the time she was born. How many more inches did she grow during the first month than during her second month? 7.NS.3, **MP** 1

Age	Length (in.)
Birth	$19\frac{3}{4}$
1 Month	$22\frac{1}{4}$
2 Month	$23\frac{1}{4}$

Ⓐ $\frac{3}{4}$ inch

Ⓑ $1\frac{1}{4}$ inches

Ⓒ $1\frac{1}{2}$ inches

Ⓓ $3\frac{1}{2}$ inches

3. Farid's family took a road trip. The circle graph shows the part of an hour that each family member drove. What fraction more of an hour did his parents drive than the rest of the family combined? 7.NS.3, **MP** 1

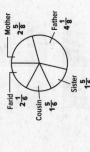

Mother $2\frac{5}{8}$

Father $4\frac{1}{8}$

Farid $1\frac{2}{6}$

Cousin $1\frac{5}{6}$

Sister $1\frac{5}{6}$

$\frac{11}{12}$ hour

2. The side measures for two sides of a triangle are shown. What is the measure, in inches, of side A if the perimeter of the triangle is 180 inches? 7.NS.3, **MP** 4

$76\frac{1}{6}$ in. $51\frac{1}{3}$ in.

A

$52\frac{1}{2}$ inches

4. **H.O.T. Problem** A point is plotted on a coordinate grid at $-7\frac{2}{3}$, $-11\frac{5}{6}$. A second point is plotted 9 units to the right and $2\frac{2}{3}$ units down. What are the coordinates of the second point? Is it in a different quadrant than the first point? Explain your reasoning. 7.NS.3, **MP** 2

$\left(1\frac{1}{3}, -14\frac{1}{6}\right)$; yes. Sample answer: The first point has a negative x-coordinate and a negative y-coordinate, so it lies in Quadrant III. The second point has a positive x-coordinate and a negative y-coordinate, so it lies in Quadrant IV.

54   Course 2 • Chapter 4 Rational Numbers

Chapter 4

NAME _____ DATE _____ PERIOD _____

Lesson 5 **Multi-Step** Problem Solving

Multi-Step Example

The table shows the makeup of the cheese tray at the DeSilva family reunion. If the family eats $6\frac{5}{6}$ pounds of the cheese, how many pounds of cheese remain on the tray? 7.NS.3, **MP** 1

Type of Cheese	Amount (lb)
Cheddar	$3\frac{1}{2}$
Provolone	$2\frac{2}{2}$
Swiss	$2\frac{1}{4}$

Ⓐ 1 pound

Ⓑ $\frac{5}{12}$ pound

Ⓒ $1\frac{1}{2}$ pound

Ⓓ $2\frac{7}{12}$ pound

Use a problem-solving model to solve this problem.

1 Analyze

Read the problem. Circle the information you know. Underline what the problem is asking you to find.

2 Plan

What will you need to do to solve the problem? Write your plan in steps.

Step 1   Determine the amount of cheese on the tray by __adding__ the mixed numbers.

Step 2   __Subtract__ the weight of cheese that was eaten from the original amount on the cheese tray.

3 Solve

Use your plan to solve the problem. Show your steps.

Determine the amount of cheese on the tray. Then subtract.

$3\frac{1}{2} + 2\frac{1}{2} + 2\frac{1}{4} = 8\frac{1}{4}$ Add.

$8\frac{1}{4} - 6\frac{5}{6} = 1\frac{5}{12}$ Subtract.

There were $1\frac{5}{12}$ pounds remaining on the cheese tray.

The correct answer is __B__. Fill in that answer choice.

> **Read to Succeed!**
> When subtracting the mixed numbers, be sure to rename them using the LCD before trying to subtract.

4 Justify and Evaluate

How do you know your solution is accurate?

Sample answer: I can add the amount eaten to the amount remaining to check my solution. $1\frac{5}{12} + 6\frac{5}{6} = 8\frac{1}{4}$ The sum is equal to the sum of the amounts of cheese on the cheese tray. So, my solution is accurate.

Course 2 • Chapter 4 Rational Numbers   53

Answers

NAME _____ DATE _____ PERIOD _____

Lesson 6 (continued)

Use a problem-solving model to solve each problem.

1 Jin took a 15-hour flight to Korea. He slept for $\frac{1}{3}$ of the flight. The table shows how Jin spent his time when he was awake. How many minutes did he spend talking? **7.EE.3, MP 1**

Activity	Fraction of Time Awake
Reading	$\frac{1}{2}$
Eating	$\frac{1}{6}$
Talking	$\frac{1}{3}$

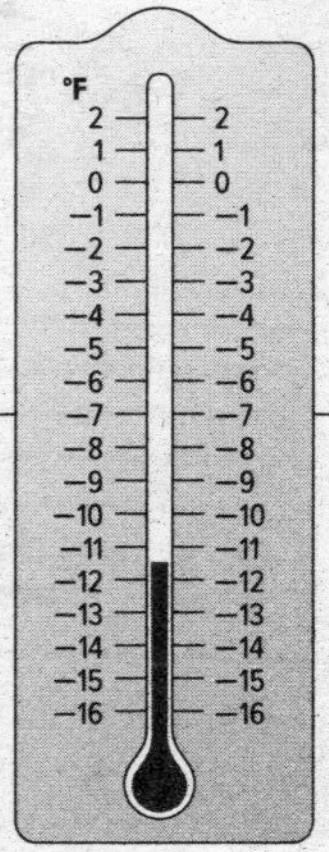

Ⓐ 100 minutes
Ⓑ 180 minutes
Ⓒ 200 minutes
Ⓓ 300 minutes

3 Rectangle 1 has a length of $2\frac{1}{2}$ inches and a width of $\frac{1}{3}$ inch. Rectangle 2 is created by multiplying each side by a factor of $1\frac{1}{2}$. Determine how many more square inches the new area is than the original area. **7.EE.3, MP 2**
$1\frac{1}{24}$ in²

2 The table shows the number of miles for each segment of a triathlon. Lina trained on a team of 5 people. Each person completed each segment of the race. How many total yards did her team swim? **7.EE.3, MP 6**

Activity	Distance (miles)
Swim	$2\frac{2}{5}$
Bike ride	112
Run	$26\frac{1}{5}$

21,120 yards

4 H.O.T. Problem The circle graph shows the breakdown of Seth's math grade. His quiz grade consists of 6 quizzes, each worth equal amounts. He missed $\frac{1}{10}$ of the possible points on his first quiz. What fraction of his overall grade do the missed points represent? Which is worth a greater fraction of his grade, Quizzes and Homework or Quizzes and Tests? Explain. **7.NS.3, MP 1**

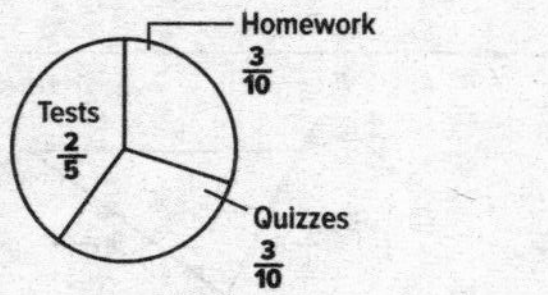

Homework $\frac{3}{10}$ · Tests $\frac{2}{5}$ · Quizzes $\frac{3}{10}$

$\frac{1}{200}$; Quizzes and Tests; Sample answer: Quizzes and Tests represent $\frac{7}{10}$ of his grade. Quizzes and Homework represent $\frac{6}{10}$ of his grade, and $\frac{7}{10} > \frac{6}{10}$.

Chapter 4

NAME _____ DATE _____ PERIOD _____

Lesson 6 Multi-Step Problem Solving

Multi-Step Example

The thermometer shows the temperature in Badger, Minnesota, at 10 P.M. The temperature decreased by $\frac{1}{3}$ of its absolute value by 4 A.M. What is the final temperature, to the nearest degree Fahrenheit? **7.EE.3, MP 1**

Ⓐ −4
Ⓑ −8
Ⓒ −15
Ⓓ −19

Use a problem-solving model to solve this problem.

1 Analyze
Read the problem. Circle the information you know. Underline what the problem is asking you to find.

2 Plan
What will you need to do to solve the problem? Write your plan in steps.
Step 1 Determine **one-third** of the absolute value of **−11$\frac{1}{2}$**.
Step 2 Then **subtract** the product from the current temperature.

3 Solve
Use your plan to solve the problem. Show your steps.
Determine the product. Then subtract from the current temperature.
$11\frac{1}{2} \times \frac{1}{3} = 3\frac{5}{6}$
$-11\frac{1}{2} - 3\frac{5}{6} = -15\frac{1}{3}$
The final temperature was about **−15** degrees Fahrenheit.
The correct answer is **C**. Fill in that answer choice.

4 Justify and Evaluate
How do you know your solution is accurate?
Sample answer: I can add the temperature change to the current temperature to determine the original temperature. $-15\frac{1}{3} + 3\frac{5}{6} = -11\frac{1}{2}$ So, my solution is accurate.

Read to Succeed! The final temperature decreased, which means the absolute value of the final temperature will be greater than the absolute value of the original temperature.

Chapter 4 Lesson 7 Answer Keys

NAME _____ DATE _____ PERIOD _____

Lesson 7 Multi-Step Problem Solving

Multi-Step Example

The students listed in the table each made a pitcher of lemonade. About how many more liters did Serena make than Kyle? 7.RP.3, MP 6

Person	Capacity
Serena	3 gal
Morgan	3,500 mL
Charity	13 quarts
Kyle	8 L

Ⓐ 0.89 liter
Ⓑ 1.4 liters
Ⓒ 3.37 liters
Ⓓ 11.37 liters

Use a problem-solving model to solve this problem.

1 Analyze

Read the problem. Circle the information you know. Underline what the problem is asking you to find.

2 Plan

What will you need to do to solve the problem? Write your plan in steps.

Step 1 Convert 3 gallons to __liters__ .

Step 2 Subtract the amount Kyle made from the amount of liters.

3 Solve

Use your plan to solve the problem. Show your steps.
Convert gallons to liters.

3 gal · $\frac{3.79 \text{ L}}{1 \text{ gal}}$ ≈ __11.37__ liters

Subtract the amount in liters of Kyle's pitcher from Serena's pitcher amount in liters.

__11.37__ − 8 = __3.37__

Serena made about __3.37__ liters more than Kyle.

So, the correct answer is __C__ . Fill in that answer choice.

Read to Succeed!
You may need to refer to the conversion chart in your book to help you convert between measurement systems.

4 Justify and Evaluate

How do you know your solution is accurate?
Sample answer: I can check by adding the difference to Kyle's pitcher amount, 8 + 3.37 to get 11.37 liters. I can divide this amount by 3.79 to convert it to gallons: 11.37 ÷ 3.79 ≈ 3 gallons. My solution is accurate.

Course 2 • Chapter 4 Rational Numbers

57

NAME _____ DATE _____ PERIOD _____

Lesson 7 (continued)

Use a problem-solving model to solve each problem.

1 Kofi and Vanessa each measured the length of their hands. In centimeters, about how much longer is Vanessa's hand compared to Kofi's? 7.RP.3, MP 6

Student	Length of Hand
Kofi	7 in.
Vanessa	19 cm

Ⓐ 1.22 cm
Ⓑ 1.5 cm
Ⓒ 12 cm
Ⓓ 17.78 cm

2 Three tables are going to be combined together in a row to make one long table. About how many feet long will the new table be? 7.RP.3, MP 6

Table	Length
A	4.5 feet
B	2.7 meters
C	2 yards

19.5 feet

3 In a sauce recipe, 2 cups of ketchup are added for every 1 cup of tomato sauce. If 2.25 cups of tomato sauce are added, about how many milliliters of ketchup should be added? Round to the nearest whole number. 7.RP.3, MP 6

1,065 mL

4 ✏ H.O.T. Problem A suitcase weighing 50 pounds contains clothes, towels, and shoes. The weight distribution is shown in the circle graph below. About how much do the clothes weigh in kilograms? Round to the nearest hundredth. 7.RP.3, MP 6

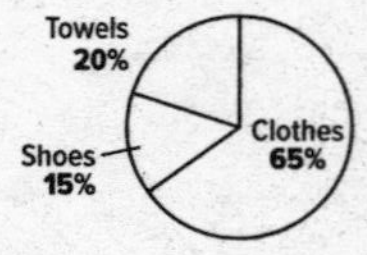

Clothes 65%
Shoes 15%
Towels 20%

14.74 kg

58 Course 2 • Chapter 4 Rational Numbers

NAME _____ DATE _____ PERIOD _____

Lesson 8 Multi-Step Problem Solving

Chapter 4

Multi-Step Example

William has $15\frac{3}{5}$ quarts of paint. He equally divided the paint into 3 two-gallon containers. How many gallons of paint are in each container? Express your answer as a decimal. 7.EE.3, MP 1

Use a problem-solving model to solve this problem.

1 Analyze

Read the problem. (Circle) the information you know. Underline what the problem is asking you to find.

2 Plan

What will you need to do to solve the problem? Write your plan in steps.

Step 1 Convert quarts to __gallons__ by dividing by 4.

Step 2 Then divide the quotient by __3__ to determine how many gallons are in each container.

> **Read to Succeed!**
> Every gallon has 4 quarts. Since you're converting from a smaller unit (quarts) to a larger unit (gallons), your answer needs to be a smaller number, so you will need to divide.

3 Solve

Use your plan to solve the problem. Show your steps.

Convert quarts to gallons.

$15\frac{3}{5} \div 4 = 3\frac{9}{10}$

Divide by 3 to determine the amount in each container.

$3\frac{9}{10} \div 3 = 1\frac{3}{10}$ or 1.3

Each container holds __1.3__ gallons of paint.

4 Justify and Evaluate

How do you know your solution is accurate?

Sample answer: I can add to determine the number of gallons of paint in all 3 containers. 1.3 + 1.3 + 1.3 = 3.9 Then I can convert this to quarts by multiplying by 4 to check my solution. 3.9 × 4 = 15.6 or $15\frac{3}{5}$.

NAME _____ DATE _____ PERIOD _____

Lesson 8 (continued)

Use a problem-solving model to solve each problem.

1. A family-sized container of macaroni holds sixteen $\frac{3}{4}$-cup servings. A chef prepares meals using $1\frac{1}{3}$ cups in each bowl. How many bowls can the chef prepare from one family-sized container? 7.EE.3, MP 1

   9 bowls

2. The side length of Cube 1 is $2\frac{1}{2}$ inches. Cube 2 has a side length of 5 inches. How many times larger is the volume of Cube 2? 7.EE.3, MP 1

   8 times

3. The table shows how much Rita paid for beans at the local market. How much more per pound will it cost to buy the most expensive beans per pound than the cheapest beans per pound? 7.NS.3, MP 2

Type	Weight (lb)	Cost ($)
Black beans	4	6
Lentil beans	$3\frac{1}{8}$	4
Kidney beans	$6\frac{1}{4}$	11

   $0.48 per pound

4. **H.O.T. Problem** Compare the mean of the data below with and without the outlier, which is the extremely high data value. Which mean represents the majority of the data more closely? Explain. 7.NS.2c, MP 2

   With the outlier, the mean is $-\frac{1}{3}$. Without the outlier, the mean is $-\frac{2}{3}$. The mean without the outlier represents the majority of the data because most of the data points are clustered around $-\frac{2}{3}$.

NAME _____ DATE _____ PERIOD _____

Lesson 1 (continued)

Use a problem-solving model to solve each problem.

1 Sonja has read 222 pages of a 350-page book. She needs to complete the book in 8 days. Write and simplify an expression to find the number of pages p that she must read per day to finish in 8 days. If Sonja skips reading on day 3, how does it affect the number of pages she needs to read on days 4–8? Explain your reasoning. *Preparation for 7.EE.1,* MP 4

Sample answer: $\dfrac{p}{8} = \dfrac{350 - 222}{8} = 16;$

16 pages a day to finish in 8 days. If Sonja skips day 3, then she has 16 additional pages to read on days 4–8, or in 5 days.

$5(16) + 16 = 96$ **pages.** $96 \div 5 = 19.2.$ **She would need to read about 19 pages a day on days 4–8.**

2 Cho has a piece of fiberboard that measures 24 centimeters by 36 centimeters. She will cut it into rectangles like the one shown below for an art project. If the area of Triangle I is 48 square centimeters, what is the greatest number of rectangles Cho can cut out of the piece of fiberboard? *Preparation for 7.EE.1,* MP 4

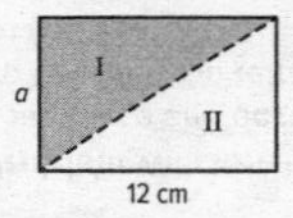

9 rectangles

3 Write a real-world problem that can be represented by the expression $49 + 8w$. *Preparation for 7.EE.1,* MP 4

Sample answer: Jamil has $49 in his savings account and plans to save $8 each week. The expression $49 + 8w$ represents the total amount of money Jamil would have in his account after w weeks.

4 🖐 **H.O.T. Problem** Richard evaluated the expressions below. He says that if $y = 6$, the value of each of the expressions will be the same. His math partner says he is wrong. Who is correct? Support your answer. *Preparation for 7.EE.1,* MP 3

$4y - 3$
$\dfrac{126}{y}$
$27 - (-y)$

Richard's math partner; Sample answer: If $y = 6$, the value of the first two expressions is 21, but the value of the third is $27 - (-6) = 27 + 6 = 33$. Richard forgot that subtracting a negative number is the same as adding its opposite.

Chapter 5

NAME _____ DATE _____ PERIOD _____

Lesson 1 Multi-Step Problem Solving

Multi-Step Example

Nelson has $65.00 to spend on some polo shirts and a jacket. One store has the shirts he likes on sale for $8.98 and a denim jacket he likes for $25.00. Write an algebraic expression that represents the cost of any number of shirts and the jacket. Use the expression to decide if Nelson has enough money to buy 4 shirts and the jacket. *Preparation for 7.EE.1,* MP 4

Use a problem-solving model to solve this problem.

1 Analyze

Read the problem. (Circle) the information you know. Underline what the problem is asking you to find.

2 Plan

What will you need to do to solve the problem? Write your plan in steps.

Step 1 Write an **algebraic** expression that represents the cost of the purchases.

Step 2 Evaluate the expression for __4__ shirts and the jacket, and compare the cost to __$65.00__.

Read to Succeed!

To determine if Nelson has enough money, you need to find a value for s that will make the total less than $65.

3 Solve

Use your plan to solve the problem. Show your steps.

Algebraic expression: **8.98s + 25** Let s represent the number of shirts.

Replace s with __4__ **8.98(4) + 25 =** __35.92__ **+ 25 =** __60.92__ **or $** __60.92__

$60.92 is __less than__ **$65.00, so Nelson has enough money to buy 4 shirts and the jacket.**

4 Justify and Evaluate

How do you know your solution is accurate?

I can subtract the cost of the items from $65.00. 65 − 25 − 4(8.98) = 4.05.

Since Nelson would have $4.05 left, my answer is accurate.

Answers

NAME _____ DATE _____ PERIOD _____

Lesson 2 Multi-Step Problem Solving

Multi-Step Example

A pet store orders a 144-box case of two new dog treats—Arffs and Yums. The table shows the total number of boxes of each brand sold at the end of each week. If the patterns continue for each brand, what will be the total number of boxes sold after 10 weeks?
Preparation for 7.EE.1, MP 7

Ⓐ 80   Ⓑ 120   Ⓒ 144   Ⓓ 200

Weeks	Arffs	Yums
1	12	8
2	24	16
3	36	24

Use a problem-solving model to solve this problem.

1 Analyze

Read the problem. Circle the information you know.
Underline what the problem is asking you to find.

2 Plan

What will you need to do to solve the problem? Write your plan in steps.

Step 1 Write algebraic expressions that can be used to find the number of boxes of each brand sold at the end of __any number__ of weeks.

Step 2 Use the expressions to find how many of each brand are sold after __10__ weeks. Add the numbers.

Read to Succeed!
Find the relationship between the numbers in the first and second, and the first and third columns. Use that relationship to write the algebraic expressions.

3 Solve

Use your plan to solve the problem. Show your steps.

If n is the number of weeks: Arffs sold = __12n__ and Yums sold = __8n__.

$12n = 12 \times \underline{10} = 120$ boxes of Arffs after 10 weeks.

$8n = 8 \times \underline{10} = 80$ boxes of Yums after 10 weeks.

Since $120 + 80 = \underline{200}$, the store will have sold 200 total boxes of treats after 10 weeks. So, the correct answer is __D__. Fill in that answer choice.

4 Justify and Evaluate

How do you know your solution is accurate?

Sample answer: I could continue the pattern for 10 weeks. 120 boxes of Arffs and 80 boxes of Yums equal 200 boxes.

NAME _____ DATE _____ PERIOD _____

Lesson 2 (continued)

Use a problem-solving model to solve each problem.

1 Laura and Shani have a summer business making bracelets. The table below shows the number of bracelets they each can make in 4 days. Patrice helps them. She can make bracelets faster than Laura can but slower than Shani. Assuming that they all work at a constant rate, which could be a number of bracelets that Patrice can make in 8 days?
Preparation for 7.EE.1, MP 7

Days	1	2	3	4
Laura	9	18	27	36
Shani	12	24	36	48

Ⓐ 42
Ⓑ 72
Ⓒ **88**
Ⓓ 96

2 Kamal is drawing columns of squares to make a design. The first column he draws has 2 squares, the second has 4 squares, and the third has 6 squares. He continues the pattern until he has 8 columns. Represent the number of squares in each column on the graph below.
Preparation for 7.EE.1, MP 7

How many squares does Kamal draw? If he shades every third square, what fraction of the squares will be shaded? Explain your reasoning.

$72, \frac{1}{3}$; Sample answer: Add the numbers on the graph: $2 + 4 + 6 + 8 + 10 + 12 + 14 + 16 = 72 \div 3 = 24$, so $\frac{24}{72} = \frac{1}{3}$ of the squares are shaded.

3 Marta has a travel and lunch budget of $45 a week. Lin's budget is $40. Both spend x dollars each school day to ride the bus to school. Marta spends $20 a week on lunches, while Lin spends $17. Write an expression for each student's expenses. Who has the most money left at the end of the week? Justify your answer. *Preparation for 7.EE.1,* MP 4

Sample answer: Marta: $45 - 20 - 5x = 25 - 5x$; Lin: $40 - 17 - 5x = 23 - 5x$; since the value $5x$ is the same in both expressions and 25 is greater than 23, Marta has more money left at the end of the week.

4 ✍ **H.O.T. Problem** Write five terms for an arithmetic sequence and describe the relationship between the terms.
Preparation for 7.EE.1, MP 1

Sample answer: 1.2, 1.5, 1.8, 2.1, 2.4, ... Each term is found by adding 0.3 to the previous term.

Chapter 5

NAME _____ DATE _____ PERIOD _____

Lesson 3 Multi-Step Problem Solving

Multi-Step Example

Janelle wants to buy a set of 24 colored drawing pencils. The table shows the brands and prices available at a local art store. Better quality pencils always cost more, but Janelle doesn't want to buy the most expensive pencils, so she uses the mean of the prices as a guide. Which brand did she buy? If this cost is 40% of her art supply budget, what is her total budget? 7.EE.1, MP 2

Brand	Cost ($)
Artistica	15
Classic Colors	22
Prism Natural	25
Prism Plus	20
True Color	18

Use a problem-solving model to solve this problem.

1 Analyze

Read the problem. (Circle) the information you know. Underline what the problem is asking you to find.

2 Plan

What will you need to do to solve the problem? Write your plan in steps.

Step 1 Find the mean of the cost of the _pencil sets_.

Step 2 Determine which brand she bought. Use this information to find her total _art supply budget_.

Read to Succeed!
If Janelle uses the mean as a guide, it suggests that she chooses the price that is the exact mean or the price that is closest to the mean.

3 Solve

Use your plan to solve the problem. Show your steps.

15 + 22 + 25 + 20 + 18

= (15 + _25_) + (22 + _18_) + 20   Use the Associative Property to reorder the addends.

= 40 + 40 + 20 = _100_   Use mental math to add and to divide.

_100_ ÷ 5 = _20_ spent on _Prism Plus_

40% = 0. _4_ , $20 × 0.4 = _$50_

So, Janelle bought Prism Plus pencils for $ _20_ , and her art budget is $ _50_ .

4 Justify and Evaluate

How do you know your solution is accurate?

Sample answer: I can use my calculator to find the mean: 15 + 22 + 25 + 20 + 18 = 100. So, Janelle bought Prism Plus at $20. If her art budget is $50, multiply 50 × 40%, or 0.4, to get $20, so my answer is accurate.

NAME _____ DATE _____ PERIOD _____

Lesson 3 (continued)

Use a problem-solving model to solve each problem.

1 Neil and Jamie went shopping at a biking discount store. Neil bought a can of bike cleaner, two pairs of shorts, a wrist brace, and a pair of sunglasses. Jamie bought the same items as Neil plus two other items. If he spent about 18% more money than Neil, what other items did he buy? Support your reasoning. 7.EE.2, MP 2

Item	Cost ($)
Bike cleaner	12
Biking shorts	20
Sunglasses	8
Tire-pressure gauge	18
Wrist brace	9
Water bottles	6

2 water bottles; Sample answer: Neil:

12 + 2(20) + 9 + 8 = 12 + 8 + 2(20) + 9 =

20 + 40 + 9 = $69; Jamie: 69 × 1.18 = 81.42;

81.42 − 69 = $12.42 more than Neil. So, Jamie must have purchased two water bottles.

2 Darla recorded and displayed the daily high and low temperatures on Monday through Saturday of one week. During the previous week, the difference between the average daily high and the average daily low was 8°F. Is this week's difference an increase over the previous week, a decrease, or is it the same? Support your answer. 7.EE.1, MP 2

	M	Tu	W	Th	F	S
High (°F)	65	67	65	70	72	63
Low (°F)	52	56	56	54	54	58

an increase: Sample answer: The mean high of the temperatures shown is 67°F and the mean low is 55°F, so the difference is 12°F.

Since 12 > 8, this is an increase over the previous week.

3 Rashida plans to build a fence around an irregularly shaped piece of land. The cost of the fencing, excluding the poles, is $38 per 20 linear feet for plain chain link and $120 per 20 linear feet for vinyl-coated chain link. How much more will it cost to use the vinyl-coated fencing for Rashida's project? 7.EE.1, MP 7

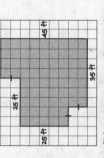

It will increase the cost of the project by $738.

4 H.O.T. Problem A student simplifies the expression as shown. He says he uses only the Commutative Property of Multiplication. Is the student correct? Support your position. 7.EE.1, MP 2

12a(5)
= 12 · a · 5
= (12 · 5) · a
= 60a

No; Sample answer: The student uses the Commutative Property to change the order in which the terms are multiplied. Then the student uses the Associative Property to change the way the terms are grouped.

Answers

NAME _____ DATE _____ PERIOD _____

Lesson 4 Multi-Step Problem Solving

Multi-Step Example

Dawit wants to buy some vintage comic books at a local shop and have them shipped to his cousin who resells them online. He buys two that are in excellent condition, four that are in good condition, and two that are in fair condition. The tax rate on the comic books is 8.25%, and the shipping cost is $5.00. What is the total cost of buying and shipping the comic books? 7.EE.2, MP 2

Vintage Comic Books Costs ($)	
Poor	2.00
Fair	4.00
Good	10.00
Excellent	18.00
Like new	26.00

A $90.83
B $95.93
C $96.34
D $100.26

Use a problem-solving model to solve this problem.

1 Analyze

Read the problem. Circle the information you know. Underline what the problem is asking you to find.

2 Plan

What will you need to do to solve the problem? Write your plan in steps.

Step 1 Write and simplify an expression to find the cost of the comic books.

Step 2 Add the __tax__ and the __shipping cost__.

Read to Succeed!
Notice that the tax rate is on the comic books alone, not on the comic books and the shipping.

3 Solve

Use your plan to solve the problem. Show your steps.

$2(18) + 4(10) + 2(4)$

$2(18 + 4) + 4(10) = 84$ Use the Distributive Property to rewrite the expression.

$84 \times 1.0825 = 90.93$ Find the tax on the cost.

$90.93 + \$5.00$ shipping $= \$95.93$ Add the tax and the shipping.

So, the correct answer is __B__. Fill in that answer choice.

4 Justify and Evaluate

How do you know your solution is accurate?

Sample answer: I can use a calculator to add the costs: $18 + 18 + 10 + 10 + 10 + 10 + 4 + 4 = 84$. Then I multiply $84 \times 0.0825 = 6.93$ to find the tax. Then I add the cost + tax + shipping: $84 + 6.93 + 5.00 = 95.93$, so my answer is accurate.

NAME _____ DATE _____ PERIOD _____

Lesson 4 *(continued)*

Use a problem-solving model to solve each problem.

1 The Puccio's have an urban farm and they sell the produce at the farmers' market. Every fall they order bulk seeds and small seed packets to plant in the early spring. The table shows what they ordered one fall. If the shipping rate is $3 per $50 ordered, which is the total cost of the seeds? 7.EE.1, MP 2

Variety	Packages Ordered
Carrots	2 @ $19.99
Collards	3 @ $19.99
Radishes	4 @ $3.49
Snow peas	10 @ $3.49
Spinach	3 @ $19.99
Sugar snap peas	10 @ $3.49

A $242.18
B $243.18
C $243.68
D $258.68

2 Kip works 65 hours a month at four part-time jobs. He works 20 hours at one company and is paid $300. He works 15 hours at his second job and is paid $8 an hour. He is paid $12 an hour at his third job. He works 15 hours at his fourth job and is paid $10.50 an hour. Complete the table to help you find his total monthly income from the four jobs. Kip puts 18% of his pay in a savings account to pay for taxes and unexpected expenses. What is his income after he deposits the 18% into savings? Round your answer to the nearest cent. 7.EE.1, MP 2

Job	Hours	Rate (hr)	Total ($)
1	20		300
2	15	$8	120
3	15	$12	180
4	15	$10.50	157.50

$757.50; $621.15

3 Yasmin bought a case of 144 beach hats. She bought them for $7 per hat and sold them for $10 per hat. Write an expression that shows her profit. Use the Distributive Property to evaluate the expression. Find the number of cases of hats Yasmin needs to buy and sell to earn $1,200 in profit. 7.EE.1, MP 2

Sample answer: $144(3) = 100(3) + 40(3) + 4(3) = 300 + 120 + 12 = 432$; $432

profit per case; $1,200 \div 432 = 2.77 = 3$;

He needs to sell 3 cases of hats to earn $1,200 profit.

4 H.O.T. Problem Towanda used algebra tiles to model an expression. Write the expression she modeled. Use the Distributive Property to rewrite the expression, and then simplify. What is true about the value of the three expressions? Support your reasoning. 7.EE.2, MP 3

$3(x + 4) = 3(x) + 3(4) = 3x + 12$; Sample answer: The expressions are equivalent because they represent the same value.

NAME _____ DATE _____ PERIOD _____

Lesson 5 Multi-Step Problem Solving

Multi-Step Example

A store is having a closeout sale on two models of televisions. The table shows each model, its discount, and the number available for sale. Which expression can be used to find the total sales for all of the televisions? **7.EE.2, MP 4**

Model	A	B
Discount	40%	25%
Available	15	18

Ⓐ (0.6a)(0.75b)   Ⓒ 15(0.4a) + 18(0.25b)

Ⓑ (1.4a) + (1.25b)   Ⓓ 15(0.6a) + 18(0.75b)

Use a problem-solving model to solve this problem.

① Analyze

Read the problem. Circle the information you know. Underline what the problem is asking you to find.

② Plan

What will you need to do to solve the problem? Write your plan in steps.

Step 1 Select variables to represent each model.

Step 2 Determine the percent of the original cost that the buyer will pay for each model.

Step 3 Write the expression for each model. Then, add.

Read to Succeed!

The cost of each television is discounted, so the buyer will pay less than 100% of the original cost.

③ Solve

Use your plan to solve the problem. Show your steps.

Use the variable _a_ to represent the original cost for Model A and _b_ to represent the original cost for Model B.

Find the percent that the buyer will pay for each model.

Model A: 100% − 40% = **60** %. Model B: 100% − 25% = **75** %.

Total sales for Model A: **15(0.6a)**   Total sales for Model B: **18(0.75b)**

Total sales for all the televisions: **15(0.6a)** + **18(0.75b)**

So, the correct answer is **D** . Fill in that answer choice.

④ Justify and Evaluate

How do you know your solution is accurate?

Sample answer: I can check that I placed the 15 and 18 with the correct discount and confirm that the decimal coefficients are correct: $\frac{100-40}{100}$

= $\frac{60}{100}$ = **0.6** and $\frac{100-25}{100}$ = $\frac{75}{100}$ = **0.75.**

NAME _____ DATE _____ PERIOD _____

Lesson 5 (continued)

Use a problem-solving model to solve each problem.

1 The tax rate in Todd's city is 6.75%. The tax rate in Anita's city is 8.25%. They both spend $36 on Blu-Rays at a national chain store. Three of the following expressions can be used to determine how much more Anita pays for her purchase. Which expression *cannot* be used? **7.EE.2, MP 4**

Ⓐ 36(0.015)

Ⓑ 36(1.0825 − 1.0675)

Ⓒ 36 − (0.825 − 0.675)

Ⓓ (36)(0.0825) − (36)(0.0675)

2 Jon has the parallelogram below. He wrote the expression $A = \frac{2m + 2(2n)}{8}$ to use to find the area of any of the smaller congruent triangles within it. Is his expression correct? Support your answer. **7.EE.2, MP 4**

No; Sample answer: The diagonals divide each half into four triangles with equal areas, so dividing by 8 is correct. Jon should multiply the length by the width to find the area of the parallelogram. A correct expression is: $\frac{m(2n)}{8}$.

3 Cecilia drew a circle graph to show how she spends her leisure time on weekends. Write an expression to use to find how much time she spends relaxing with family and friends, where *t* is equal to her total leisure time. If she has 16 hours of leisure time, how much time does she spend relaxing with family and friends? Round your answer to the nearest half hour. Show your work. **7.EE.1, MP 6**

Relaxing with Family 25%

Relaxing with Friends 21%

Training Dog 16%

Outdoor Activities 38%

about $7\frac{1}{2}$ **hours; Sample answer: 0.25t +**

0.21t = 0.46t. If t = 16, then 0.46(16) =

7.36 hours. 60 minutes × 0.36 = 21.6

minutes, so she spends about $7\frac{1}{2}$ **hours**

relaxing with family and friends.

4 🔲 **H.O.I. Problem** Kenji says that the following expressions are equivalent. Is he correct? If not, explain the possible error in thinking. **7.EE.1, MP 3**

5x(x − 7)
5x² − 35x
5x(x) − 5x(7x)

No. Sample answer: Using the Distributive Property, the first two expressions are equivalent. The third expression simplifies to 5x² − 35x². He incorrectly simplified 5x(7x) as 35x.

Answers

NAME _____ DATE _____ PERIOD _____

Lesson 6 Multi-Step Problem Solving

Multi-Step Example

The Drama Club is selling tickets for their latest production. They are also accepting additional cash donations. They plan to save 20% of the money from all ticket sales and donations for their spring trip. Ticket sales and donations from adults are represented by $(92a + 109)$, and ticket sales and donations from students are represented by $(34m + 13)$. If adult tickets cost $9 and student tickets cost $5, how much money will the Drama Club have available for their spring trip. 7.EE.1, MP 6

Ⓐ $224   Ⓒ $937
Ⓑ $896   Ⓓ $1,120

Use a problem-solving model to solve this problem.

1 Analyze
Read the problem. Circle the information you know. Underline what the problem is asking you to find.

2 Plan
What will you need to do to solve the problem? Write your plan in steps.

Step 1 Write an algebraic expression that represents total adult and student ticket sales and donations.

Step 2 Find __20__ % of the total ticket sales and donations.

Read to Succeed!
Read the question carefully. The Drama Club can only use 20% of total ticket sales and donations for their spring trip.

3 Solve
Use your plan to solve the problem. Show your steps.

$(92a + 109) + (34m + 13)$

$(92 \times \underline{9} + 109) + (34 \times \underline{5} + 13)$ Substitute the values of a and m.

$937 + 183 = \underline{1{,}120}$ Simplify.

$0.2(\underline{1{,}120}) = \$ \underline{224}$ saved.   Find 20% of the sum.

The correct answer is __A__. Fill in that answer choice.

4 Justify and Evaluate
How do you know your solution is accurate?

Sample answer: I could simplify the expression by adding all the donations together: $92a + 34m + 122$. Then I could substitute in the price of adult and student tickets and find 20% of the total: $0.2(92 \cdot 9) + 34(5) + 122) =$

$0.2(1{,}120) = 224$, so my answer is accurate.

Course 2 • Chapter 5 Expressions   71

NAME _____ DATE _____ PERIOD _____

Lesson 6 (continued)

Use a problem-solving model to solve each problem.

1 Alberto gets an allowance of $10 a week. His older brother gets a $15 allowance a week. They also are paid c dollars for each household chore they do. One week, Alberto does 8 chores and his brother does 3. They would like to combine their weekly money to buy a video game. Which linear expression in simplest form represents their total earnings for that week? 7.EE.1, MP 2

Ⓐ $(10 + 8c)(15 + 3c)$
Ⓑ $10(8c) + 15(3c) = 80c + 45c$
Ⓒ $10 + 15 + c + 8 + 3 = 31 + c$
Ⓓ $(10 + 8c) + (15 + 3c) = 25 + 11c$

2 Lakisha has a triangular flower garden. She wants to put a small fence around it to keep her dogs out. The fencing she likes costs $4.25 per foot. Write and simplify a linear expression to represent the cost of the fencing. 7.EE.1, MP 4

(triangle with sides $(6x + 2)$ ft, $(5x - 3)$ ft, $(5x + 1)$ ft)

4.25(16x); Sample answer: The perimeter in feet is $(5x - 3) + (6x + 2) + (5x + 1) =$ $(5x + 6x + 5x) + (-3 + 2 + 1) = 16x;$ **multiply by the cost per foot.**

3 Larry and some friends are playing a game. Two of the rules for the game are shown. 7.EE.1, MP 2

Move	Score	Bonus
Capture	x points	+ 10 points if done in one move
Rescue	y points	+ 5 points if done in one move

Larry has two captures, one of which took one move, and two rescues, both of which took one move. If $x = 2$ and $y = 2x$, how many points did he score? Support your answer by writing and simplifying an expression.

23; Sample answer: $(x + 10) + x + (y + 5) +$ $(y + 5) = 2x + 10 + 2y + 10 = 2x + 2y +$ $20 = 2(2) + 2(4) + 20 = 4 + 8 + 20 = 32$

4 ♨ **H.O.T. Problem** If x is an integer, will the linear expression $(x + 1) + (x - 1)$ always simplify to a positive value for x? If your answer is no, include a counterexample. 7.EE.1, MP 3

No; Sample answer: Suppose $x = -5$. This simplifies to $(-5 + 1) + (-5 - 1).$ $(-4) + (-6) = -10.$

72

Course 2 • Chapter 5 Expressions

NAME _____ DATE _____ PERIOD _____

Lesson 7 (continued)

Use a problem-solving model to solve each problem.

1 The table shows the attendance at a home football game, where $a = 250$. About what percent more of the crowd at the game were home fans than were visitors? 7.EE.1, MP 1

Team	Attendance
Home	$8a + 3$
Visitors	$6a - 5$

Ⓐ 15%
Ⓑ 25%
Ⓒ 33%
Ⓓ 57%

2 The perimeter of the triangular reception room shown is $12x + 4$ feet. Find the missing side length in terms of x. If $x = 3$, what is the perimeter of the room to the nearest tenth of a yard? 7.EE.1, MP 1

$5x + 4$

$2x - 4$ feet, 13.3 yards

3 Marcy has the following scores on three rounds of a game: $4x - 3$, $3x + 5$, and $2x + 8$. Jose scores are $3x + 6$, $4x + 9$, and $3x - 14$. If $x = 10$, by how much does Marcy need to increase her score to win? Support your answer. 7.EE.1, MP 2

2 points; Marcy's total score is $9x + 10$, and Jose's is $10x + 1$. Jose's score is $x - 9$ greater than Marcy's, or 1 point. So Marcy needs to increase her score by 2 points to win.

4 🔶 **H.O.T. Problem** Susana correctly subtracted the expression on the left. Without actually subtracting, what is the difference of the expression on the right? Explain why. 7.EE.1, MP 7

$$3x + 2 \qquad 2x - 8$$
$$\underline{-2x - 8} \qquad \underline{-3x + 2}$$
$$x + 10 \qquad ?$$

$-x - 10$; Sample answer: You are doing an opposite subtraction, so both signs in the difference are opposite.

74

NAME _____ DATE _____ PERIOD _____

Lesson 7 Multi-Step Problem Solving

Multi-Step Example

Bonnie owns a T-shirt shop. She tracks the sales of plain T-shirts and T-shirts with a design each week to be sure she has enough stock. If $t = 25$, the sales of T-shirts with a design total how much more than the sales of plain T-shirts? 7.EE.1, MP 1

Ⓐ $780 more
Ⓑ $984 more
Ⓒ $1,230 more
Ⓓ $2,050 more

Sales in One Week		
Style	Cost ($)	Number Sold
Plain	12	$5t - 4$
Design	15	$8t + 3$

Use a problem-solving model to solve this problem.

1 Analyze

Read the problem. Circle the information you know. Underline what the problem is asking you to find.

2 Plan

What will you need to do to solve the problem? Write your plan in steps.

Step 1 **Subtract** the expressions that represent the number of T-shirts sold.

Evaluate the difference using $t = $ **25** .

Step 2 **Multiply** the product by $ **15** .

3 Solve

Use your plan to solve the problem. Show your steps.

$(8t + 3) - (5t - 4)$

$$\begin{array}{r} 8t + 3 \\ (+)\ -5t + 4 \\ \hline 3t + 7 \end{array}$$

The additive inverse of $5t - 4$ is $(-5t + 4)$.

$3(\ \underline{25}\ ) + 7 = (\ \underline{82}\ )$ · Substitute the value given for t. Simplify.

$(\$ \underline{15}\ )(\ \underline{82}\ ) = \$ \underline{1,230}$ · Multiply the cost by the number of shirts.

So, **C** is the correct answer. Fill in that answer choice.

Read to Succeed!

The answer to the question represents the difference between the total sales of T-shirts with and without a design. Careful: The variable t is not a dollar amount.

$3t + 7$ more design T-shirts

4 Justify and Evaluate

How do you know your solution is accurate?

Sample answer: I can add $3t + 7$ to $5t - 4$ to get $8t + 3$, so my subtraction is correct. Then I can substitute the value of t and multiply: $15[(3)(25) + 7] =$

$15(82) = 1,230$, so my answer is accurate.

73

Answers

NAME _____ DATE _____ PERIOD _____

Lesson 8 (continued)

Use a problem-solving model to solve each problem.

1 A rectangular strip of land is divided into four equal garden plots. One is planted with flowers and the other three with vegetables. If the total area of the garden in square feet is $(20x + 300)$, what are the possible dimensions of the garden? **7.EE.1, MP 2**

$20x$	300

Ⓐ 4 feet by $(5x + 72)$ feet
Ⓑ 5 feet by $(4x + 50)$ feet
Ⓒ 10 feet by $(2x + 20)$ feet
Ⓓ 20 feet by $(x + 15)$ feet

2 Ruben, Theresa, and Arnold raised money for improvements to their local park. Ruben raised d dollars. Theresa raised $75 more than Ruben, and Arnold raised 25% more than Ruben. Write an expression to represent the amount each student earned. If Ruben raised $178, what is the total amount the students raised? Support your answer. **7.EE.1, MP 4**

$653.50; Sample answer: $d + d + 75 +$
$1.25d = 3.25d + 75; 3.25(178) + 75 =$
$653.50; 653.50

3 A group of eight students went rock climbing. They paid eight admission fees and $10 to park their van. Yolanda paid for herself and her sister with a $20 bill. What was her change in terms of x? **7.EE.2, MP 1**

$20 - 2(x + 1.25),$ or $20 - 2x - 2.50,$ or
$17.50 - 2x$

4 ♨ H.O.T. Problem Two students factor the expression $\frac{3}{8}x + 24$. The table shows their results. **7.EE.1, MP 3**

Student 1	$\frac{3}{8}(x + 64)$
Student 2	$\frac{3}{8}\left(x + \frac{1}{64}\right)$

Which student is correct? Justify your answer.

Student 1; Sample answer: Because
$\frac{3}{8} \times \frac{1}{64} \neq 24$ **Student 2's answer is not logical. The product of a fraction multiplied by a fraction is always less than one.**

NAME _____ DATE _____ PERIOD _____

Lesson 8 Multi-Step Problem Solving

Chapter 5

Multi-Step Example
The expressions in the table show Mr. Owusu's and Mr. Carson's monthly income, where x is the number of hours worked. Which expression represents the difference in their monthly income? If $x = 8$, what is the actual difference? **7.EE.1, MP 1**

Mr. Owusu	$14x - 16$
Mr. Carson	$10x + 8$

Ⓐ $4(x - 6)$, $8   Ⓒ $4(x - 8)$, $24
Ⓑ $4(x + 6)$, $38   Ⓓ $4(x + 8)$, $40

Use a problem-solving model to solve this problem.

1 Analyze
Read the problem. Circle the information you know. Underline what the problem is asking you to find.

2 Plan
What will you need to do to solve the problem? Write your plan in steps.

Step 1 Subtract to find the difference of their income.
Step 2 Factor the difference.
Step 3 Find the actual difference.

> **Read to Succeed!**
> The expressions in the answers are in a different form than the ones in the table. You may need to use factoring.

3 Solve
Use your plan to solve the problem. Show your steps.

$(14x - 16) - (10x + 8)$

$\quad 14x - 16$
$(+) -10x - 8$ The additive inverse of $10x + 8$ is $(-10x - 8)$.
$\quad\overline{\quad 4x - 24}$

The GCF of 4 and 24 is __4__, so $4x - 24 =$ __4__ $(x - 6)$.   Factor the expression.

$4(x - 6) =$ __8__   Substitute the value of x.

So, __A__ is the correct answer. Fill in that answer choice.

4 Justify and Evaluate
How do you know your solution is accurate?

I can add $4x - 24 + 10x + 8 = 14x - 16$, so my subtraction is correct. I can substitute 8 into both expressions and simplify: $4x - 24 = 32 - 24 = 8$, and $4(x - 6) = 4(2) = 8$. Since the values are the same, my answer is accurate.

Chapter 6 Lesson 1 Answer Keys

NAME _____ DATE _____ PERIOD _____

Lesson 1 Multi-Step Problem Solving

Multi-Step Example

Devin recorded the weight of his empty backpack and some items he put in it. He found it weighed 15.65 pounds. Janet packed exactly the same items in an identical backpack, but her laptop weighs 1.1 pounds less than Devin's. What is the weight of Janet's laptop? **7.EE.4a, MP 1**

Item	Weight (lb)
Empty backpack	1.75
Math book	3.2
Science book	3.5
Water bottle	1.0
Laptop	x

A) 5.1 lb
B) 6.2 lb
C) 7.3 lb
D) 9.45 lb

Use a problem-solving model to solve this problem.

1 Analyze

Read the problem. Circle the information you know. Underline what the problem is asking you to find.

2 Plan

What will you need to do to solve the problem? Write your plan in steps.

Step 1 Determine the value of __x__ by writing an equation.

Step 2 Determine the weight of __Janet's laptop__.

Read to Succeed!
The only difference between the weight of the two backpacks and the items in them is the weight of the laptops.

3 Solve

Use your plan to solve the problem. Show your steps.

$1.75 + 3.2 + 3.5 + 1.0 + x = 15.65$

$9.45 + x = 15.65$, so $x =$ __6.2__   Write and solve an equation.

$6.2 - $ __1.1__ $ = $ __5.1__   Find the weight of Janet's laptop.

So, __A__ is the correct answer. Fill in that answer choice.

4 Justify and Evaluate

How do you know your solution is accurate?

Sample answer: The weight of the backpacks without the laptops is 9.45 lb. I can subtract the weights of the backpacks and see if the difference is 1.1 lb:

$15.65 - (9.45 + 5.1) = 15.65 - 14.55 = 1.1$ lb, so my answer is accurate.

Course 2 • Chapter 6 Equations and Inequalities   77

NAME _____ DATE _____ PERIOD _____

Lesson 1 (continued)

Use a problem-solving model to solve each problem.

1 Devin recorded the percent humidity Monday through Saturday as shown on the graph. The total of the humidity readings for Friday through Sunday is 195. How many percentage points higher was the humidity on Monday than on Sunday? **7.EE.4a, MP 1**

Humidity

A) 11
B) 13
C) 14
D) 20

2 The table shows how much Prisha read on Saturday and Sunday. If she read at the same rate on Sunday as she did on Saturday, what time did she start reading Sunday night? **7.RP.3, MP 4**

Day	Start Time	End Time	Pages Read
Saturday	12:00 PM	12:30 PM	60
Sunday	?	8:40 PM	40

8:20 P.M.

3 Josiah and Perry were painting their bedroom walls, which have a surface area of 196 square feet. Josiah can paint 16 square feet in 4 minutes, while Perry can paint 7 square feet in 2 minutes. After 10 minutes, how much more total area will Josiah and Perry have left to paint? **7.RP.3, MP 2**

121 sq ft

4 H.O.T. Problem The maximum speed of the El Toro roller coaster is 70 miles per hour. The difference in speeds of El Toro and the T-Express roller coaster is 5 miles per hour. Using s to represent the speed of T-Express, write and solve two equations that could represent this situation and tell what they mean. What additional information is needed to determine the most appropriate equation for the problem situation? **7.EE.3, MP 6**

Sample answer: $s + 5 = 70$, $s = 65$, which means that the speed of T-Express is 65 mph and it is slower than El Toro; $s - 5 = 70$, $s = 75$, which means that the speed of T-Express is 75, and it is faster than El Toro. To determine the most appropriate equation, I would need to know which roller coaster is faster.

Course 2 • Chapter 6 Equations and Inequalities

78

Answers

NAME _____ DATE _____ PERIOD _____

Lesson 2 Multi-Step Problem Solving

Multi-Step Example

Elisa drove 340 miles to visit her cousins. She drove 65 miles per hour for 4 hours. If she drove 40 miles per hour during the rest of the trip, how long did it take her to drive the 340 miles? 7.EE.4a, MP 1

Ⓐ 5 hours
Ⓑ 6 hours
Ⓒ 7 hours
Ⓓ 8 hours

Use a problem-solving model to solve this problem.

1 Analyze

Read the problem. (Circle)the information you know.
Underline what the problem is asking you to find.

2 Plan

What will you need to do to solve the problem? Write your plan in steps.

Step 1 Write an equation that sets the following equal to __340__ miles:

Distance driven in __4__ hours plus distance driven at __40__ miles per hour.

Step 2 __Add__ the numbers of hours driven at each rate.

3 Solve

Use your plan to solve the problem. Show your steps.

$65 \cdot (4) + 40 \cdot (x) = 340$ $x = (2)$ Let x represent the hours driven at 40 mph.

Add the hours: __4__ hours + __2__ hours = __6__ hours.

So, the correct answer is __B__. Fill in that answer choice.

> **Read to Succeed!**
>
> Elisa drives at two different rates. Add the number of hours that she drove at each rate.

4 Justify and Evaluate

How do you know your solution is accurate?

Sample answer: I can substitute 2 for x in my equation, simplify, and see if I get 340. 65(4) + 40(2) = 340; 260 + 80 = 340, so my solution is accurate.

NAME _____ DATE _____ PERIOD _____

Lesson 2 (continued)

Use a problem-solving model to solve each problem.

1 Mrs. Watson works as a sales representative and earns a base salary of $300 each week. She also receives a commission, which is a percentage of her total sales. One week she had $5,225 in sales and total pay of $1,083.75. What is her commission rate (R)? 7.EE.4a, MP 1

Ⓐ $R = 15\%$
Ⓑ $R = 20\%$
Ⓒ $R = 25\%$
Ⓓ $R = 30\%$

2 Mr. Levy stopped at the grocery store on his way home. He spent $10.50 to buy two loaves of bread, eggs, juice, and milk. Using the information in the table, write and solve an equation that shows how much Mr. Levy spent on each loaf of bread. 7.EE.4, MP 2

Item	Bread	Eggs	Juice	Milk
Cost ($)		1.25	2.50	3.25

Sample answer: $2b + 1.25 + 2.5 + 3.25 =$

10.5, $b = 1.75$. Each loaf of bread costs

$1.75.

3 Lara's business has orders for a large number of rectangular tabletops from three stores. Each tabletop has an area of 16 square feet. If a bucket of paint will cover 1,000 square feet, how many buckets will Lara need to paint all the tabletops? Write an equation and solve. 7.EE.4a, MP 6

Store	Tabletops Ordered
New Look	30
Deco Depot	50
Retro Room	90

3 buckets; Sample answer:

$$\frac{(30 + 50 + 90)(16)}{1,000} = b; \frac{2,720}{1,000} = 2.72,$$

which rounds up to 3 buckets.

4 ✏ **H.O.T. Problem** Roberto drove 18 minutes to get to the highway. Once on the highway, he drove the same amount of time but covered twice the distance. Compare the average rate Roberto drove on the highway to the average rate he drove before getting on the highway. Justify your solution. 7.EE.4, MP 4

Sample answer: The rate Roberto drove on the highway is two times the rate he drove to get to the highway. If his original rate can be represented by $r = d \div t$, then his highway rate can be represented by $r = 2 \times d \div t$. To determine his rate on the highway, his rate getting to the highway must be multiplied by 2. Therefore, his average highway speed is two times his average speed before getting on the highway.

NAME _____ DATE _____ PERIOD _____

Lesson 3 Multi-Step Problem Solving

Multi-Step Example

The upper quartile of the data set represented in the box plot at the right is the product of three-fourths and the median. The lower quartile is the quotient of the median and four-sevenths. What is the interquartile range? 7.EE.4a, MP 1

[box plot: −8 −7 −6 −5 −4 −3 −2]

Use a problem-solving model to solve this problem.

1 Analyze
Read the problem. Circle the information you know. Underline what the problem is asking you to find.

2 Plan
What will you need to do to solve the problem? Write your plan in steps.

Step 1 Use equations to determine the **median** and **lower quartile**.

Step 2 Subtract the upper quartile from the **lower quartile**.

Read to Succeed!
Recall that the interquartile range is the distance between the first and third quartiles.

3 Solve
Use your plan to solve the problem. Show your steps.

Use equations to determine the median and lower quartile.

$-3 = \frac{3}{4}m$ median = **−4**

$m \div \frac{4}{7} = q$ lower quartile = **−7**

Determine the interquartile range.

$\underline{-7} - \underline{-3} = \underline{4}$ Subtract.

The interquartile range is **4**.

4 Justify and Evaluate
How do you know your solution is accurate?

Sample answer: Work backward to check. $-4 \times \frac{3}{4} = -3$ and $-7 \times \frac{4}{7} = -4$.

The difference between the absolute values of the lower and upper quartile is 7 − 3 or 4. My solution is accurate.

NAME _____ DATE _____ PERIOD _____

Lesson 3 (continued)

Use a problem-solving model to solve each problem.

1 Kimberly's weight on Venus is approximately 0.38 times her weight on Jupiter. Her weight on the Earth is approximately the quotient of her weight on Venus divided by 0.9. Her weight on the Earth is 100 pounds. What is her weight in pounds on Jupiter, rounded to the nearest whole number? 7.EE.4a, MP 1

237

2 A point on a number line moves to the right $\frac{1}{2}$ unit, to the left $5\frac{1}{2}$ units, and to the right 2 units, landing on the number line as shown. Where does the point start? Express your answer as a decimal. 7.EE.4a, MP 2

[number line: −5 −4 −3 −2 −1 0 1 2 3 4 5, point at −2.5]

0.5

3 Tevon designates 40% of his income for spending. If he makes $10 per hour, how many hours per week does he have to work to have $100 to spend weekly? 7.EE.4a, MP 1

25

4 H.O.T. Problem The table below shows the withdrawals and deposits for a checking account. The ending balance is $51.20. Determine the starting balance. Explain. 7.EE.4a, MP 4

Transaction	Amount
Withdrawal	$30
Deposit	$10.20
Deposit	$45.50
Withdrawal	$60

$85.50; Sample answer: Add each amount.

The sum is $(-30 + 10.20 + 45.50 - 60) = -34.30$. Since the overall effect of the transactions is a withdrawal of $34.30, I used the equation $s - \$34.30 = \$51.20$ to solve for s. The starting balance was $51.20 + $34.30 or $85.50.

Answers

Lesson 4   (continued)

Use a problem-solving model to solve each problem.

1 An electrician charges his customers an hourly rate plus a service fee of $30. The table shows the amount of money the electrician earned from his last four customers. What equation represents a customer's charge, C, for x hours of service? 7.EE.4a, MP 4

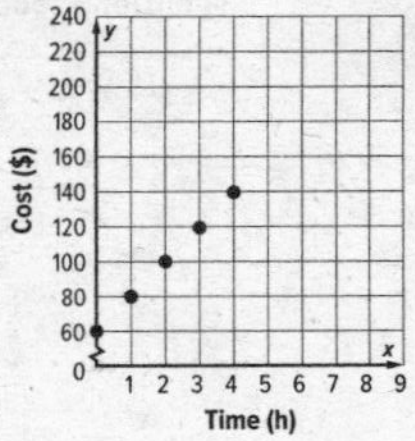

Customer	Hours	Charge ($)
Smith	3	94.50
Jones	2	73.00
Travers	6	159.00
Johnson	7	180.50

Ⓐ $C = 30x + 21.50$

Ⓑ $C = 21.50x + 30$

Ⓒ $C = 25.50x + 30$

Ⓓ $C = 30x + 25.50$

2 Valerie works at a local amusement park. She earns $9.80 per hour. She is also paid $7.00 for meals and $3.00 for transportation each day. Last Friday, Valerie earned $88.40. Write and solve an equation to determine how many hours Valerie worked on Friday. 7.EE.4a, MP 2

$88.40 = $9.80h + $7.00 + $3.00; h = 8;$

8 hours

3 Write and solve an equation to determine the measures of the angles in the triangle below. 7.EE.4a, MP 4

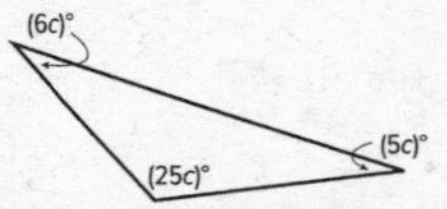

(60)°   (25x)°   (5x)°

$180 = 5c + 6c + 25c; 25°; 30°, 125°$

4 🖐 **H.O.T. Problem** A seventh grade class is playing a game of *Guess My Rule*. As a student makes a guess, the teacher tells what number the rule gives back. Is it possible for a student to guess 10 with the teacher response being 3? Write a two-step equation that describes the rule to justify your answer. 7.EE.4a, MP 3

Student Guess (x)	Teacher Response (y)
2	−1
5	8
0	−7
6	11

No; Sample answer: The equation that
describes the rule is $y = 3x − 7$. If a student
guesses the number 10, the teacher
response should be 23, not 3.

Lesson 4   Multi-Step Problem Solving

Multi-Step Example

The graph shows the amount of money customers are charged to rent a moon bounce for an event. Write an equation to represent the total cost. Then use it to determine the cost for renting the moon bounce for 8.5 hours. 7.EE.4a, MP 4

Ⓐ $200

Ⓑ $220

Ⓒ $230

Ⓓ $240

[Graph: Cost ($) vs Time (h), y-axis 0 to 240 by 20, x-axis 0 to 9]

Use a problem-solving model to solve this problem.

1 Analyze

Read the problem. Circle the information you know. Underline what the problem is asking you to find.

2 Plan

What will you need to do to solve the problem? Write your plan in steps.

Step 1 Determine the cost per **hour** to rent the moon bounce.

Step 2 Determine the **total cost** for 8.5 hours.

Read to Succeed!

The cost for 0 hours is $60. This must mean there is a rental fee plus an hourly rate to rent the moon bounce.

3 Solve

Use your plan to solve the problem. Show your steps.

There is a **$60** rental fee and the rate of change is **20**.

$20 h + 60 = t$ Let h represent hours and t represent total cost.

$20 (8.5) + 60 = t$ Replace h with 8.5.

$230 = t$

The cost for renting the moon bounce for 8.5 hours is **$230**.

The correct answer is **C**. Fill in that answer choice.

4 Justify and Evaluate

How do you know your solution is accurate?

Sample answer: The graph shows that the cost for 8 hours is $220 and the
cost for 9 hours is $240. The cost for 8.5 hours would be the middle of these
costs, or $230. So, my solution is accurate.

NAME _____ DATE _____ PERIOD _____

Lesson 5 Multi-Step Problem Solving

Multi-Step Example

Pierre uses two rectangular pieces of paper as bookmarks. The width of the larger bookmark is equal to the length of the smaller bookmark. The length of the larger bookmark is equal to half the perimeter of the smaller bookmark which is 14 inches. What is the perimeter of the larger bookmark? 7.EE.4a, MP 2

Pierre's Bookmarks

$2\frac{1}{2}$ in.

Ⓐ 32 in.   Ⓒ 26 in.
Ⓑ 30 in.   Ⓓ 23 in.

Use a problem-solving model to solve this problem.

1 Analyze

Read the problem. Circle the information you know.
Underline what the problem is asking you to find.

2 Plan

What will you need to do to solve the problem? Write your plan in steps.

Step 1 Use the perimeter to determine the __length__ of the smaller bookmark.

Step 2 Determine the __perimeter__ of the larger bookmark.

3 Solve

Use your plan to solve the problem. Show your steps.

Determine the length of the smaller bookmark.

$14 = 2\left(2\frac{1}{2}\right) + 2(\ell)$ $\ell = \underline{4\frac{1}{2}}$ cm

Determine the perimeter of the larger bookmark. The length is 7 inches, half of 14 inches.

$P = 2\left(4\frac{1}{2}\right) + 2(7)$ $P = \underline{23}$ cm

The perimeter of the larger bookmark is __23__ inches.

So, the correct answer is __D__. Fill in that answer choice.

Read to Succeed!
Use the width of the smaller bookmark to solve the equation for the larger bookmark to determine the perimeter.

4 Justify and Evaluate

How do you know your solution is accurate?

Sample answer: The perimeter of the smaller bookmark is $2\left(2\frac{1}{2}\right) + 2\left(4\frac{1}{2}\right)$, **or 14 inches, and the perimeter of the larger bookmark is** $2\left(4\frac{1}{2}\right) + 2(7)$, **or 23 inches.**

NAME _____ DATE _____ PERIOD _____

Lesson 5 (continued)

Use a problem-solving model to solve each problem.

1 Wendell and Katie have bedrooms with the same perimeter. Katie's bedroom has a width $1\frac{1}{3}$ times the width of Wendell's bedroom. How many feet long is Katie's bedroom? 7.EE.4a, MP 2

Wendell's Bedroom

11 ft (ℓ)

9 ft (w)

Katie's Bedroom

ℓ

w

Ⓐ 8 ft   Ⓒ 12 ft
Ⓑ 10 ft   Ⓓ 14 ft

2 Diego and two friends are going skating and will choose between two skating rinks. Skate-O-Rama charges $5 admission plus a skate rental fee, which comes to $20.25 for Diego and his friends. Ice Stars charges one dollar less for admission but twice the skate rental fee. If all three friends plan to rent skates, how much more will they spend, in dollars, at Ice Stars than at Skate-O-Rama? 7.EE.4a, MP 1

$2.25

3 Ella solved the equation $0.5(3 + x) = 2.5$ and then the equation $0.25(4 + y) = x$. If the value of x is the same for both equations, what is the value of y? 7.EE.4, MP 1

4

4 🖐 **H.O.T. Problem** Write and solve a real-world problem based on the equation $5\left(1\frac{3}{8} + x\right) = 8\frac{3}{4}$. 7.EE.4, MP 4

Sample answer: Jack is making 5 costumes that each require $1\frac{3}{8}$ yard of blue fabric and a certain amount of red fabric. If he will use $8\frac{3}{8}$ yards in all, how much red fabric is needed for each costume? $\frac{3}{8}$ yard

Answers

NAME _____ DATE _____ PERIOD _____

Lesson 6 *(continued)*

Use a problem-solving model to solve each problem.

1 Ogima has $12.94 left on a music download gift card. He has the following in his online shopping cart: six $0.99 downloads and three $1.29 downloads. Which additional downloads can Ogima buy using the card? **7.EE.4b, MP 6**

Ⓐ one $0.99, two $1.29
Ⓑ two 0.99, one $1.29
Ⓒ two $1.29
Ⓓ four $0.99

2 Roland plans to spend no more than $50 at the grocery store and $25 at the hardware store. His shopping lists include the following.

Grocery Store List	Hardware Store List
Milk — $3.50	Duct tape — $3.95
Cereal — $2.95	Hammer — $4.75

What is the difference, in dollars, between the maximum amounts Roland has left to spend at each store? **7.EE.3, MP 1**

$27.25

3 Blanca solves the inequality $-6 \geq n - 5$ and represents the solution on a number line as shown.

Her friend says the arrow should be pointing the other direction because the solution is $-1 \geq n$. Who is correct? Support your reasoning. **7.EE.4b, MP 3**

Blanca; Sample answer: The solution $-1 \geq n$ is equal to $n \leq -1$, so the arrow points to the left.

4 ✎ **H.O.T. Problem** Write an addition inequality and a subtraction inequality that both have the solution $y > 6$. Include a negative integer in both inequalities. **7.EE.4b, MP 4**

Sample answer: $y + (-3) > 3$, $y - 10 > -4$

NAME _____ DATE _____ PERIOD _____

Chapter 6

Lesson 6 **Multi-Step** Problem Solving

Multi-Step Example

The maximum weight capacity of the elevator in Maia's apartment building is 900 pounds. One morning she and five other people are on the elevator. Then two more passengers get on the elevator. If Maia weighs 108 pounds, which could be the weights of the two additional passengers without exceeding the maximum weight capacity? **7.EE.4b, MP 4**

Ⓐ 93 lb, 117 lb
Ⓑ 115 lb, 74 lb
Ⓒ 118 lb, 203 lb
Ⓓ 152 lb, 110 lb

Passenger	Weight (lb)
1	126
2	182
3	78
4	135
5	63

Use a problem-solving model to solve this problem.

1 Analyze

Read the problem. Ⓒircle the information you know. Underline what the problem is asking you to find.

2 Plan

What will you need to do to solve the problem? Write your plan in steps.

Step 1 **Add** the weights of the first six passengers.

Step 2 **Subtract** the sum from **900**.

Step 3 Compare the difference to the **total** weight in each answer choice.

> **Read to Succeed!**
> The phrase "without exceeding" means including but not more than 900 pounds. Use the less than or equal to symbol, $\leq$.

3 Solve

Use your plan to solve the problem. Show your steps.

Write an inequality that sets the sum of the weights as $\leq$ **900**.

Use x and y as the unknowns.

$108 + 126 + 182 + 78 + 135 + 63 +$ **x** and **y** ≤ 900.

$692 + x + y \leq 900$

Subtract to find $x + y$. $900 - 692 = 208$

$x + y \leq$ **208**

The only answer choice with a sum less than or equal to 208 is $115 + 74 =$ **189**, so the correct answer is **B**. Fill in that answer choice.

4 Justify and Evaluate

How do you know your solution is accurate?

I can substitute the weights into the inequality and see if it is still true.

$692 + 189 \leq 900$; $881 \leq 900$, so my solution is accurate.

NAME _____ DATE _____ PERIOD _____

Lesson 7 Multi-Step Problem Solving

Chapter 6

Multi-Step Example

To get the grade she wants in her English class, Elspeth needs an average of 85% from her quiz scores. Each quiz is worth 20 points. The scores of her first four quizzes are shown in the table. There will be one more quiz. What is the minimum score she can receive to earn at least an 85% grade? 7.EE.4b, MP 2

Quiz	Score
1	18
2	16
3	19
4	14

Ⓐ at least 15 points   Ⓒ at least 17 points
Ⓑ at least 16 points   Ⓓ at least 18 points

Use a problem-solving model to solve this problem.

1 Analyze
Read the problem. Circle the information you know. Underline what the problem is asking you to find.

2 Plan
What will you need to do to solve the problem? Write your plan in steps.

Step 1 Determine the __total score__ she earned on the first four quizzes.

Step 2 Write an inequality to determine what she must score on the __fifth quiz__.

Read to Succeed!
To write an inequality, first express the minimum score needed, 85%, as a decimal.

3 Solve
Use your plan to solve the problem. Show your steps.

$18 + 16 + 19 + 14 = 67$ Add the scores for quizzes 1–4.

Write and solve an inequality, where x is the score she needs to earn.

$\frac{67 + x}{100} \geq 0.85$ $x \geq$ __18 points__

Elspeth needs to earn at least __18__ points on her fifth quiz.

So, the correct answer is __D__. Fill in that answer choice.

4 Justify and Evaluate
How do you know your solution is accurate?

Sample answer: If she scores 18, her total score would be $18 + 16 + 19 + 14 +$ __18__, or __85__ points. Divide her points earned by the total points of the quizzes, $5(20)$ or 100 points. $85 \div 100 = 0.85$ or 85% so my solution is accurate.

NAME _____ DATE _____ PERIOD _____

Lesson 7 (continued)

Use a problem-solving model to solve each problem.

1 Phong and Janice are collecting action cards for a strategy game. They want to collect more than 30 new action cards. Action cards come in packs of 5. What is the least number of packs of action cards they will need to buy to have at least 30 new action cards? 7.EE.4, MP 2

Ⓐ at least 6
Ⓑ at least 5
Ⓒ at least 4
Ⓓ at least 3

2 Ling earns $9 per hour at the public library. She saves $7 of her earnings from every hour worked for college. How many hours does she have to work each week to save at least $105 for college? Write and solve an inequality to show how many hours she must work each week to save at least $100 for college. 7.EE.4, MP 2

__at least 15 hours; $7x \geq 105$__

3 Edwardo is painting the rectangle, which has a rectangular hole in the middle. The rectangular hole in the center is less than 40% of the area of the larger rectangle. What is the greatest possible length of the rectangular hole, to the nearest tenth? 7.EE.4b, MP 2

__7.1 feet__

4 🖐 H.O.T. Problem Write and solve a real-world problem involving the multiplication inequality below. Then, graph it on a number line. 7.EE.4b, MP 6

$2m \leq 15$

0 1 2 3 4 5 6 7 8 9 10

__Sample answer: Kelsey has $15 to spend on supplies to make bracelets. If supplies cost $2 per bracelet, how many bracelets can Kelsey make?; $x \leq 7$__

NAME _____ DATE _____ PERIOD _____

Lesson 8 Multi-Step Problem Solving

Multi-Step Example

Benjamin cannot exceed 10 hours of watching television in a week. He plans to watch a $2\frac{1}{2}$ hour movie on Friday night and not watch any television on Saturday. He writes an inequality to determine how much time he can spend watching television on the other days of the week, if he watches the same amount each day. Which number line represents the solution set of the inequality? 7.EE.4b, MP 4

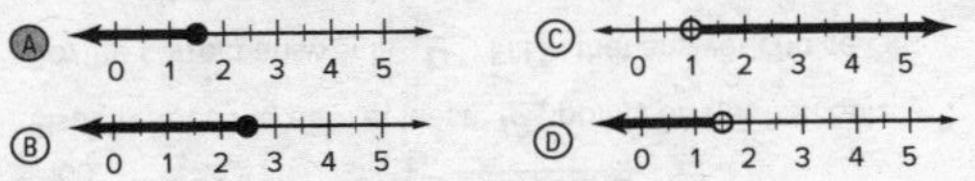

(A) 0 1 2 3 4 5
(B) 0 1 2 3 4 5
(C) 0 1 2 3 4 5
(D) 0 1 2 3 4 5

Use a problem-solving model to solve this problem.

1 Analyze

Read the problem. Circle the information you know.
Underline what the problem is asking you to find.

2 Plan

What will you need to do to solve the problem? Write your plan in steps.

Step 1 Write an __inequality__ to represent the situation.

Step 2 Solve the inequality and compare __graphs__.

Read to Succeed!
Determine the appropriate inequality symbol to use.
He cannot exceed 10 hours, which means he can watch less than or equal to 10 hours of television.

3 Solve

Use your plan to solve the problem. Show your steps.

Write an inequality to represent the situation where x is the amount of time he can watch television on the other five days in the week.

$2\frac{1}{2} + 5x \le 10$ $x \le 1\frac{1}{2}$ hours

The graph that represents the solution set for the inequality is __A__.

The correct answer is __A__. Fill in that answer choice.

4 Justify and Evaluate

How do you know your solution is accurate?

Sample answer: If he watches television for 1.5 hours for 5 days, that equals 7.5 hours. Add the movie, 2.5 + 7.5, which is a total of 10 hours. This is equal to the maximum number of hours he can watch television.

Chapter 6

NAME _____ DATE _____ PERIOD _____

Lesson 8 (continued)

Use a problem-solving model to solve each problem.

1 Peta has studied $2\frac{1}{2}$ hours for a test and plans to continue studying at the rate of $\frac{3}{4}$ hour per day. She writes an inequality to determine how many more days she needs to study to meet her goal of at least 7 hours total. Which number line represents the solution set of the inequality? 7.EE.4b, MP 4

(A) 0 1 2 3 4 5 6 7 8
(B) 0 1 2 3 4 5 6 7 8
(C) 0 1 2 3 4 5 6 7 8
(D) 0 1 2 3 4 5 6 7 8

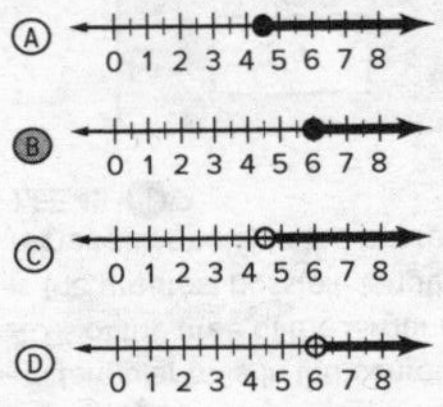

2 Jala wrote and correctly solved the two inequalities shown below and then compared their solution sets. What whole number is a solution in both inequalities? 7.EE.4b, MP 6

Jala's Inequalities
$\frac{1}{2}a + 5 \le 6\frac{1}{2}$
$3b - 2 > 4$

3

3 Reggie solved the inequality $1.2x + 4 \le 10$. Faith solved the inequality $5x - 3 \ge 14$. What is the difference between the greatest value of x in Reggie's solution and the least value of x in Faith's solution? 7.EE.4b, MP 6

1.6

4 H.O.T. Problem Stephanie is solving $-11 < 3x - 3.5$ and $3x - 3.5 \le 14.5$. Help her solve each inequality and graph the solution sets. Then write the complete whole-number solution set. 7.EE.4b, MP 6

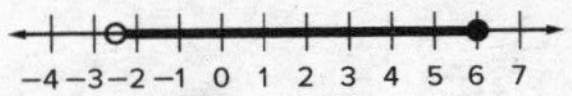

-4 -3 -2 -1 0 1 2 3 4 5 6 7

-2, -1, 0, 1, 2, 3, 4, 5, 6

NAME _____ DATE _____ PERIOD _____

Lesson 1 Multi-Step Problem Solving

Multi-Step Example

The value of the variable in the angle measure in the circle is also equal to the radius r of the circle. If a circle's diameter is twice its radius, what is the diameter of the circle? 7.G.5, MP 4

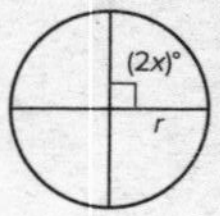

$(2x)°$

Ⓐ 22.5 units

Ⓑ 45 units

Ⓒ 90 units

Ⓓ 112.5 units

Use a problem-solving model to solve this problem.

1 Analyze

Read the problem. Circle the information you know. Underline what the problem is asking you to find.

2 Plan

What will you need to do to solve the problem? Write your plan in steps.

Step 1 Determine the value of __x__ by solving an equation.

Step 2 Determine the __diameter__ of the circle.

3 Solve

Use your plan to solve the problem. Show your steps.

Write and solve an equation.

$$2x = 90$$

$$\frac{2x}{2} = \frac{90}{2}$$

$$x = 45$$

$$d = 2r$$

$$d = 90$$

The diameter of the circle is __90__ units.

So, the correct answer is __B__. Fill in that answer choice.

4 Justify and Evaluate

How do you know your solution is accurate?

Sample answer: In the right angle shown, the value of x is 45 degrees because $2(45) = 90$. If the radius is equal to the value of x, then the diameter is $2(x) = 2(45) = 90$. So, my solution is accurate.

NAME _____ DATE _____ PERIOD _____

Lesson 1 *(continued)*

Use a problem-solving model to solve each problem.

1 Write and solve an equation to determine the value of x. 7.G.5, MP 4

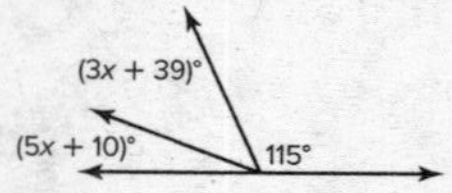

$(3x + 39)°$

$(5x + 10)°$

$115°$

Ⓐ 2

Ⓑ 7

Ⓒ 21

Ⓓ 34

2 The time shown on a clock is 6:00 P.M. The seconds hand is at 11 seconds. The angles formed between the seconds hand and the hour and minute hands are adjacent angles. At what time will those adjacent angles be equal? 7.G.5, MP 1

6:00 P.M. with the seconds hand at

15 seconds

3 A class of students was asked for their favorite color. The circle graph shows the results. The sum of the vertical angles for yellow and red in the circle graph is 40° and represents $\frac{1}{9}$ of the students. There are 360° in a circle and 18 students in the class. How many students chose yellow? 7.G.5, MP 2

Favorite Color

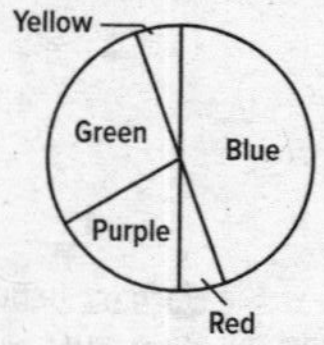

Yellow / Green / Blue / Purple / Red

Read to Succeed!

The angle symbol in the circle represents a right angle. All right angles measure 90°. Use this to solve the equation.

1 student

4 H.O.T. Problem An obtuse angle is divided into a right angle and ∠A. If the measures of the angles are whole numbers, what are the possible measures of ∠A? 7.G.5, MP 3

Sample answer: Since it is an obtuse angle, the sum of the measures of the right angle and ∠A must be between 91° and 179°.

Since the measure of the right angle is 90°, the measure of ∠A can range from 1° to 89°.

Answers

NAME _____ DATE _____ PERIOD _____

Lesson 2 Multi-Step Problem Solving

Multi-Step Example

The angle shown represents a building support joist. Engineers determined that the measure of angle x needs to be about 7% less to be more supportive. What is the measure of the new angle rounded to the nearest tenth? 7.G.5, MP 1

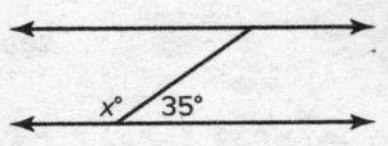

(A) 134.9°   (C) 155.2°

(B) 145°   (D) 165.9°

Use a problem-solving model to solve this problem.

1 Analyze

Read the problem. Circle the information you know. Underline what the problem is asking you to find.

2 Plan

What will you need to do to solve the problem? Write your plan in steps.

Step 1 Determine the value of __x__ by solving an equation.

Step 2 Determine __7%__ of the measure of angle x.

3 Solve

Use your plan to solve the problem. Show your steps.

Write and solve an equation.

$35 + x = 180$ $x = $ __145__

Determine 7% of the measure of angle x.

__145__ × 0.07 = __10.15__

__145__ − __10.15__ = __134.85__

The measure of the new angle is __134.9__ degrees.

So, the correct answer is __A__. Fill in that answer choice.

Read to Succeed!

The angles shown above form a supplementary angle. The sum of their measures is 180°.

4 Justify and Evaluate

How do you know your solution is accurate?

Sample answer: Add 10.2°, 7% of 145, and 134.9°, measure of the new angle, to get a sum of 145.1°, which is close to the measure of the measure of angle x. The sum of 145° and 35° is equal to 180°.

NAME _____ DATE _____ PERIOD _____

Lesson 2 (continued)

Use a problem-solving model to solve each problem.

1 Two angles are complementary. The measure of one angle is 25% the measure of the other. What is the measure of the smaller angle? 7.G.5, MP 2

(A) 4.5°

(B) 18°

(C) 36°

(D) 72°

2 The time on a clock is 10:00 A.M. The second hand creates a supplementary angle to the angle formed by the hour and minute hands on a clock. What time, in seconds, does the second hand point to? 7.G.5, MP 1

20 seconds or 30 seconds

3 What is the measure, in degrees, of the angle x that is complementary to the angle with a measure (160y)°? 7.G.5, MP 1

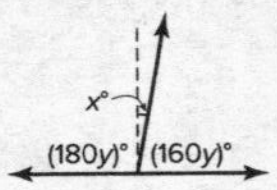

10°

4 H.O.T. Problem Two lines intersect to form vertical angles that are supplementary. What do you know about the measures of the four angles formed by the lines? 7.G.5, MP 4

Each of the four angles has a measure of 90°.

Chapter 7 Lesson 3 Answer Keys

Top portion (Lesson 3 continued)

NAME _____ DATE _____ PERIOD _____

Lesson 3 (continued)

Use a problem-solving model to solve each problem.

1 Half of an isosceles triangle is shown below. Move point C to (−1, −3) and label the new vertex D. If the measure of angle ADB is 54 degrees, what is the measure of angle DAB? 7.G.5, **MP** 4

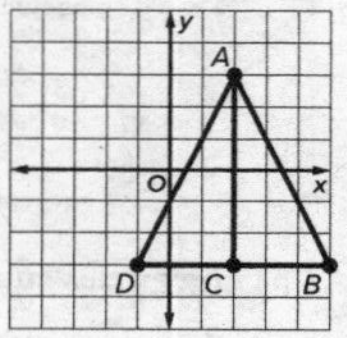

Ⓐ 36°
Ⓑ 54°
Ⓒ 63°
Ⓓ 72°

2 What is the value of x in the triangle shown? 7.G.5, **MP** 2

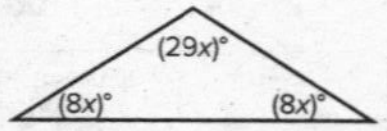

$(8x)°$ $(29x)°$ $(8x)°$

4

3 What is the measure of the smallest angle in the largest triangle in the figure shown? 7.G.5, **MP** 2

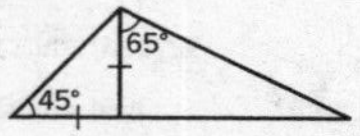

65°
45°

25°

4 ♧ **H.O.T. Problem** What is the measure of ∠A? 7.G.5, **MP** 2

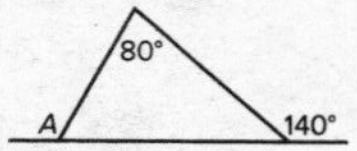

80° 140°
A

120°

98   Course 2 • Chapter 7 Geometric Figures

Bottom portion (Multi-Step Problem Solving)

NAME _____ DATE _____ PERIOD _____

Chapter 7

Lesson 3 Multi-Step Problem Solving

Multi-Step Example

Amie drew an acute triangle as shown. If she moves point C to (0, −3), what are the new measures of angle A and angle C? 7.G.2, **MP** 4

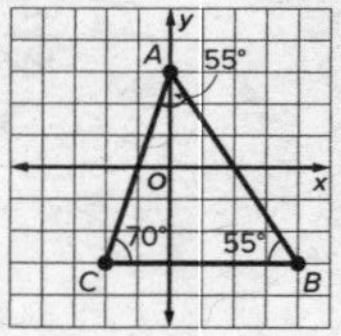

Ⓐ 25°   Ⓒ 55°
Ⓑ 35°   Ⓓ 90°

55°
70° 55°

Use a problem-solving model to solve this problem.

1 Analyze

Read the problem. Circle the information you know. Underline what the problem is asking you to find.

2 Plan

What will you need to do to solve the problem? Write your plan in steps.

Step 1 Determine the ___measure___ of angle C after moving it.

Step 2 Determine the ___measure___ of new angle A.

Read to Succeed!
Point C is located at (−2, −3). To move it to (0, −3), move two units to the right.

3 Solve

Use your plan to solve the problem. Show your steps.

If you move point C to _(0, −3)_, it will form a ___right___ triangle.

The new measure of angle C is ___90°___ because side AC is now ___perpendicular___ to side CB.

The new measure of angle A is ___180°___ − 90° + ___55°___ = ___35°___

So, the correct answer is ___B___. Fill in that answer choice.

4 Justify and Evaluate

How do you know your solution is accurate?

Sample answer: If m∠B is 55°, and does not change, m∠C is 90° because its two rays are perpendicular, and m∠A is 35°. 55 + 90 + 35 = 180, so my answer is accurate.

97   Course 2 • Chapter 7 Geometric Figures

Answers

NAME _____ DATE _____ PERIOD _____

Lesson 4 *(continued)*

Use a problem-solving model to solve each problem.

1 Cory is drawing a housing plan for his architecture class. He is making a scale model of one of the bedrooms. If the scale is 3 inches represents 1 foot, what is the area of the actual room? 7.G.1, MP 4

27 in.

15 in.

- (A) 45 square feet
- (B) 48 square feet
- (C) 54 square feet
- (D) 63 square feet

2 Shantel wants to know the area of the gymnasium floor at her school. She found a scale drawing that shows the square gym measured $4\frac{1}{2}$ inches long. If the scale is 1 inch = 5 feet, what is the actual area of the gym in square feet? 7.G.1, MP 4

$506\frac{1}{4}$ sq ft

3 Elisha was born in Aruba but now lives in the U.S. She wants to determine the length of the island of Aruba. Using the scale map below, determine the length of Aruba in yards, from Cudarebe to Ceru Colorado. 7.G.1, MP 4

Sample answer: 52,800 yd

Cudarebe
Noord
Santa Cruz
Oranjestad
Barcadera
Sabaneta
Ceru Jamonota
Ceru Colorado

0   3   6 mi
1 cm = 6 mi

4 ✏️ H.O.T. Problem Tevon plans to tile a friend's kitchen. On a scale drawing, the rectangular kitchen is 6 inches by 8 inches. The scale shows that 1 inch equal $1\frac{1}{2}$ feet. Use this information to determine how much it would cost to use Travertine, in dollars. 7.G.1, MP 4

Tile Style	Cost per Square feet ($)
Ceramic	6.50
Marble	8.00
Travertine	9.75

$1,053.00

NAME _____ DATE _____ PERIOD _____

Lesson 4 Multi-Step Problem Solving

Multi-Step Example

William is building a storage shed. The blueprint shown uses a scale of 1 inch = 3 feet. How many square feet of storage room will William have? 7.G.1, MP 4

$3\frac{1}{2}$ in.

$2\frac{1}{4}$ in.

- (A) $23\frac{5}{8}$ ft²
- (B) $55\frac{1}{8}$ ft²
- (C) $65\frac{7}{8}$ ft²
- (D) $70\frac{7}{8}$ ft²

Use a problem-solving model to solve this problem.

1 Analyze

Read the problem. Circle the information you know. Underline what the problem is asking you to find.

2 Plan

What will you need to do to solve the problem? Write your plan in steps.

Step 1 Use the **scale factor** to determine the actual dimensions of the storage shed.

Step 2 Multiply the length by the width to determine the **area**.

> **Read to Succeed!**
> Make sure you use the scale factor to determine the dimensions of the shed before calculating the area.

3 Solve

Use your plan to solve the problem. Show your steps.

$\frac{1\text{ in.}}{3\text{ ft}} = \frac{3\frac{1}{2}\text{ in.}}{\ell\text{ ft}}$ $\ell = 10\frac{1}{2}$ $\frac{1\text{ in.}}{3\text{ ft}} = \frac{2\frac{1}{4}\text{ in.}}{w\text{ ft}}$ $w = 6\frac{3}{4}$

Determine the area.

$10\frac{1}{2} \times 6\frac{3}{4} = 70\frac{7}{8}$

The area of William's storage shed is $70\frac{7}{8}$ square feet.

So, the correct answer is **D**. Fill in that answer choice.

4 Justify and Evaluate

How do you know your solution is accurate?

Sample answer: Estimate the length would be 4 feet and the width in width.

The actual length in feet would be 12 feet and the width would be 6 feet. The area is about 12 × 6, or 72 square feet which is close to my solution.

Chapter 7

NAME _____ DATE _____ PERIOD _____

Lesson 5 Multi-Step Problem Solving

Multi-Step Example

Armando is making a barbeque using cube-shaped bricks that measure 6 inches per side. The diagram shows top, side, and front views of the bricks he has stacked so far. He needs to save some money to purchase the rest of the bricks. If the bricks cost $2.50 each and Armando needs a total of 40 bricks, how much money does he need to save? *Preparation for 7.G.3,* MP 2

Ⓐ $25 Ⓒ $75
Ⓑ $55 Ⓓ $100

Top Side Front

Use a problem-solving model to solve this problem.

1 Analyze
Read the problem. Circle the information you know. Underline what the problem is asking you to find.

2 Plan
What will you need to do to solve the problem? Write your plan in steps.
Step 1 Determine the number of bricks Armando has **already** stacked.
Step 2 Determine the number of bricks he **needs**. Then **multiply** to find the cost of those bricks.

3 Solve
Use your plan to solve the problem. Show your steps.
Use the top, side, and front views to draw a **corner** view of the stacked bricks. The top layer has **2** bricks, the middle layer has **2** bricks, and the bottom layer has **6** bricks, so Armando has already stacked **10** bricks.
40 − 10 = **30** bricks needed. 2.5 × 30 = **75**
Armando needs to save $75, so, **C** is the correct answer. Fill in that answer choice.

Read to Succeed!
Sometimes a problem contains extra information. The dimensions of the bricks are not needed to answer the question.

4 Justify and Evaluate
How do you know your solution is accurate?
Sample answer: I can check my figure against the top, side, and front views to be certain it is correct and that I have counted the bricks correctly. Then I can subtract the cost of these bricks from the total cost. 40 × 2.50 = 100.
10 × 2.50 = 25. 100 − 25 = 75, so my answer is accurate.

Course 2 • Chapter 7 Geometric Figures   101

NAME _____ DATE _____ PERIOD _____

Lesson 5 *(continued)*

Use a problem-solving model to solve each problem.

1 Maka has been asked to design a sculpture to be placed in the center of an open courtyard, allowing visitors to walk around all sides of the sculpture. Below is a sketch of the sculpture she will build. On the actual sculpture, if Maka paints every side of one cube, she will use 4.5 pints of paint per cube. However, she plans to paint only the sides that are visible. Which expression, when simplified, will show the amount of paint Maka will use? *Preparation for 7.G.3,* MP 2

Ⓐ (23)(4.5)   Ⓒ (40)(4.5)
Ⓑ (23)(0.75)   Ⓓ (40)(0.75)

2 The figure below shows a three-dimensional view of a building. Sketch and label front, top, and side views of the building. Then use the appropriate sketch to find the perimeter of the building in feet. *Preparation for 7.G.3,* MP 2

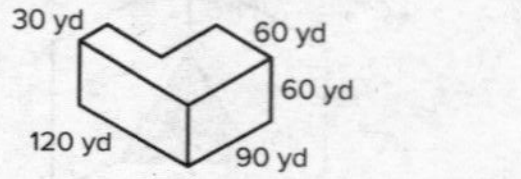

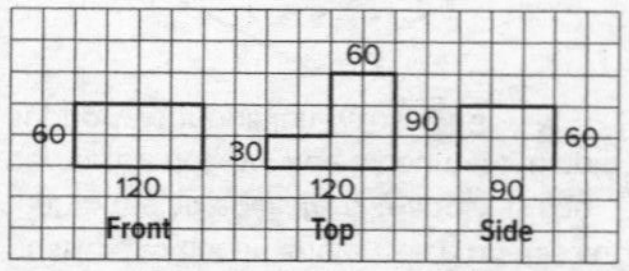

perimeter of building = 420 yd = 1,260 ft

3 Each cube on the figure shown measures 2 centimeters per side. Darnell divides the figure into two congruent parts, as indicated by the arrows. Write and simplify an expression that gives the area of one of the new faces formed when the two congruent parts are separated. *Preparation for 7.G.3,* MP 4

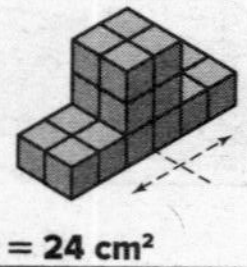

6 × (2 × 2) = 24 cm²

4 H.O.T. Problem Kang and Ileana viewed the three drawings shown. Kang says the front, top, and side views are the same. Ileana says that only the top and side views are the same. Are either of them correct? Support your answer. *Preparation for 7.G.3,* MP 3

Figure A   Figure B   Figure C

Ileana is correct. Sample answer: The top view of each figure is a row of three squares. The side view of each figure is a column of two squares. The front view of each figure does have a bottom row of three squares but the second row for each front view is different.

Course 2 • Chapter 7 Geometric Figures

102

Answers

Course 2 • Chapter 7 Geometric Figures   **195**

NAME _____ DATE _____ PERIOD _____

Lesson 6 Multi-Step Problem Solving

Multi-Step Example

The figure shown has a rectangular base and top, and the lengths of its sides are congruent. Draw a horizontal cross section on the figure. Describe the shape of the cross section. Then write two inequalities that compare the cross section's perimeter p to the perimeters of the base and the top. 7.G.3, MP 4

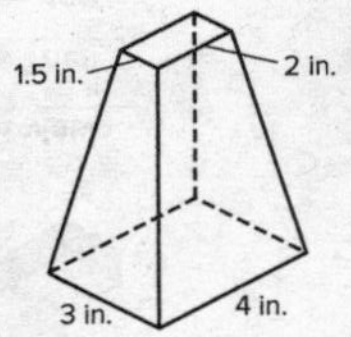

Use a problem-solving model to solve this problem.

1 Analyze
Read the problem. Circle the information you know. Underline what the problem is asking you to find.

2 Plan
What will you need to do to solve the problem? Write your plan in steps.

Step 1 Draw and name the cross section.

Step 2 Find the **perimeter** of the base and the top of the given figure.

Step 3 Write two **inequality** statements to compare the perimeters.

Read to Succeed!
The sides of a horizontal cross section will be parallel to the sides of the base and top.

3 Solve
Use your plan to solve the problem. Show your steps.

The cross section is a(n) **rectangle**.

The perimeter of the base is 2(**3** + **4**) = **14** inches.

The perimeter of the top is 2(**1.5** + **2**) = **7** inches.

So, **Sample answer: $p > 7$ and $p < 14$ inches.**

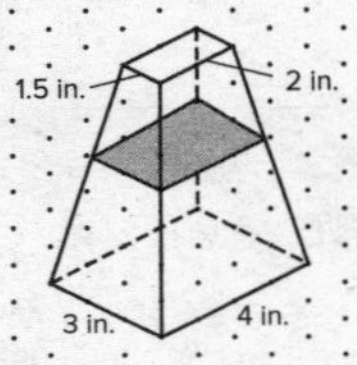

4 Justify and Evaluate
How do you know your solution is accurate?

Sample answer: The rectangular base, cross section, and top lay in the same plane, so their corresponding sides become proportionally shorter. The perimeter of the cross section must be smaller than the perimeter of the base but larger than the perimeter of the top.

NAME _____ DATE _____ PERIOD _____

Lesson 6 (continued)

Use a problem-solving model to solve each problem.

1 Dartrin cuts a cross section through the rectangular prism from AB to DC. Shade the cross section and describe its shape. Then use the area of the resulting shape to find the area of triangle ADC. Describe your thinking. 7.G.3, MP 1

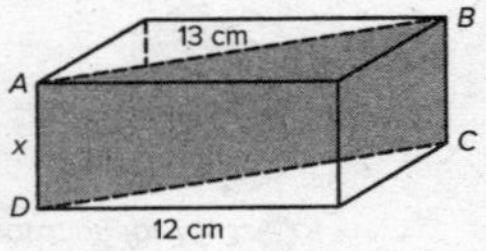

Perimeter of front face = 34 cm

rectangle, 32.5 cm²; Sample answer: Since

$2x + 2(12) = 34$, $x = 5$. So the area of the rectangular cross section is $5(13) = 65$ cm².

Triangle ADC is one half the area of rectangle ABCD, so its area is 32.5 cm².

2 Describe the shape resulting from a vertical, horizontal, and angled cross section of a cone. 7.G.3, MP 4

Vertical   Horizontal   Angled

triangle, circle, oval

3 The perimeter of a vertical cross section of a box is 20 inches. If the length of the box is 1.5 times its width, what are the dimensions of the cross section? 7.G.3, MP 2

4 in. by 6 in.

4 H.O.T. Problem Lorri says that it is not possible to cut an angled slice on this cube that forms an equilateral triangle. Is she correct? If not, provide a counterexample to support your opinion. 7.G.3, MP 3

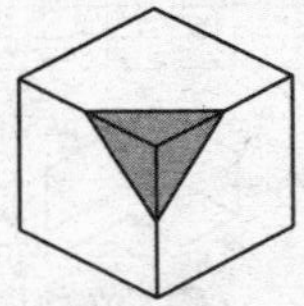

She is not correct.

NAME _____ DATE _____ PERIOD _____

Lesson 1 (continued)

Use a problem-solving model to solve each problem.

1 Bart used string to make this necklace. The diagram below represents the string Bart used. Meg made a necklace with a diameter that was $\frac{1}{2}$ foot longer. How much string did Meg use? Use 3.14 for π. Round to the nearest tenth. 7.G.4, MP 4

9 in.

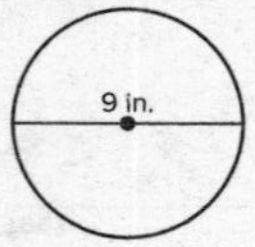

- Ⓐ 28.3 inches
- Ⓑ 29.8 inches
- Ⓒ 40.8 inches
- **Ⓓ 47.1 inches**

3 The radii for a penny and a nickel are shown. What is the difference in circumferences, in millimeters? Use 3.14 for π. Round to the nearest hundredth. 7.G.4, MP 4

9.525 mm   10.605 mm

6.78 mm

2 Diego ran around this track one and one-half times. Then he ran 50 more feet. How far did Diego run? Use 3.14 for π. Round to the nearest tenth. 7.G.4, MP 2

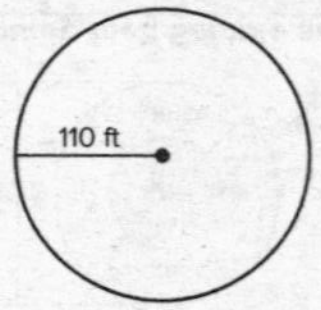

110 ft

1,086.2 feet

4 🧠 **H.O.T. Problem** If the radius of a circle is tripled, what would happen to its circumference? Explain and give an example. 7.G.4, MP 6

Sample answer: The circumference would triple. A circle with radius 4 has a circumference of 2 × 4 × π, or 8π. If the radius were tripled, the circumference would be 2 × 12 × π, or 24π. This is 3 times as much as 8π.

106

NAME _____ DATE _____ PERIOD _____

Lesson 1 Multi-Step Problem Solving

Chapter 8

Multi-Step Example

Kama uses landscape edging to border his circular garden. The diagram at the right represents Kama's garden. His neighbor has a garden that has a diameter that is 24 inches larger. How much landscape edging does his neighbor need to border their garden? Use 3.14 for π. Round to the nearest tenth. 7.G.4, MP 4

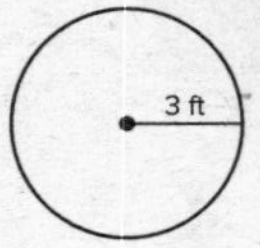

3 ft

- Ⓐ 15.7 feet
- Ⓒ 26 feet
- **Ⓑ 25.1 feet**
- Ⓓ 31.4 feet

Use a problem-solving model to solve this problem.

1 Analyze

Read the problem. Circle the information you know. Underline what the problem is asking you to find.

2 Plan

What will you need to do to solve the problem? Write your plan in steps.

Step 1 Determine the **diameter** of his neighbor's garden.

Step 2 Determine the **circumference** of his neighbor's garden.

3 Solve

Use your plan to solve the problem. Show your steps.

Ramon's garden has a diameter of 6 feet. So, his neighbor's garden is 24 inches or __2__ feet greater.

6 + __2__ = __8 ft__

Determine the circumference.

3.14 × 8 ≈ **25.1 ft**

Ramon's neighbor will need __25.1__ feet of landscaping border.

So, the correct answer is __B__. Fill in that answer choice.

Read to Succeed!

The diameter of his neighbor's garden is 24 inches larger. Make sure you add this distance to Ramon's diameter, not the radius.

4 Justify and Evaluate

How do you know your solution is accurate?

Sample answer: I can check my solution by estimating the diameter of his neighbor's garden. Divide 25 by 3 to get a diameter of about 8 feet. This is 2 feet or 24 inches greater than Ramon's garden, so my solution is accurate.

105

Answers

NAME _____ DATE _____ PERIOD _____

Lesson 2 Multi-Step Problem Solving

Multi-Step Example

Julian and Ava are raking the leaves around a tree in their backyard. The tree is 2 feet in diameter and is surrounded by a circle of leaves that is 24 feet in diameter. What is the area in square feet of the ground covered by leaves? Use 3.14 for π. 7.G.4, MP 4

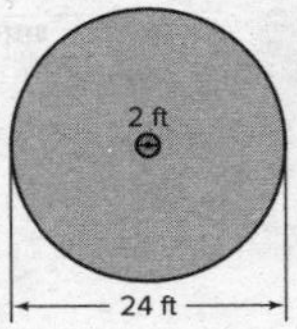

Use a problem-solving model to solve this problem.

1 Analyze

Read the problem. (Circle) the information you know. Underline what the problem is asking you to find.

2 Plan

What will you need to do to solve the problem? Write your plan in steps.

Step 1 Determine the **area** of **both circles.**

Step 2 Subtract the area of the **smaller circle** from the area of the **larger circle.**

3 Solve

Use your plan to solve the problem. Show your steps.

Write and solve equations to determine both areas.

$A = \pi r^2$ $A = \pi (1^2)$ $A \approx$ __3.14__

$A = \pi r^2$ $A = \pi (12^2)$ $A \approx$ __452.16__

__452.16__ − __3.14__ = __449.02__   Subtract.

The area of the ground covered by leaves is about __449.02__ square feet.

4 Justify and Evaluate

How do you know your solution is accurate?

Sample answer: I used my calculator, including the π key to check my answer. Rounded to the nearest hundredth, the area covered by leaves is **449.25 square feet, which is close to my answer.**

Read to Succeed!

Determine the area of the larger circle. Then subtract the area of the trunk of the tree to determine the area where they will rake.

NAME _____ DATE _____ PERIOD _____

Lesson 2 (continued)

Use a problem-solving model to solve each problem.

1 On a clear day, the light from a certain lighthouse can be seen from 10 miles away in any direction, measured from the center of the lighthouse's base. On a cloudy day, the light can be seen from only half the distance. What is the difference, in square miles, between the area that the light is visible on a clear day and on a cloudy day? Use 3.14 for π. 7.G.4, MP 2

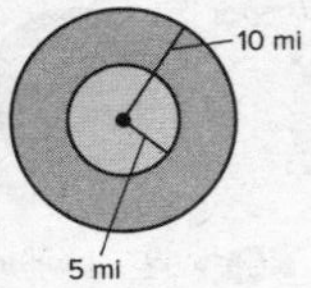

__235.5 square miles__

2 Two semicircles are drawn in a rectangle as shown.

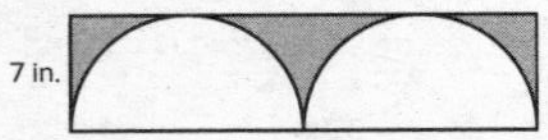

Determine the area of the shaded region in the figure shown. Use $\frac{22}{7}$ for π. 7.G.4, MP 1

__42 square inches__

3 Carter has 88 feet of fencing to make a dog pen in his yard. He is trying to decide whether to make the pen circular or square. Assuming he uses all of the fencing, what is the difference between the area of the circular pen and the square pen? Use $\frac{22}{7}$ for π. 7.G.4, MP 1

__132 square feet__

4 🐾 **H.O.T. Problem** Brian is performing in a play at the community theater. The theater is round with a seating area around a circular stage as shown below. One quarter of the seating area is taken up by the orchestra and the rest is for audience seating. What is the area of the audience seating? Use 3.14 for π. Explain your method. 7.G.4, MP 1

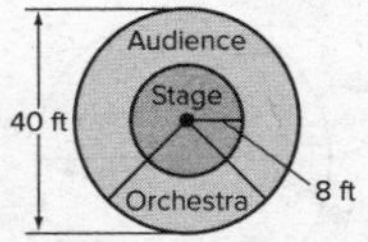

791.28 square feet; Sample answer: Determine $\frac{3}{4}$ the total area of the theater, which is 942 square feet. Subtract $\frac{3}{4}$ the area of the stage, 150.72, to equal 791.28 square feet.

NAME _____ DATE _____ PERIOD _____

Lesson 3 (continued)

Use a problem-solving model to solve each problem.

1 Juliana is making a cartoon about space travel, and drew this design for the Moon and sky as seen through a spaceship's window. Determine the area of the shaded region of her design. Use 3.14 for π. 7.G.6, MP 4

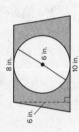

Ⓐ 39.87 square inches

Ⓑ 31.74 square inches

Ⓒ 28.26 square inches

Ⓓ 25.74 square inches

2 The figure shows the dimensions of a home plate for baseball, rounded to the nearest half-inch. If the plate is cut from a two-foot square piece of plastic, what is the area of the unused plastic? 7.G.6, MP 1

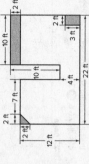

359.25 square inches

3 Felipe's backyard has a two-foot walkway with outside dimensions of 64 feet long and 36 feet wide. He wants to seed a lawn inside the area enclosed by the walkway. There is a pool, with dimensions shown, at one end of the yard. What is the total area in square feet of the lawn Felipe will plant? Use 3.14 for π. 7.G.6, MP 1

1,591.07 square feet

4 🖐 **H.O.T. Problem** The floor plan shows Carmen's studio apartment. She is installing new carpeting, which will cover the entire area except a triangular entertainment center, a closet, and a 10-foot wall with kitchen appliances as shown in the sketch. How many square feet of carpet will Carmen need? Show your calculations. 7.G.6, MP 2

232 ft²; 12(9) = 108; 4(3) = 12; 10(14) = 140;

108 + 12 + 140 = 260. $\frac{1}{2}$(2 × 2) = 2;

3(2) = 6; 10(2) = 20; 2 + 6 + 20 = 28;

260 − 28 = 232 square feet

NAME _____ DATE _____ PERIOD _____

Chapter 8

Lesson 3 Multi-Step Problem Solving

Multi-Step Example

Erin is putting wallpaper on her bedroom wall shown at the right. Determine the area of wallpaper needed for the wall shown. 7.G.6, MP 1

Ⓐ 63 square feet   Ⓒ 84 square feet

Ⓑ 75 square feet   Ⓓ 96 square feet

Use a problem-solving model to solve this problem.

1 Analyze

Read the problem. Circle the information you know. Underline what the problem is asking you to find.

2 Plan

What will you need to do to solve the problem? Write your plan in steps.

Step 1 Determine the __area__ of the entire larger rectangle.

Step 2 Subtract __areas__ of the two smaller rectangles.

3 Solve

Use your plan to solve the problem. Show your steps.

The area of the entire wall is 12 × 8 or __96__ square feet.

The area of the window is 3 × 4 or __12__ square feet.

The area of the door is 3 × 7 or __21__ square feet.

Subtract the window and door area from the wall area.

__96__ − __12__ − __21__ = __63__

The area of the wall that will need wallpaper is __63__ square feet.

So, the correct answer is __A__. Fill in that answer choice.

4 Justify and Evaluate

How do you know your solution is accurate?

Sample answer: Add the area of the doorway and window to the area of the

wallpaper area, 21 + 12 + 63, or 96 square feet. This is the area of the entire

wall. So, my solution is accurate.

Read to Succeed!

Erin will not put wallpaper over the window or doorway. You will need to subtract those areas from the area of the wall.

Chapter 8 Lesson 4 Answer Keys

Lesson 4 (continued)

Use a problem-solving model to solve each problem.

1 Timothy poured vegetable broth into the container shown. If the container is now 75% full, about how many cups of broth did he have? (*Hint:* 1 cup ≈ 14.4 cubic inches) 7.G.6, **MP** 1

10 in.
12 in.
6 in.

Ⓐ 12.5 cups
Ⓑ 15.25 cups
Ⓒ 18.75 cups
Ⓓ 25 cups

3 The base of a triangular prism has dimensions with a base of 3 meters and a height of 2.5 meters. If the volume of the triangular prism is 5.625 cubic meters, what is the height of the triangular prism? 7.G.6, **MP** 1

1.5 meters

2 Thema has a raised garden bed in her backyard that is a rectangular prism with dimensions 6 feet by 3 feet by $\frac{2}{3}$ feet. How many bags of soil should Thema buy to fill the bed if each bag holds 960 cubic inches of soil? 7.G.6, **MP** 2

22 bags

4 🏆 **H.O.T. Problem** Compare the volume of the two triangular prisms shown. What do you notice? Explain. 7.G.6, **MP** 6

4 cm
6 cm
6 cm
6 cm

12 cm
4 cm
3 cm

Sample answer: The volumes are equal. The height of each triangle is equal. The base of the first prism is twice the length of the second prism and the height of the first prism is half the height of the second prism.

112   Course 2 · Chapter 8 Measure Figures

Lesson 4 Multi-Step Problem Solving

Multi-Step Example

A drink cooler is in the shape of a rectangular prism. How many liters of lemonade will it hold if half of the volume is taken up by ice? (*Hint:* 1 L = 1,000 cm³) 7.G.6, **MP** 2

20 cm
15 cm
15 cm

Ⓐ 1.65 L   Ⓒ 4.5 L
Ⓑ 2.25 L   Ⓓ 9 L

Use a problem-solving model to solve this problem.

1 Analyze

Read the problem. Circle the information you know. Underline what the problem is asking you to find.

2 Plan

What will you need to do to solve the problem? Write your plan in steps.

Step 1 Determine the **volume** of the rectangular prism.

Step 2 Determine half of the volume, then **convert** to liters.

Read to Succeed!

To convert cubic centimeters to liters, you will need to divide the volume in cubic centimeters by 1,000.

3 Solve

Use your plan to solve the problem. Show your steps.

The volume of the cooler is 15 × 15 × 20 or **4,500** cubic centimeters.

Half of the volume is **4,500** ÷ 2, or **2,250** cubic centimeters.

Convert cubic centimeters to liters.

2,250 ÷ 1,000 = **2.25**

The cooler will hold **2.25** liters of lemonade.

So, the correct answer is **B**. Fill in that answer choice.

4 Justify and Evaluate

How do you know your solution is accurate?

Sample answer: I can use another method by determining half of the volume of the cooler by multiplying $\frac{1}{2}$ × 15 × 15 × 30 to equal 2,250. Divide 2,250 by 1,000 to equal 2.25 liters. So, my solution is accurate.

Course 2 · **Chapter 8** Measure Figures   111

200   Course 2 · **Chapter 8** Measure Figures

NAME _____ DATE _____ PERIOD _____

Lesson 5 Multi-Step Problem Solving

Multi-Step Example

Yukiko has 10,000 cubic centimeters of sand. She pours it into the pyramid shown. What fraction of the pyramid can she fill with sand? 7.G.6, MP 4

60 cm, 30 cm, 40 cm

(A) $\frac{1}{2}$
(B) $\frac{5}{9}$
(C) $\frac{3}{4}$
(D) $\frac{5}{6}$ (circled)

Use a problem-solving model to solve this problem.

1 Analyze
Read the problem. Circle the information you know. Underline what the problem is asking you to find.

2 Plan
What will you need to do to solve the problem? Write your plan in steps.

Step 1 Determine the **volume** of the triangular pyramid.

Step 2 Determine the **fraction** of the pyramid that is filled.

Read to Succeed!
The pyramid shown is a triangular pyramid. Use the formula for the triangle with determining the base B.

3 Solve
Use your plan to solve the problem. Show your steps.

Determine the volume.

$V = \frac{1}{3}Bh$ $V = \frac{1}{3}\left(\frac{1}{2}\cdot 40 \cdot 30\right)\cdot 60$ $V = 12{,}000$ cm³

Write the volume of sand Yukiko has over the volume of the pyramid.

$\frac{10{,}000}{12{,}000}$ or $\frac{5}{6}$

The pyramid will be $\frac{5}{6}$ full.

So, the correct answer is **D**. Fill in that answer choice.

4 Justify and Evaluate
How do you know your solution is accurate?
Sample answer: Determine $\frac{5}{6}$ of the volume of the pyramid, or 12,000 cubic centimeters. The result is 10,000, which is the amount of sand that Yukiko has to fill the pyramid. So, my solution is accurate.

NAME _____ DATE _____ PERIOD _____

Lesson 5 *(continued)*

Use a problem-solving model to solve each problem.

1 The solid cube below fits inside a hollow triangular pyramid. The triangular base of the pyramid has a base of $7\frac{1}{2}$ in. and a height of 4 in. The height of the pyramid is 5 in. What percent of the pyramid's volume is filled by the cube? Round your answer to the nearest thousandth, if necessary. 7.G.6, MP 2

2 in.

(A) 5%
(B) 16.7%
(C) 25%
(D) 32% (circled)

2 A square pyramid trophy is being shipped in a rectangular prism shaped package. The square pyramid has a base edge of 6 inches and height of 8 inches. What is the minimum volume that the package must be in order for the trophy to fit inside? 7.G.6, MP 1

288 cubic inches

3 The rectangular pyramid block shown was cut in half. What is the volume of each half of the pyramid block? 7.G.6, MP 4

10 in.   12 in.   14 in.

280 in³

4 H.O.T. Problem A triangular pyramid is placed on top of a triangular prism with a congruent base. If the volumes are equal, and the height of the prism is 1 unit, what is the total height of the both figures? Explain. 7.G.6, MP 6

4 units; Sample answer: Since the bases are congruent, their areas are equal. For the volumes to be equal, one-third of the pyramid height must equal the prism height. The pyramid height must be 3 units, or 3 times the prism height. So, the total height is 4 units.

Answers

NAME _____ DATE _____ PERIOD _____

Lesson 6 (continued)

Use a problem-solving model to solve each problem.

1 Mrs. Reno is preparing a project for 22 students to make bird houses. The dimensions of the bird house are shown in the sketch.

5 in. 8 in. 5 in. 6 in. 6 in. 6 in. 12 in.

If wood costs $1 for 3 square feet, what is the cost of the wood needed for the project? 7.G.6, MP 2

Ⓐ $16   Ⓒ $104
Ⓑ $48   Ⓓ $191

2 Refer to the problem on the previous page. The builder will cover the roof with shingles that cost $30 per bundle. Three bundles of shingles cover 100 square feet. How much will the builder spend on shingles? 7.G.6, MP 1

$936

3 Kareem plans to make a tent in the shape of a triangular prism, as shown. He will use nylon fabric for the walls and floor of the tent. When ordering the fabric, Kareem ordered an extra 10%. If the fabric costs $0.50 per square foot, how much will the fabric cost to the nearest dollar? 7.G.6, MP 2

5 ft 10 ft 6 ft 4 ft

$101

4 ✏️ **H.O.T. Problem** Sarah is a packaging technology student at a community college. Her teacher writes the following assignment on the board:

> Assignment: Design a rectangular box with all whole number dimensions that has a volume of 60 cubic inches and has the least possible surface area.

What is the surface area of the box that meets the requirements? Explain. 7.G.6, MP 6

94 square inches; Sample answer: The prime factorization of 60 is 2 × 2 × 3 × 5. I used that to list all the ways to get a volume of 60 in³, using whole numbers:

60 = 4 × 3 × 5, 60 = 2 × 6 × 5,

60 = 2 × 3 × 10, and 60 = 2 × 2 × 15.

Then I found the surface area for each option, and the least surface area is 94 in².

Course 2 • Chapter 8 Measure Figures   116

NAME _____ DATE _____ PERIOD _____

Chapter 8

Lesson 6 Multi-Step Problem Solving

Multi-Step Example

The drawings show two views of a house a builder is covering with vinyl siding. The builder will subtract 160 square feet for windows and doors and then cover the remaining parts of the walls with vinyl siding that costs $200 per square. What is the minimum amount the builder can spend on siding? (Hint: 1 square = 100 ft²). 7.G.6, MP 1

Ⓐ $3,632   Ⓒ $3,072
Ⓑ $3,312   Ⓓ $3,000

13 ft 12 ft 40 ft 13 ft 24 ft
Front View 12 ft 24 ft 13 ft 17 ft

Use a problem-solving model to solve this problem.

1 Analyze

Read the problem. Circle the information you know. Underline what the problem is asking you to find.

2 Plan

What will you need to do to solve the problem? Write your plan in steps.

Step 1 Determine the **total area** of the house to be covered.

Step 2 Determine the **cost** of **vinyl siding** needed.

3 Solve

Use your plan to solve the problem. Show your steps.

The area of the house consists of four **rectangles** and two **triangles**, less **160** square feet for windows and doors.

The area is **1,536** + **120** − **160** or **1,496** square feet.

Each square of siding covers **100** square feet. The builder needs to order **15** squares. The cost of the siding will be **15** (**$200**) or **$3,000** .

So, the correct answer is **D** .

📖 **Read to Succeed!**
Don't forget to subtract the area of the windows and doors when calculating the area of the walls to be covered by siding.

4 Justify and Evaluate

How do you know your solution is accurate?

Sample answer: Choice A added an extra 160 square feet, B did not subtract 160 square feet, and C only included the rectangular portion of the walls.

Course 2 • Chapter 8 Measure Figures   115

NAME _____ DATE _____ PERIOD _____

Lesson 7 Multi-Step Problem Solving

Multi-Step Example

A team of students will make a square pyramid, for the set for the school play. They will paint every surface, and then paste glitter on the lateral surfaces. One gallon of paint costs $62 and will cover about 75 square feet. A $\frac{1}{4}$-pound bag of glitter costs $5 and will cover about 38 square feet. About how much will it cost to paint and glitter the pyramid? 7.G.6, MP 4

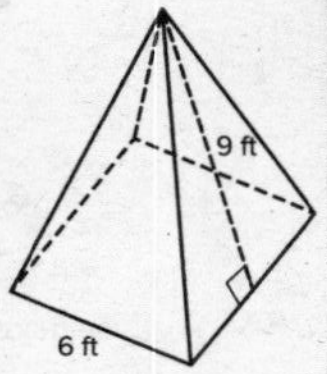

A $139
B $144
C $191
D $195

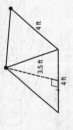

Use a problem-solving model to solve this problem.

1 Analyze

Read the problem. Circle the information you know. Underline what the problem is asking you to find.

2 Plan

What will you need to do to solve the problem? Write your plan in steps.

Step 1 Find the surface area that will be **glittered** and its cost.

Step 2 Find the surface area that will be **painted** and its cost.

Step 3 Find the total cost.

3 Solve

Use your plan to solve the problem. Show your steps.

Glittered area: $L.A. = \frac{1}{2}P\ell = \frac{1}{2}($ 24 $)($ 9 $) = $ 108 ft²

108 ft² ÷ 38 ft² per bag ≈ 2.8 bags

(3)($ 5) = ($ 15) cost of glitter

Painted area: $L.A. + B = $ 108 + 36 = 144 ft²

144 ft² ÷ 75 ft² per can ≈ 1.9 cans (2)($ 62) = $ 124 cost of paint

Total cost: $ 139 so, A is the correct answer. Fill in that answer choice.

Read to Succeed!
They will paint the entire pyramid but will put glitter on the sides only. Use different areas to find the cost of the paint and the glitter.

4 Justify and Evaluate

How do you know your solution is accurate?

Sample answer: I can work backward: Three bags of glitter cover 114 ft², 150 > 144. $15 + $124 = $139
114 > 108 ft². Two gallons of paint cover 150 ft², 150 > 144. $15 + $124 = $139

Course 2 • Chapter 8 Measure Figures
117

NAME _____ DATE _____ PERIOD _____

Lesson 7 (continued)

Use a problem-solving model to solve each problem.

1. Omar has a small garden for lettuce that measures 4 feet by 4 feet, as shown. He placed a pyramid-shaped net tent over it to keep the rabbits out. The netting cost $1.40 per square foot, and the framework to support it cost $12. How much did Omar spend to build the net tent? 7.G.6, MP 4

   A $32.80
   B $39.20
   C $51.20
   D $73.60

2. The Great Pyramid in Egypt was built using a measure called a *royal cubit*, which is about 1.7 feet. Its apex, or capstone, is missing so it does not come to a point. The diagram shows some suggested dimensions of the missing capstone in royal cubits. What is the lateral surface area of the missing capstone in square feet? Round to the nearest tenth. 7.G.6, MP 1

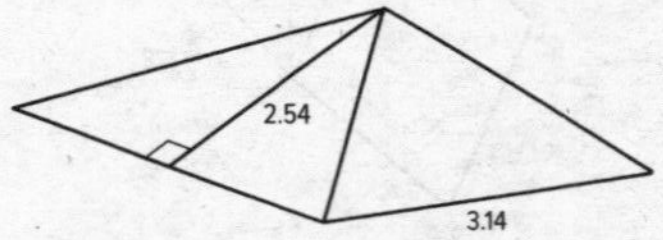

   about 46.1 ft²

3. A garden ornament is shaped like a rectangular pyramid with a base that measures 17.9 centimeters by 16.2 centimeters. Its slant height is 15 centimeters. Ama orders 24 of the ornaments and plans to completely cover $\frac{2}{3}$ of them with a waterproof covering. She should buy enough spray to cover how many square meters? Round to the nearest tenth. 7.G.6, MP 4

   1.3 m²

4. H.O.T. Problem Suppose you have a regular triangular pyramid with base sides of 2 units and a slant height of 1.5 units. Without using the formula $L.A. = \frac{1}{2}P\ell$, describe another way to find the lateral surface area of the pyramid. Support your method by using the given dimensions, then check using the standard formula. 7.G.6, MP 3

   Sample answer: I could apply the formula for the area of a triangle to find the area of each triangular side $\frac{1}{2}bh$, and then multiply the area by the number of sides. $\frac{1}{2}(2)(1.5)(3) = 4.5$. To check, I could use the formula for the lateral area of a pyramid: $\frac{1}{2}(2)(1.5)(3) = (1.5)(3) = 4.5$, so my method works.

Course 2 • Chapter 8 Measure Figures
118

Answers

NAME _____ DATE _____ PERIOD _____

Lesson 8 *(continued)*

Use a problem-solving model to solve each problem.

1 The structure shown is used in a performance. It backs up against a solid wall, and all the visible parts are covered with burlap. The burlap costs $0.29 per square foot. To the nearest dollar, what was the cost of covering the structure? 7.G.6, MP 1

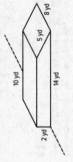

Ⓐ $125
Ⓑ $128
Ⓒ $376
Ⓓ $438

2 Pam makes tables from several types of wood. The diagram shows the design for a square-topped model. Curly maple weighs 45 pounds per cubic foot and cherry weighs 36 pounds per cubic foot. How much more will this table weigh in curly maple than cherry? Round to the nearest tenth. 7.G.6, MP 2

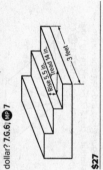

about 3.9 lb more

3 Steps are made up of a *tread* that you step on, and a *rise*, which is the height. On the steps shown, the depth of the tread is 14 inches and the rise is 5.5 inches. If the concrete used to make the steps cost $2.78 per cubic foot, what was the cost of the concrete for these steps to the nearest dollar? 7.G.6, MP 7

$27

4 🔑 **H.O.T. Problem** The diagram shows a composite solid figure. If each length is multiplied by 2, the volume of the figure is multiplied by what scale factor? Support your answer. 7.G.6, MP 5

a factor of 8; Sample answer: The volume of the figure is 106.875 cm³. If each length is doubled, the volume is 855 cm³.

120

Course 2 · Chapter 8 Measure Figures

NAME _____ DATE _____ PERIOD _____

Chapter 8

Lesson 8 Multi-Step Problem Solving

Multi-Step Example

The Garcia's built the garden shed shown. The frame and walls cost $368. Now they will paint it and shingle the roof. Mr. Garcia estimates that it will cost about $0.10 per square foot for the paint. A bundle of shingles costs $20 and covers about 32 square feet. What is the approximate total cost of the project? Round to the nearest ten dollars. 7.G.6, MP 1

Ⓐ $630
Ⓑ $640
Ⓒ $650
Ⓓ $670

Use a problem-solving model to solve this problem.

1 Analyze

Read the problem. Circle the information you know. Underline what the problem is asking you to find.

2 Plan

What will you need to do to solve the problem? Write your plan in steps.

Step 1 Determine the total surface area of the **sides** that will be painted and the total surface area of the **roof**.

Step 2 Determine the total cost of the **paint** and **shingles**.

3 Solve

Use your plan to solve the problem. Show your steps.

The surface area of the sides is $4 \times \underline{108}$ square feet $- \underline{24}$ square feet $= \underline{408}$ square feet. The area of the roof is $\frac{1}{2}Pℓ = \frac{1}{2} \times 48 \times 16 = \underline{384}$ square feet.

The cost of the paint will be about $\underline{40.80}$. He will need $\underline{12}$ bundles of shingles.

The total cost of the shed is $40.80 + $240 + $368 = $648.80. So, **C** is the correct answer. Fill in that answer choice.

4 Justify and Evaluate

How do you know your solution is reasonable?

Sample answer: $650 − $368 = $282 for the paint and shingles. Twelve bundles of shingles cover about 384 sq ft and cost $240. The area of the sides shows $40.80 is reasonable. $240 + $40 = $280, so my solution is reasonable.

Course 2 · **Chapter 8** Measure Figures

119

NAME _____ DATE _____ PERIOD _____

Lesson 1 (continued)

Use a problem-solving model to solve each problem.

1 Suppose you spin the spinner one time. How much greater is the probability that the spinner will land on A compared to C or D? 7.SP.7, MP 1

Ⓐ 12.5%

Ⓑ 25%

Ⓒ 37.5%

Ⓓ 50%

2 These six numbered squares are placed in a bag. If you randomly select one square from the bag, how much greater is the probability that you select an even number than an odd number? Express your answer as a fraction, percent, and decimal. 7.SP.7a, MP 2

| 255 | 256 | 260 | 263 | 264 | 270 |

$\frac{1}{3}$; about 33%, or about 0.33

3 The bar graph shows the number of colored candies in a bag. Blaze's favorite colored candy is blue. If he chooses one candy from the bag without looking, how much greater is the probability that he will choose a green, yellow, or orange candy compared to a red or blue candy? Express your answer as a fraction, percent, and decimal. 7.SP.5, MP 2

Blaze's Favorite Candy

$\frac{1}{10}$; 10%, or 0.1

4 H.O.T. Problem What is the probability that a randomly chosen number from 1 to 100 is *not* a multiple of 5? Express your answer as a fraction, percent, and decimal. 7.SP.5, MP 2

$\frac{4}{5}$; 80%, or 0.8

NAME _____ DATE _____ PERIOD _____

Chapter 9

Lesson 1 Multi-Step Problem Solving

Multi-Step Example

The table shows Bobby's number of hits for his entire baseball season. How much greater is the probability that Bobby hit a single or double compared to a triple or homerun? 7.SP.7, MP 1

Result	Number of Times
Singles	41
Doubles	13
Triples	14
Homeruns	7

Ⓐ $\frac{9}{25}$

Ⓑ $\frac{2}{5}$

Ⓒ $\frac{11}{25}$

Ⓓ $\frac{18}{25}$

Use a problem-solving model to solve this problem.

1 Analyze

Read the problem. Circle the information you know. Underline what the problem is asking you to find.

2 Plan

What will you need to do to solve the problem? Write your plan in steps.

Step 1 Determine the **probability** of each event.

Step 2 Combine the probabilities, then determine the **difference**.

3 Solve

Use your plan to solve the problem. Show your steps.

$P(\text{single or double}) = \frac{54}{75}$ or $\frac{18}{25}$ $P(\text{triple or homerun}) = \frac{21}{75}$ or $\frac{7}{25}$

Determine the difference between the probabilities.

$\frac{18}{25} - \frac{7}{25} = \frac{11}{25}$

The probability of Bobby hitting a single or double is $\frac{11}{25}$ greater than hitting a triple or homerun.

So, the correct answer is **C** . Fill in that answer choice.

Read to Suceeed!

Add the number of favorable outcomes for each type of hit before expressing it as a fraction and determining the probability.

4 Justify and Evaluate

How do you know your solution is accurate?

Sample answer: The two events are complementary, so the sum of the two probabilities is equal to 1 or 100%. $\frac{18}{25} + \frac{7}{25}$ is equal to $\frac{25}{25}$ or 1. So, my

solution is accurate.

Answers

Lesson 2 (continued)

Use a problem-solving model to solve each problem.

1. Mary performed an experiment where she flipped three coins 20 times. The table shows her results. How much greater is the probability that the result will be at least two tails compared to at least two heads? 7.SP.7a, MP 2

Result	Number of Occurrences
3 heads	2
2 heads, 1 tail	6
1 head, 2 tails	11
3 tails	1

Ⓐ $\frac{4}{5}$ Ⓑ $\frac{7}{10}$ Ⓒ $\frac{2}{5}$ Ⓓ $\frac{1}{5}$

2. Yesterday, 75 orchard customers bought apples and 15 of those customers bought gala apples. If 300 customers buy apples tomorrow, predict the number of customers you would expect to buy gala apples. 7.SP.7, MP 7

60 customers

3. High school students were asked to report their favorite lunch combo option. The chart shows the survey results. Predict the number of students who will have to purchase a lunch combo for the school to sell 140 bowls of soup? 7.SP.7b, MP 2

Lunch Combo Preference

Number of Students: 0, 5, 10, 15, 20, 25, 30
Soup and Sandwich · Soup and Salad · Salad and Sandwich

240 students

4. ✎ **H.O.T. Problem** The probability of spinning red on a spinner is $\frac{1}{8}$, the probability of blue is $\frac{1}{2}$, and the probability of yellow is $\frac{1}{4}$. There are 3 sections that are green. What is the minimum number of total sections on the spinner? Explain. 7.SP.7b, MP 7

24; Sample answer: The probability of each color is a multiple of the fraction $\frac{1}{8}$.

124 ... Course 2 • Chapter 9 Probability

Lesson 2 Multi-Step Problem Solving

Chapter 9

Multi-Step Example

Jarvis is playing a board game with his brother. The table shows the results of his number cube rolls throughout the game. If his next roll is an odd number, he will win the game. How much greater is the probability that he will win? 7.SP.7a, MP 2

Number	Number of Occurrences
1	4
2	5
3	7
4	5
5	3
6	1

Ⓐ $\frac{11}{25}$ Ⓒ $\frac{1}{5}$

Ⓑ $\frac{2}{5}$ Ⓓ $\frac{3}{25}$

Use a problem-solving model to solve this problem.

1 Analyze

Read the problem. Circle the information you know. Underline what the problem is asking you to find.

2 Plan

What will you need to do to solve the problem? Write your plan in steps.

Step 1 Determine the **probability** of each event.

Step 2 Determine the **difference** of the probabilities.

Read to Succeed!
You can use a tree diagram, list, or table to help determine the outcomes for this problem.

3 Solve

Use your plan to solve the problem. Show your steps.

$P(\text{odd}) = \frac{14}{25}$ $P(\text{even}) = \frac{11}{25}$

Determine the difference between the probabilities.

$\frac{14}{25} - \frac{11}{25} = \frac{3}{25}$

The probability of Jarvis winning is $\frac{3}{25}$ times greater than losing.

So, the correct answer is __D__. Fill in that answer choice.

4 Justify and Evaluate

How do you know your solution is accurate?

Sample answer: The two events are complementary, so the sum of the two probabilities is equal to 1 or 100%. $\frac{14}{25} + \frac{11}{25} = \frac{25}{25}$ is equal to $\frac{25}{25}$ or 1. So, my solution of $\frac{3}{25}$ is accurate.

Course 2 • Chapter 9 Probability 123

NAME _____ DATE _____ PERIOD _____

Lesson 3 Multi-Step Problem Solving

Multi-Step Example

Morgan rolls a number cube, twice. If the number 1 shows up at least once, Morgan wins. Otherwise, Jaclyn wins. How much greater is the probability that Morgan will win compared to Jaclyn winning? 7.SP.8b, MP 1

Ⓐ $\frac{1}{3}$ Ⓑ $\frac{7}{18}$ Ⓒ $\frac{4}{9}$ Ⓓ $\frac{2}{3}$

Use a problem-solving model to solve this problem.

1 Analyze

Read the problem. Circle the information you know.
Underline what the problem is asking you to find.

2 Plan

What will you need to do to solve the problem? Write your plan in steps.

Step 1 Make a list to determine the **sample space**

Step 2 Determine the **probability** for Morgan and Jaclyn. Then **subtract**.

3 Solve

Use your plan to solve the problem. Show your steps.

Use a list.

11, 12, 13, 14, 15, 16, 21, 22, 23, 24, 25, 26, 31, 32, 33, 34, 35, 36, 41, 42, 43, 44, 45, 46, 51, 52, 53, 54, 55, 56, 61, 62, 63, 64, 65, 66

Determine the probabilities and then subtract.

$P(\text{Morgan wins}) = \frac{11}{36}$ $P(\text{Jaclyn wins}) = \frac{25}{36}$

$\frac{25}{36} - \frac{11}{36} = \frac{14}{36}$ or $\frac{7}{18}$

The probability of Jaclyn winning is $\frac{7}{18}$ times greater than Morgan winning.

So, the correct answer is **B** . Fill in that answer choice.

Read to Succeed!
A number cube has six sides that are numbered 1 through 6. Use this information to help make a list.

4 Justify and Evaluate

How do you know your solution is accurate?

Sample answer: A tree diagram shows there are 36 outcomes with 11 outcomes that include a 1. The probability of Morgan winning is $\frac{11}{36}$ and $\frac{25}{36}$ is the probability of Jaclyn winning. The difference in the probabilities is $\frac{18}{18}$.

NAME _____ DATE _____ PERIOD _____

Lesson 3 (continued)

Use a problem-solving model to solve each problem.

1 Nicolás tosses a coin three times. If heads appears at least once, he wins. Otherwise, Manny wins. How much greater is the probability that Nicolás will win compared to Manny winning? 7.SP.8a, MP 1

Ⓐ $\frac{1}{8}$
Ⓑ $\frac{1}{2}$
Ⓒ $\frac{3}{4}$
Ⓓ $\frac{7}{8}$

2 The table shows the colors of socks, shoes, and belts that Landon owns. If he randomly selects a pair of socks, a pair of shoes, and a belt, what is the probability that the colors will all match? Write the probability as a decimal rounded to the nearest hundredth. 7.SP.8, MP 2

Socks	Shoes	Belt
Navy	Brown	Brown
Brown stripes	Black	Black leather
Black		Black nylon
Brown dots		
Tan		

$0.1\overline{3}$

3 Jarek randomly selects a card from a pile of 3 unique cards, replaces it, and randomly selects again. What is the probability of selecting any card three times in a row? Write the probability as a percent, rounded to the nearest tenth. 7.SP.8a, MP 1

11.1%

4 H.O.T. Problem Dakotah was randomly assigned a computer password, where each number can be any digit 0 through 9, but digits will not repeat. The first three digits are shown. If he randomly guesses the last two digits, what is the probability he will guess correctly? Explain. 7.SP.8a, MP 2

7	3	1	?	?

$\frac{1}{42}$; Three of the ten possible digits, 0–9, have been used. So, the first guess will be one of the seven remaining digits. Once one of those 7 digits is guessed, the last guess will be one of the six remaining digits. Each of the 7 possibilities can be paired with six possibilities, resulting in 42 possibilities. Only one is correct.

Answers

NAME _____ DATE _____ PERIOD _____

Lesson 4 (continued)

Use a problem-solving model to solve each problem.

1 Marlene conducts a simulation. She rolled a number cube, twice. The sum of 8 or greater showed up 21 times, each resulted in a win for her. Ashton won all the other games. Based on the simulation, what percent more did Marlene win compared to Ashton winning? Write your answer as a percent rounded to the nearest tenth. 7.SP.8, MP 1

16.7%

2 There is a 25% chance of rain every day this week. Sandra set up a spinner to simulate the probability of rain. She spun the spinner below 7 times and her experimental probability was $\frac{2}{7}$. How much greater was the experimental probability compared to the theoretical probability? 7.SP.8, MP 2

Chances of Rain

$\frac{1}{28}$

3 Rebecca received a $50 check from her grandmother for her birthday. She used the money to buy some new clothes. If she spent $49.75, how many ways could she receive change if no pennies are used? 7.SP.8, MP 4

4 ways

4 H.O.T. Problem Juan is playing basketball. During a game, he is fouled 8 times. Each time, he goes to the free-throw line to shoot two shots. A simulation was conducted to determine the experimental probability of making a free-throw shot. Compare the experimental probability, $\frac{3}{8}$, to the theoretical probability, 50%. 7.SP.8, MP 2

Sample answer: The experimental probability is $\frac{1}{8}$ or 12.5% less than the theoretical probability.

128

NAME _____ DATE _____ PERIOD _____

Chapter 9

Lesson 4 Multi-Step Problem Solving

Multi-Step Example
Rico conducts a simulation. He spun a spinner with four equal sections labeled A, B, C, and D, twice. The letter D showed up five times, each resulted in a win for Rico. Natasha won all the other games. Based on the simulation, what percent more did Natasha win compared to Rico winning? Write your answer as a percent. 7.SP.8, MP 1

Use a problem-solving model to solve this problem.

1 Analyze
Read the problem. (Circle) the information you know. Underline what the problem is asking you to find.

2 Plan
What will you need to do to solve the problem? Write your plan in steps.

Step 1 Determine the **sample space**.

Step 2 Determine the **experimental probability** for Rico and Natasha. Then **subtract**.

Read to Succeed!
Use a list or tree diagram to help determine the total number of outcomes for the simulation.

3 Solve
Use your plan to solve the problem. Show your steps.

There are a total of **16** outcomes.

Determine the probabilities and then subtract.

$P(\text{Rico won}) = \frac{5}{16}$ $P(\text{Natasha won}) = \frac{11}{16}$

$\frac{11}{16} - \frac{5}{16} = \frac{6}{16}$ or $\frac{3}{8}$ which is equal to **37.5%**

Natasha won **37.5%** more than Rico.

4 Justify and Evaluate
How do you know your solution is accurate?

Sample answer: Write the number of wins for Rico over the total outcomes, $\frac{5}{16}$. The difference is $\frac{11}{16}$. Natasha's probability is the complement of Rico's, so it is $\frac{11}{16}$. $\frac{3}{8}$ which can be expressed as 0.375 or 37.5%. So, my solution is accurate.

127

NAME _____ DATE _____ PERIOD _____

Lesson 5 Multi-Step Problem Solving

Multi-Step Example

Zaku is going to buy a fresh fruit smoothie and a personal pizza for lunch. For the smoothie, he can choose one of five different fruits, one of six different types of juice, and either milk or ice cream. For Zaku's pizza, he can choose one of three crusts and one of four toppings. How many different pizza and smoothie choices does Zaku have for his lunch? 7.SP.8, MP 2

Ⓐ 12　　Ⓑ 60　　Ⓒ 72　　Ⓓ 720

Use a problem-solving model to solve this problem.

Read to Succeed!
When reading the problem, identify different categories and how many choices are in each category.

1 Analyze
Read the problem. Circle the information you know. Underline what the problem is asking you to find.

2 Plan
What will you need to do to solve the problem? Write your plan in steps.

Step 1　Identify how many possible options there are for each category.

Step 2　Calculate the total number of **combinations**.

Step 3　**Multiply** the total number of pizza and smoothie combinations.

3 Solve
Use your plan to solve the problem. Show your steps.

Possible smoothie outcomes: **5 × 6 × 2 = 60**

Possible pizza outcomes: **3 × 4 = 12**

Multiply the options together to find the amount of different meal options for Zaku for a total of **720**.

The correct answer is **D**. Fill in that answer choice.

4 Justify and Evaluate
How do you know your solution is accurate?
Sample answer: If I create a tree diagram and count the different outcomes, there will be 60 different choices for smoothies and 12 for pizzas. Each smoothie choice has 12 different pizza choices, which is why I multiply 60 by 12.

NAME _____ DATE _____ PERIOD _____

Lesson 5 (continued)

Use a problem-solving model to solve each problem.

1 Alana goes to a school that requires her to wear a uniform. Girls are allowed to wear a polo style shirt in one of four colors; khaki pants, blue pants, or a khaki skirt; and either tennis shoes or dress shoes. From how many different types of outfits can girls choose? 7.SP.8, MP 2

Ⓐ 3
Ⓑ 9
Ⓒ 24
Ⓓ 54

2 Kitan would like to order from the children's menu at Jonny John's Burger Haven. The kid's menu allows her to choose from five different types of burgers, eight different drinks, seven different sides, and either a girl's toy or a boy's toy. How many unique types of children's meals does Jonny John's offer? 7.SP.8, MP 1

560 different children's meals

3 The menu for Sam's Scoops lists the following different cones and toppings.

Cones	Toppings
Cake	None
Sugar	Chocolate sprinkles
Waffle	Nuts
Chocolate waffle cone	Multi-colored sprinkles
	Sugar sprinkles
	Caramel sauce
	Chocolate sauce
	Cookie crumbles
	Chocolate chips

If Sam's Scoops claims they can make 828 different ice cream cones with up to one topping, how many different ice cream flavors do they offer? 7.SP.8b, MP 2

23 flavors

4 H.O.T. Problem Determine the number of possible outcomes for rolling one number cube, two number cubes, three number cubes, and four number cubes. Write a rule for rolling n number cubes if each number cube has six different numbers. Explain how you determined your rule. 7.SP.8a, MP 4

6, 36, 216, 1,296; 6^n. One number cube was 6^1 or 6, two number cubes was 6^2 or 36, and three number cubes was 6^3 or 216, so the pattern indicates that for n cubes the rule would be 6^n.

Answers

NAME _____ DATE _____ PERIOD _____

Lesson 6 Multi-Step Problem Solving

Multi-Step Example

Jimena, Jade, and Jaqui all raced in the 100-yard dash. How many different ways could they place first, second, and third? 7.SP.8, MP 2

Ⓐ 3   Ⓑ 6   Ⓒ 12   Ⓓ 16

Use a problem-solving model to solve this problem.

1 Analyze

Read the problem. Circle the information you know. Underline what the problem is asking you to find.

2 Plan

What will you need to do to solve the problem? Write your plan in steps.

Step 1 Identify that the problem is interested in the different ways something can be __ordered__.

Step 2 Identify **how many** items are being ordered.

Step 3 Find the __factorial__ of the number of items.

Read to Succeed!
When determining the total combinations of different items, it is important to determine if order matters.

3 Solve

Use your plan to solve the problem. Show your steps.

The problem is interested in how many different orders the girls could finish the race.

There are __3__ different girls who raced and __3__ ways they can finish.

The total number of different ways the girls could place in the race is __3 × 2 × 1 = 6__. The correct answer is __B__. Fill in that answer choice.

4 Justify and Evaluate

How do you know your solution is reasonable?

Sample answer: If I make a list of all of the different ways the girls could finish the race, I get 6 different outcomes.

Chapter 9

NAME _____ DATE _____ PERIOD _____

Lesson 6 *(continued)*

Use a problem-solving model to solve each problem.

1. The five starting players for the school basketball team line up to shake hands with their opponents. In how many ways can the five players line up? 7.SP.8, MP 2

   Ⓐ 5
   Ⓑ 15
   Ⓒ 25
   Ⓓ 120

2. Five talented boys are auditioning for the lead role in the school play. One boy will be selected as the lead actor and one will be selected as the understudy, or replacement in case of illness. Find the probability that Sanjay gets the lead and Eli is the understudy. 7.SP.8a, MP 2

   $\frac{1}{20}$

3. The Mount Clair School Fair currently offers vanilla, chocolate, and strawberry ice cream. If the school adds one more flavor of ice cream, how many more ways could the ice cream be arranged in the display case if order is important? 7.SP.8a, MP 7

   18

4. ⚡ **H.O.T. Problem** The new state license plates will each have six characters. The first three characters on the plates must be letters and the second three must be numbers 0–9, with no repeat of any letter or number. Will the department of motor vehicles be able to make enough unique license plates for a population that registers 14 million vehicles? Explain your answer. 7.SP.8, MP 8

   No, there would not be enough unique license plates because

   26 × 25 × 24 × 10 × 9 × 8 = 11,232,000;

   11,232,000 < 14,000,000.

NAME _____ DATE _____ PERIOD _____

Lesson 7 Multi-Step Problem Solving

Multi-Step Example

Wesley exercises about 3% of the number of hours in a week. Suppose he is tracking the hours he exercises in a year or 52 weeks. Which prediction could represent the number of hours you would expect Wesley to exercise rounded to the nearest tenth? 7.SP.8a, MP 1

Ⓐ 52.1 hours Ⓒ 252 hours
Ⓑ 162.1 hours Ⓓ 262.1 hours

Use a problem-solving model to solve this problem.

Read to Succeed!
You can express 3% as a decimal or a fraction in order to solve this problem.

1 Analyze

Read the problem. Circle the information you know. Underline what the problem is asking you to find.

2 Plan

What will you need to do to solve the problem? Write your plan in steps.

Step 1 | Determine the number of **hours** he works out each week.

Step 2 | **Multiply** the hours he exercises each week by **52** weeks.

3 Solve

Use your plan to solve the problem. Show your steps.

There are 24 hours in a day. Multiply that by 7 to determine the hours in a week.

$24 \times 7 = $ **168**

Wesley exercises 3% or $\frac{3}{100}$ of a week. Multiply by the hours in a week.

$\frac{3}{100} \times$ **168** $=$ **5.04 hours**

Multiply by the number of weeks in a year, 52.

$5.04 \times 52 =$ **262.1**

Wesley would exercise about **262.1** hours in a year.

So, the correct answer is **D** . Fill in that answer choice.

4 Justify and Evaluate

How do you know your solution is accurate?

Sample answer: I can work backward to check my solution. Divide 262.1 by 52 to equal 5.04 and 5.04 divided by 168 is about $\frac{3}{100}$ or 3%. So, my solution is accurate.

NAME _____ DATE _____ PERIOD _____

Lesson 7 (continued)

Use a problem-solving model to solve each problem.

1 One letter tile is selected and the spinner is spun. What is the probability that the tile will be a vowel and the spinner will land on a consonant? 7.SP.8, MP 1

Ⓐ $\frac{1}{4}$

Ⓑ $\frac{3}{1}$

Ⓒ $\frac{1}{6}$

Ⓓ $\frac{1}{12}$

2 Sonya has a bag with 4 green, 7 orange, and 9 blue marbles. She randomly selects one marble and then another. What is the probability that Sonya picks two blue marbles? Express your answer as a percent, rounded to the nearest tenth. 7.SP.8a, MP 2

18.9%

3 Deepak wants a new video game but is not sure which one to buy. His choices are 5 sports games, 3 role-playing games, and 8 action games. He writes the game titles on pieces of paper and puts them all in a bag. He randomly selects one piece of paper from the bag, does not replace it, and selects another piece of paper. What is the probability that Deepak selects two sports games? Express your answer as a percent, rounded to the nearest hundredth. 7.SP.8, MP 2

8.33%

4 H.O.T. Problem Tyrell is rolling two number cubes. He rolls them both at the same time. What is the probability that the sum of the two outcomes will be an even number? 7.SP.8, MP 2

$\frac{1}{2}$

Answers

Chapter 10 Lesson 1 Answer Keys

Lesson 1 Multi-Step Problem Solving

Multi-Step Example

Adrian's class surveyed 150 students to determine their favorite ice cream flavors. The results are shown in the circle graph at the right. How many more students favored vanilla than mint chocolate chip? 7.SP.1, MP 2

Favorite Ice Cream

- 26% Chocolate
- 24% Vanilla
- 12% Strawberry
- 18% Mint Chocolate Chip
- 20% Cookie Dough

Use a problem-solving model to solve this problem.

1 Analyze

Read the problem. Circle the information you know. Underline what the problem is asking you to find.

2 Plan

What will you need to do to solve the problem? Write your plan in steps.

Step 1 Determine **24%** of 150 and **18%** of 150.

Step 2 Then subtract the **products** .

3 Solve

Use your plan to solve the problem. Show your steps.

Determine 24% of 150.   Determine 18% of 150.

$0.24 \times 150 = $ **36** $0.18 \times 150 = $ **27**

$\frac{36 - 27 = \quad 9}{\text{Subtract.}}$

There are **9** more students who favor vanilla than mint chocolate chip.

Read to Succeed!

You can use another method by subtracting the percents first before multiplying by 150.

4 Justify and Evaluate

How do you know your solution is accurate?

Sample answer: Another method is to subtract 18% from 24%, which is equal to 6%. Then determine 6% of 150, which is 0.09 × 150 or 9. So, my solution is accurate.

Course 2 • Chapter 10 Statistics

135

Lesson 1 (continued)

Use a problem-solving model to solve each problem.

1 All the seventh graders in Carla's school voted on where to go for their class trip. There are a total of 350 students in the seventh grade. How many fewer students voted for the two least popular choices than for the two most popular choices? 7.SP.1, MP 2

Field Trip Votes

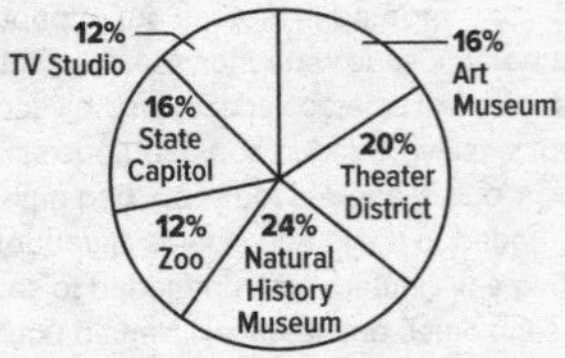

- 16% Art Museum
- 20% Theater District
- 24% Natural History Museum
- 12% Zoo
- 16% State Capitol
- 12% TV Studio

70

2 Billy spent $500 on his dog last year, and he made a circle graph to show how he spent the money. This year, he spent $100 less on the veterinarian but the same amount on every other category. This year, what percent of dog expenses was spent on the veterinarian? 7.SP.1, MP 2

Dog Expenses

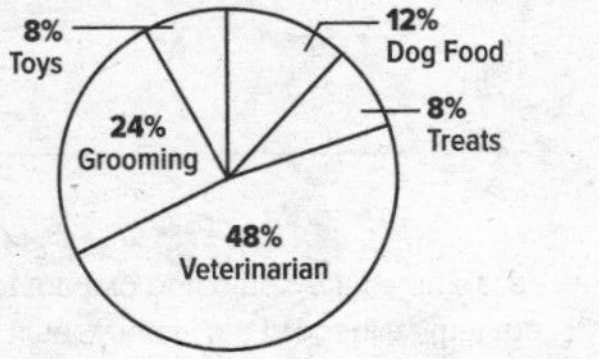

- 12% Dog Food
- 8% Treats
- 48% Veterinarian
- 24% Grooming
- 8% Toys

35%

3 Kya and Nicholas each kept a list of trees that their class saw during a nature project. To show their results, Kya made a circle graph and Nicholas made a table. If Kya's circle graph represents 27 beech trees, how many more total trees are represented on her graph than on Nicholas's table? 7.SP.1, MP 2

Trees Counted

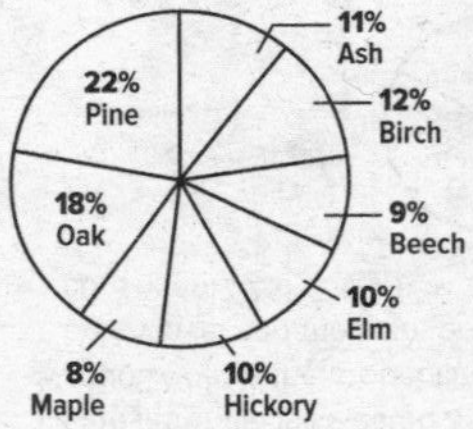

- 11% Ash
- 12% Birch
- 9% Beech
- 10% Elm
- 10% Hickory
- 8% Maple
- 18% Oak
- 22% Pine

Trees Counted	
Tree	Number
Ash	33
Birch	29
Beech	27
Elm	30
Hickory	30
Maple	20
Oak	52
Pine	22

57 trees

4 H.O.T. Problem Look at the divisions on the circle graph. Assign approximate percents to each section. Then, write a real-world problem about the graph. 7.SP.2, MP 6

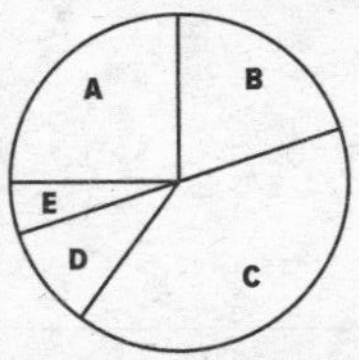

(Circle graph with sections A, B, C, D, E)

Sample answer: A 25%, B 20%, C 40%, D 10%, E 5%; See students' work.

136   Course 2 • Chapter 10 Statistics

212

Chapter 10 Lesson 2 Answer Keys

NAME _____ DATE _____ PERIOD _____

Lesson 2 Multi-Step Problem Solving

Multi-Step Example
The table shows the results of a survey of students in Janette's class about their favorite pencil-and-paper puzzles. If there are 360 students in Janette's grade, predict how many more favor word searches compared to word scrambles. **7.SP1, MP 2**

Ⓐ 36   Ⓒ 144
Ⓑ 72   Ⓓ 216

Kind of Puzzle	Students
Crossword	6
Sudoku	8
Word Search	14
Word Scramble	7

Use a problem-solving model to solve this problem.

1 Analyze
Read the problem. Circle the information you know. Underline what the problem is asking you to find.

2 Plan
What will you need to do to solve the problem? Write your plan in steps.

Step 1 Determine how many more students favor **word searches** compared to **word scrambles** written as a fraction.

Step 2 Determine the __fraction__ out of 360 students.

3 Solve
Use your plan to solve the problem. Show your steps.

There were 35 students surveyed. Write the number of students that prefer each puzzle over 35. Then subtract.

$$\frac{14}{35} - \frac{7}{35} = \frac{7}{35} \text{ or } \frac{1}{5}$$ Subtract.

$$\frac{1}{5} \times 360 = 72$$ Multiply.

There would be __72__ students more that favor word searches.

So, the correct answer is __B__ . Fill in that answer choice.

4 Justify and Evaluate
How do you know your solution is accurate?
Sample answer: Another method would be to determine $\frac{14}{35}$ or $\frac{2}{5}$ of 360, or 144. Then subtract $\frac{7}{35}$ or $\frac{1}{5}$ of 360, or 72. So, 144 − 72 is equal to 72 students. So, my solution is accurate.

> **Read to Succeed!**
> You can also express the difference as a decimal before multiplying. One-fifth is equal to 0.2 or 20%.

NAME _____ DATE _____ PERIOD _____

Lesson 2 (continued)

Use a problem-solving model to solve each problem.

1 The table shows the results of a student survey at a shopping mall in which they asked people what store they were visiting first. During the survey, the students observed 30 shoppers entering the mall. If 390 people were surveyed, predict how many more would have said they were visiting the electronics store or clothing store compared to the bookstore. **7.SP1, MP 2**

Store	Shoppers
Bookstore	8
Electronics	11
Clothing	7
Sporting Goods	4

Ⓐ 234   Ⓒ 130
Ⓑ 195   Ⓓ 104

2 Jack surveyed two classes in his school to determine how many students had savings accounts. The circle graphs show his results. If there are 250 total seventh-graders and 220 eighth-graders in Jack's school, predict the difference in the number of students who have savings accounts between the two grades. **7.SP1, MP 2**

Seventh-Graders: 38% No Savings Account, 62% Savings Account
Eighth-Graders: 30% No Savings Account, 70% Savings Account

1 student

3 Kristen at the Yummy Lunch restaurant kept track of how many people ordered different dishes in one day. She used the results to predict how many orders the restaurant would receive during the following week. If 750 people visited Yummy Lunch that week, predict how many more people ordered salad than soup. **7.SP.2, MP 2**

Orders at Yummy Lunch
Soup 48%, Salad 60%, Sandwich 72%, Dessert 42%

90 people

4 H.O.T. Problem The graph shows the results of a survey of families in the town of Jefferson about their household's newspaper subscriptions. If there are a total of 4,300 households in Jefferson, predict how many more families subscribe to State Telegram or Jefferson Gazette compared to County Journal or The City Sentinel. **7.SP1, MP 2**

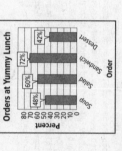

Newspaper Subscriptions
State Telegram 22, County Journal 15, The City Sentinel 18, Jefferson Gazette 20

516 families

NAME _____ DATE _____ PERIOD _____

Lesson 3 *(continued)*

Use a problem-solving model to solve each problem.

1 A toy store sells three different versions of a popular game as a board game, electronic, or a travel-size version. The store workers survey 120 customers at random about their favorite version of the game. The table shows the results of this survey. If 420 games are ordered, about how many more should be electronic than travel-size?
Extension of 7.SP1, MP 1

Game Type	Number
Board	42
Electronic	50
Travel-Size	28

Ⓐ 273   Ⓒ 98
Ⓑ 175   Ⓓ 77

3 Two pharmacies on opposite sides of town each surveyed a random sample of customers in their store about what type of cold medicine they prefer. If store A and store B each order 150 units of cold medicine, make an inference to determine how many more should be in the pill form for store A compared to store B.
Extension of 7.SP1, MP 2

Medicine Form	Store A	Store B
Pill	33	38
Syrup	10	15
Spray	2	4

about 10 orders

2 A sporting goods store sells three different versions of athletic shoes. The store workers surveyed 200 customers at random. The results are shown in the table. Out of 500 shoes they ordered, 220 were cross trainers. Based on the survey, make an inference about how many cross trainers they will still need.
Extension of 7.SP1, MP 2

Shoe Type	Number in Survey
Cross Trainer	100
High Top	24
Tennis Shoes	76

30 shoes

4 🖉 **H.O.T. Problem** A jewelry store wanted to survey customers to determine if they preferred silver, gold, or platinum chain. The store surveyed 67 customers who made a purchase and 23 customers who did not make a purchase. Explain why neither of the data collection methods is valid, and what would be a better way to collect the data.
Extension of 7.SP1, MP 4

Sample answer: Each sample is not a random sample. Customers who have already made a purchase may not provide useful information as they may not buy another chain. Also, the sample size for customers who did not make a purchase is very small. A better method would be to survey every 5th person who comes into the store about their chain preference.

140

Course 2 • Chapter 10 Statistics

NAME _____ DATE _____ PERIOD _____

Lesson 3 Multi-Step Problem Solving

Multi-Step Example

A furniture store sells wood, metal, and wicker chairs. The store workers survey 80 customers at random about their favorite type of chair. The table shows the results of this survey. If 200 chairs are ordered, about how many more should be wood than metal?
Extension of 7.SP1, MP 1

Chair Type	Number
Wood	45
Metal	27
Wicker	8

Ⓐ 18   Ⓒ 68
Ⓑ 45   Ⓓ 113

Use a problem-solving model to solve this problem.

1 Analyze

Read the problem. Circle the information you know.
Underline what the problem is asking you to find.

2 Plan

What will you need to do to solve the problem? Write your plan in steps.

Step 1 Determine how many more people favor __wood__ compared to __metal__ written as a fraction.

Step 2 Determine the __fraction__ out of 200 chairs.

3 Solve

Use your plan to solve the problem. Show your steps.

There were 80 people surveyed. Write the number of people that prefer each chair type over 80. Then subtract.

$$\frac{45}{80} - \frac{27}{80} = \frac{18}{80} \text{ or } \frac{9}{40} \quad \text{Subtract.}$$

$$\frac{9}{40} \times 200 = \textbf{45} \quad \text{Multiply.}$$

The store would expect about __45__ more wood chair orders than metal.

So, the correct answer is __B__. Fill in that answer choice.

> **Read to Succeed!**
> You can also express the difference as a decimal before multiplying. It can be expressed as 0.225 or 22.5%.

4 Justify and Evaluate

How do you know your solution is accurate?
Sample answer: Another method would be to determine $\frac{45}{80}$ **or** $\frac{9}{16}$ **of 200,**
or 112.5. **Then subtract** $\frac{27}{80}$ **of 200, or** 67.5. **So,** $112.5 - 67.5$ **is equal to**
45 orders. So, my solution is accurate.

Course 2 • Chapter 10 Statistics

139

   Course 2 · Chapter 10 Statistics

Chapter 10 Lesson 4 Answer Keys

NAME _____ DATE _____ PERIOD _____

Lesson 4 Multi-Step Problem Solving

Multi-Step Example

Four models of televisions are on sale this week at the local electronic store. In their advertisement, the store claims that their average price for a television is $2,106.25. The sale prices of the televisions are shown in the graph. By how much should they increase this amount to give a more accurate representation of the average price, in dollars, of the televisions on sale? 7.SP.4, MP 2

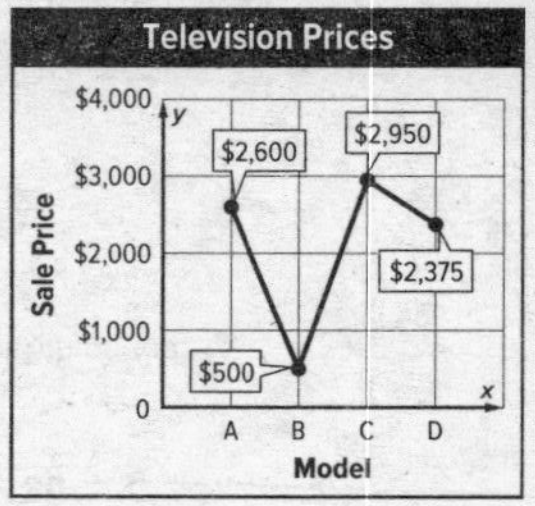

Television Prices

$$\begin{array}{l}\$4,000\\ \$3,000 \quad \boxed{\$2,950}\\ \$2,000 \quad \boxed{\$2,600} \quad \boxed{\$2,375}\\ \$1,000 \quad \boxed{\$500}\\ \quad A \quad B \quad C \quad D\end{array}$$

Sale Price / Model

Ⓐ $381.25   Ⓒ $535.42
Ⓑ $450.50   Ⓓ $575.00

Use a problem-solving model to solve this problem.

1 Analyze

Read the problem. (Circle) the information you know.
Underline what the problem is asking you to find.

2 Plan

What will you need to do to solve the problem? Write your plan in steps.

Step 1 Determine the more appropriate __measure__ to describe to data.

Step 2 Determine the __difference__ between the mean and median.

3 Solve

Use your plan to solve the problem. Show your steps.

The median is the more appropriate measure. Determine the median.

$2,375 + $2,600 = **$4,975** $4,975 ÷ 2 = **$2,487.50**

$2,487.50 − $2,106.25 = **$381.25**   Subtract

The more accurate price would be the median that is **$381.25** greater than the mean.

So, the correct answer is __B__. Fill in that answer choice.

4 Justify and Evaluate

How do you know your solution is accurate?

Sample answer: Since the mean is much lower than the median, it is misleading.

The median of $2,487.50 is a more accurate representation of the data.

The median is $2,487.50 − $2,106.25, or $381.25 greater than the mean.

NAME _____ DATE _____ PERIOD _____

Lesson 4 (continued)

Use a problem-solving model to solve each problem.

1 A certain thrift store claims they will buy used jewelry at an average of $48 per necklace. The amounts the store has paid for the last four necklaces are shown in the graph. Based on these data, how much less than the store's advertised average is the more appropriate representation of the average payment? 7.SP.4, MP 2

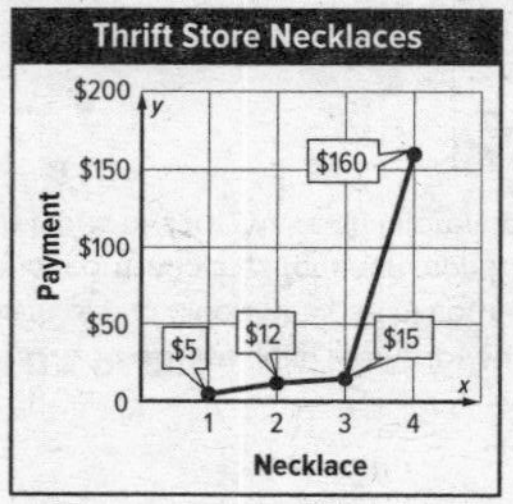

Thrift Store Necklaces

$$\begin{array}{l}\$200 \quad y\\ \$150 \quad \boxed{\$160}\\ \$100\\ \$50 \quad \boxed{\$5} \quad \boxed{\$12} \quad \boxed{\$15}\\ \quad 0 \quad 1 \quad 2 \quad 3 \quad 4 \quad x\end{array}$$

Necklace

Ⓐ $13.50   Ⓒ $34.50
Ⓑ $25.75   Ⓓ $61.50

2 The table shows the times, in minutes, of the jogs that Fernando and Nakita ran last week. What is the difference, in minutes, between the measures that best describe Fernando's running times and Nakita's running times? 7.SP.4, MP 1

Running Times (in min)	
Fernando	Nakita
16	5
20	20
12	23

__4 minutes__

3 🔥 **H.O.T. Problem** A ski resort claims they have an average of 190,000 visitors per year. The circle graph shows the number of visitors to the resort during each of the four seasons. Explain why 190,000 is a misleading descriptor of the average number of visitors. What would be a better way to convey the appropriate information? 7.SP.4, MP 6

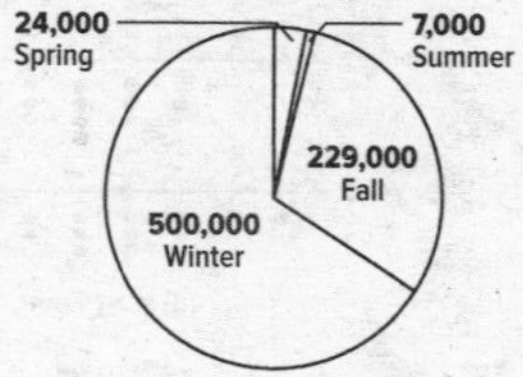

Ski Resort Visitors by Season

- Spring 24,000
- Summer 7,000
- Fall 229,000
- Winter 500,000

Sample answer: The ski resort is most active during the winter. They should say they had 500,000 customers last winter. This number is more representative of how busy the resort is during the peak time customers want to be there.

Read to Succeed!

There is no mode for the data. You should only compare the mean and median to determine which is more appropriate for the data.

Answers

NAME _____ DATE _____ PERIOD _____

Lesson 5 Multi-Step Problem Solving

Multi-Step Example

The double box plot shows the test scores for two different math classes. Use the information to determine which of the following inferences is *not true*. *Extension of 7.SP1,* MP 2

Test Scores (percent)
5th period
1st period
50 60 70 80 90 100

Ⓐ Only one of the data sets is symmetric.

Ⓑ The median test score in 1st period is greater than 5th period.

Ⓒ The highest test score is the same in both periods.

Ⓓ The interquartile range of 1st period is larger than 5th period.

Use a problem-solving model to solve this problem.

1 Analyze

Read the problem. Circle the information you know. Underline what the problem is asking you to find.

2 Plan

What will you need to do to solve the problem? Write your plan in steps.

Step 1 Determine the **shapes, centers, and spreads** of the two scores.

Step 2 Determine which inference is _not true_.

3 Solve

Use your plan to solve the problem. Show your steps.

The 1st period is **symmetric**, but the 5th period is **not symmetric**.

The median for 1st period is _85_. The median for 5th period is _80_.

Both periods have a high test score of **100%**.

The interquartile range for 1st period is _20_, and it is _25_ for 5th period.

So, the correct answer is _D_. Fill in that answer choice.

Read to Succeed!

Recall that box plots separate data into four parts. Each part contains 25% of the data.

4 Justify and Evaluate

How do you know your solution is accurate?

Sample answer: All of the inferences listed are true except for answer choice D.

The 1st period interquartile range is 20 which is smaller than the interquartile range for 5th period.

NAME _____ DATE _____ PERIOD _____

Lesson 5 *(continued)*

Use a problem-solving model to solve each problem.

1 The box plots below show the wait times in minutes for two popular rides at an amusement park. Use the data to determine which of the statements below is *not correct*. *Extension of 7.SP1,* MP 2

Wait Time (min)
Red Racer
Wild Viper
10 20 30 40 50 60

Ⓐ The median wait time for both rides is 35 minutes.

Ⓑ The Red Racer has a shorter maximum wait time than the Wild Viper.

Ⓒ The Wild Viper has a larger range of wait times than the Red Racer.

Ⓓ The Red Racer has a larger interquartile range than the Time Warp.

2 The double dot plot below shows the number of hours Kayla and Carmen studied during a two week period in college. Determine the most appropriate measure of variation for each data set. What is the difference between the centers? *Extension of 7.SP1,* MP 2

Study Time (h)
Kayla
Carmen
1 2 3 4 5 6 7 8

0.5 hour

3 🧠 **H.O.T. Problem** Juan works for an agricultural company and is studying the growth of two different types of corn. The table below shows the growth of each type of corn in inches for each month. Compare the shapes, centers, and spreads for both types of corn. Make an inference based on your findings. *Extension of 7.SP1,* MP 6

	Corn A	Corn B
1st month	20	28
2nd month	20	19
3rd month	26	15
4th month	18	7
5th month	13	26

Sample answer: Corn A – median 20, IQR 7.5; Corn B – median 19, IQR 16;

The median of Corn A is slightly greater than that of Corn B, which

indicates a slightly larger amount of growth. The variation of Corn B is

significantly greater than that of Corn A making growth prediction less

accurate and more difficult.

Chapter 10 Performance Task Rubric

Part	Max Points	
B	2	**Full Credit:** Sample answer: The top two sports were volleyball and basketball. Volleyball: $\frac{12}{15} = \frac{x}{145}$; $x = 70$ seventh-graders Basketball: $\frac{7}{25} = \frac{x}{145}$; $x = 41$ seventh-graders Your sample would be biased since most seventh-graders have completely different interests than twelfth-graders. An unbiased sample would be to survey two students from every lunch table in the cafeteria provided the school is grades 7–12. **Partial Credit** will be given for correct ratios for the seventh grade class OR for accurate discussion on biased and unbiased data. **No credit** will be given for incorrect answers.
C	2	**Full Credit:** Sample graph: Our box plot of class arm spans looks like this: 50 52 54 56 58 60 62 64 66 68 70 72 74 76 78 Sample answer: Our IQR is $72 - 60 = 12$ (variation). Their IQR is $64 - 56 = 8$. Our median is 68 and their median is 60. Our class's median and IQR suggest that, in general, our students have a larger arm span than the other class's students. **Partial Credit** will be given for correct box plot OR accurate analysis of differences in class data. **No credit** will be given for incorrect answers.
D	1	**Full Credit:** Sample answer: Outliers, such as the student(s) who have an arm span of 74 inches, skew the mean. The median is a much better representation of the average student. From the box plot, we can determine that their median is 60 inches, so this would provide a more accurate answer. In our class, 68 is the median. It would be a good representation of the arm span of the average student. **No credit** will be given for incorrect answers.
TOTAL	9	

PT19 Playing Favorites

Note to teacher: Prior to completing this task, have students collect data to use for the task. In this task, students survey others for favorite sport for intramurals. They also measure arm spans of classmates. Have students compile and share the results.

All answers are sample answers with a class of 25 students and an entire seventh grade of 145 students.

CCSS Content Standard(s)	7.SP.1, 7.SP.2, 7.SP.4
Mathematical Practices	MP2, MP3, MP4, MP6, MP8
Depth of Knowledge	DOK2, DOK3

Scoring Rubric

Part	Max Points	
A	4	**Full Credit:** Sample graphs: **Favorite Sport** 48% Volleyball 28% Basketball 20% Softball 4% Soccer **Favorite Sport** Soccer Softball Basketball Volleyball **Sample questions:** • How many total students were surveyed? Bar graph; 25 • What percentage of students favor either volleyball or basketball? Circle graph; 76% • What is the ratio of students who preferred volleyball to those who preferred softball? Bar graph; 12:5 **Partial Credit** (2 points) will be given for correct displays of the data OR for writing three appropriate sample questions that can be answered using the displays. **No credit** will be given for incorrect answers.

Chapter 9 Performance Task Rubric

Page PT17 College Ball

CCSS Content Standard(s)	7.SP.5, 7.SP.7a, 7.SP.7b, 7.SP.8a, 7.SP.8b, 7.SP.8c
Mathematical Practices	MP1, MP2, MP3, MP4, MP7
Depth of Knowledge	DOK2, DOK3, DOK4

Part	Max Points	Scoring Rubric
A	1	**Full Credit:** Evan's total field goals made are the sum of his 2-pointers and 3-pointers made. He made 38 field goals out of 71 attempts. Therefore, he missed 33 field goals. $\frac{33}{71} \approx 0.465$ or 46.5% chance he will miss an attempted field goal. This is an example of experimental probability because it is based on data that have already been gathered. No credit will be given for incorrect answers.
B	2	**Full Credit:** If Evan attempts five of each type of shot for three games, he will be attempting 15 total of each. Make ratios comparing his shot chart to how many he would make out of 15 attempts. 2-pointers: $\frac{25}{40} = \frac{x}{15}$; $x \approx 9.4$; Evan could make nine 2-pointers. 3-pointers: $\frac{13}{31} = \frac{x}{15}$; $x \approx 6.3$; Evan could make six 3-pointers. Free throws: $\frac{68}{74} = \frac{x}{15}$; $x \approx 13.8$; Evan could make 13 free throws. Statistically, this means he is on pace to score 49 points for the rest of the regular season. He has already scored 157 points. So, yes, statistically, Evan could be expected to reach the milestone of 200 points this season. Partial Credit will be given for correctly calculating the probability of scoring each type of shot in the last three games OR determining he can reach his milestone of 200 points with explanation. No credit will be given for incorrect answers.
C	2	**Full Credit:** Evan has at least a 10% chance of making those three shots. Changing the order of the shots would not change the probability because multiplication is commutative. Evan's shot chart tells us he has a $\frac{13}{31}$ chance of making each of the 3-pointers. He has a $\frac{5}{8}$ chance of making the 2-pointer. $\frac{13}{31} \times \frac{13}{31} \times \frac{5}{8} = \frac{845}{7,688} \approx 0.11$ or 11%. Partial Credit will be given for only one correct answer with explanation. No credit will be given for incorrect answers.
D	1	**Full Credit:** Evan is incorrect; If 10 players have already been lined up, then there are only 5 players remaining. The amount of remaining sequences can be represented by 5! = 5 × 4 × 3 × 2 × 1 = 120 photos. If each photo takes 15 seconds, we get 120(15) = 1,800 total seconds, which is 1,800 ÷ 60 = 30 minutes. The players do not have to leave for practice for another 35 minutes. They would have enough time to take the additional photos. No credit will be given for incorrect answers.
E	2	**Full Credit:** The highlight footage is 4(60) = 240 seconds long. That means there are 240 ÷ 5 = 48 highlights. Evan's probability of having one of his made shots included at the state banquet is $\frac{4}{48}$ or $\frac{1}{12}$ or about 8%. A probability model could be a bag of 48 colored marbles where each color represents a different player. For example, Evan's made shots could be represented by 4 black marbles. The coach would take one of the marbles out of the bag to represent his selection. This experiment could be repeated a number of times and results could be recorded in a table. As the number of trials increase, the relative frequency of the event is closer to the theoretical probability of $\frac{1}{12}$. Partial Credit will be given for only one correct answer with explanation. No credit will be given for incorrect answers.
TOTAL	8	

Performance Task Rubrics

Part	Max Points	Scoring Rubric
		Full Credit: Sample answer: Esperanza could get a rough estimate of the number of bricks used by multiplying 10,480 by 4. She will need to subtract the area of the garage door ($10 \times 15 = 150$ ft²). She will also need to know the dimensions of the doors and windows on the other three sides of the house so she can subtract that area when calculating the number of bricks used.
		Partial Credit will be given the correct number of bricks and explanation OR thorough explanation of how to estimate number of bricks for entire house.
		No credit will be given for incorrect answers.
D	2	**Full Credit:** We need the total area of the backyard minus the areas of the basketball court and shed. The area of the backyard is $80 \times 55 = 4,400$ ft². The area of the shed is $11 \times 11 = 121$ ft². The area of the basketball court is the sum of the semi-circle and the adjacent rectangle. The area of a semi-circle is $\frac{\pi \times r^2}{2}$. We know from the width of the adjacent rectangle that the diameter of the semi-circle is 8 feet, so the radius of the circle is $8 \div 2 = 4$ feet. $$\frac{\pi \times (4)^2}{2} = \frac{3.14 \times 16}{2} = \frac{50.24}{2} \approx 25.1 \text{ ft}^2.$$ The area of the adjacent rectangle is $8 \times 20 = 160$ ft². So, the area of the basketball court is $25.1 + 160 = 185.1$ ft². Our final square footage that needs grass is $4,400 - 121 - 185.1 = 4,093.9$ ft². Each bag of grass seed covers 1,500 ft², so $4,093.9 \div 1,500 \approx 2.7$. She will need 3 bags of grass seed. No; The new area is $160 \times 110 = 17,600$ ft². The dimensions of the basketball court and shed will stay the same, so the area to be covered by grass would be $17,600 - 121 - 185.1 = 17,293.9$. Compared to the original area that needed grass, 4,093.9 ft², she would need more than double the amount grass seed. She would need $17,293.9 \div 1,500 = 11.5$ or about 12 bags of grass seed.
		Partial Credit will be given for only one correct answer with explanation.
		No credit will be given for incorrect answers.
TOTAL	**8**	

Page PT15   Home Sweet Home

CCSS Content Standard(s)	7.G.4, 7.G.6, 7.NS.3
Mathematical Practices	MP3, MP4, MP6, MP7, MP8
Depth of Knowledge	DOK2, DOK3

Part	Max Points	Scoring Rubric
A	2	**Full Credit:** Yes; The volume of cement needed for the driveway is $8.5 \times 60 \times 0.5 = 255$ ft³ $= 9.\overline{4}$ yd³ or about 9.5 yd³. Yes; there will be about 0.5 yd³ or 13.5 ft³ remaining. The amount of cement needed for the bike area is $6 \times 4 \times 0.5 = 12$ ft³, so there will be enough cement left over to fill this space. **Partial Credit** will be given for the volume of cement for the driveway and explanation OR the correct volume of cement for the bike area and explanation. **No credit** will be given for incorrect answers.
B	2	**Full Credit:** Based on the dimensions of the house, the area of one of the floors is $50 \times 45 = 2,250$ ft². Doubling this because there are two floors yields $2,250 \times 2 = 4,500$ ft². The area of the kitchen is $20 \times 18 = 360$ ft² and the area of each bathroom is $8 \times 7.5 = 60$ ft². Our final carpeted area becomes $4,500 - 360 - 60 - 60 = 4,020$ ft². An equation for the total cost for carpeting is $c = 2.49f + 900$, where c represents total cost and f represents the number of square feet. The total carpet cost is $4,020 \times 2.49 + 900 = 10,909.80$; $10,909.80. **Partial Credit** will be given for the correct square footage needing carpeting and explanation OR a correct equation and cost of carpeting with an explanation. **No credit** will be given for incorrect answers.
C	2	**Full Credit:** The area of the wall is $45 \times 30 = 1,350$ ft². The area of the wall minus the window is $1,350 - 40 = 1,310$ ft². Each brick covers $0.5 \text{ ft} \times 0.25 \text{ ft}$ or 0.125 ft². So, $1,310 \div 0.125 = 10,480$ bricks.

Part	Max Points	Scoring Rubric
C	2	**Full Credit:** Sample answer: The sum of all three interior angles of a triangle equals 180°. So, angle F + angle G + angle H = 180°. Since angle H = 180°. So, angle F + angle G + angle H = 180°. Since angle F = 5(angle H + (−2)), we get 5(H − 2) + H + 90 = 180; H = 16.$\overline{6}$°. So, angle F = 5(16.$\overline{6}$ − 2) = 5(14.$\overline{6}$) = 73.$\overline{3}$°. Because angle G is 90°, angle F must be less than 90° in order for the sum of the three angles to still be 180°. Therefore, the largest measurement that angle F could have is 89.9°. Partial Credit will be given for a correct measurement for angle F and explanation OR for correct answer of largest measure of angle F with explanation. No credit will be given for an incorrect answer.
D	2	**Full Credit:** Sample answer: The sum of the three angles needs to be 180°, and the two unknown angles need to be the same because it is an isosceles triangle. 2x + 120 = 180; 2x = 60; x = 30° The triangle is an obtuse isosceles triangle. It is not possible for one of the other angles to be obtuse because the sum of the three angles would be more than the 180° inside of a triangle. The shape would not be a triangle. Partial Credit will be given for correct angle measures of roof and classification of triangle OR correct explanation about more than one obtuse angles in triangle with explanation. No credit will be given for an incorrect answer.
E	2	**Full Credit:** Since the building is a cube, the horizontal cross section is a square. Yes, the architect is correct. The building is a cube, but the roof makes the building taller such that the side view is a rectangle. The front view of the building is a pentagon, and the top view is a square. Partial Credit will be given for correctly identifying shape of the horizontal cross section OR for correctly identifying the side view, front view, and top view of the building with an explanation. No credit will be given for an incorrect answer.
TOTAL	9	

Page PT13   *Geometry in Buildings*

CCSS Content Standard(s)	7.G.1, 7.G.2, 7.G.3, 7.G.5
Mathematical Practices	MP2, MP3, MP4, MP6, MP7
Depth of Knowledge	DOK2, DOK3, DOK4

Part	Max Points	Scoring Rubric
A	1	**Full Credit:** Sample answer: When two lines intersect, the vertical (opposite) angles formed are always equal. So, angles A and C must be equal because they are vertical angles. When two lines intersect, the adjacent angles formed always sum to 180°. This tells us that these angles must equal 180°. However, 70° + 105° = 175°. Therefore, one or both of the measurements must be incorrect. No credit will be given for an incorrect answer.
B	2	**Full Credit:** Sample answer: Set up ratios and cross multiply to determine the height of the elevator shaft. $\dfrac{2}{9} = \dfrac{7}{x}$ $2x = 63$ $x = 31.5$ So, the elevator shaft will be 31.5 feet tall. Also, $\dfrac{4}{9} = \dfrac{7}{x}$ $4x = 63$ $x = 15.75$ So, doubling the left side of the scale equation would *halve* the height of elevator shaft instead of doubling it. Partial Credit will be given for the finding the correct height of the elevator shaft OR a correct explanation of the impact of doubling the left side of the scale equation. No credit will be given for an incorrect answer.

Chapter 6 Performance Task Rubric

PT11 Bank Statement

CCSS Content Standard(s)	7.EE.4, 7.EE.4a, 7.EE.4b
Mathematical Practices	MP1, MP2, MP3, MP6, MP7, MP8
Depth of Knowledge	DOK2, DOK3

Part	Max Points	Scoring Rubric
A	1	**Full Credit:** $7{,}456.43 + 2{,}010.55 + 2{,}378.09 = \$11{,}845.07 \qquad x = 1{,}154.93$ No, he is not correct; Mario must deposit $1,154.93 to reach his goal. This is less than $1,200. No credit will be given for an incorrect answer.
B	2	**Full Credit:** $5m + 75 \le 2{,}378.09 \qquad m \le 460.60$ $2{,}378.09 - 5(460) = 78.09$ He can donate up to $460 to each charity. He will have at least $78.09 left. Partial Credit will be given for a correct inequality OR the correct whole dollar amount donated to each charity and the correct amount left if he donates that amount to each charity. No credit will be given for an incorrect answer.
C	1	**Full Credit:** $45x = 2{,}989.45 \qquad x \approx 66.4$ Paying $45 per month for 66 months would not quite pay off the debt, so it would take at least 67 months, or a little more than 5½ years. Partial Credit will be given for the correct equation with explanation OR the correct number of years to pay off the debt. No credit will be given for an incorrect answer.
D	1	**Full Credit:** Since Mario wants to keep 85% of the money in his checking account, he is allowing himself to spend no more than 15% of the money in his checking account. $0.15(7{,}456.43) = \$1{,}118.46 \qquad 0.05(19{,}080) = \$954$ Since $954 < $1,118.46, he was able to purchase the car and still keep 85% of the money in his checking account. No credit will be given for an incorrect answer.
E	2	**Full Credit:** Mario's current savings account balance is $2,010.55 + $4,000.00 = $6,010.55. His down payment for the condo would be $70{,}000(0.2) = 14{,}000$; $14,000. Let x represent the number of months that Mario saves his money. The inequality for the number of months it will take him to save up enough for a down payment on the condo is: $6{,}010.55 + 350x \ge 14{,}000 \qquad x \ge 22.827$ Therefore, Mario will need to wait at least 22.9 months. 20 21 22 23 24 25 26 Partial Credit will be given for the correct answer and justification without the number line. No credit will be given for an incorrect answer.
F	3	**Full Credit:** Sample answer: Let e represent the total electric bill each month. $1{,}450 - \left(700 + 250 + 80 + e + \tfrac{1}{5}\,e\right) \ge 250 \qquad e \le 141.67$ If Mario wants to have at least $250 left for groceries and expenses, his electric bill can be no higher than $141.67, and his water bill can be no higher than $\tfrac{1}{5}(\$141.67) = \$28.33$. Partial Credit (2 points) will be given for an inequality and justification to solve the problem OR (1 point) for the correct amounts for the electric bill and water bill. No credit will be given for an incorrect answer.
TOTAL	10	

Chapter 5 Performance Task Rubric

Page PT9 Cell City

CCSS Content Standard(s)	7.EE.1, 7.EE.2
Mathematical Practices	MP1, MP2, MP3, MP6, MP7
Depth of Knowledge	DOK2, DOK3

Part	Max Points	Scoring Rubric
A	2	**Full Credit:** Danielle's weekly income can be written as: $90 + 5(5.5x) = 90 + 27.5x$ For one month, we need to multiply this by 4. $4(90 + 27.5x) = 360 + 110x$ Using our one month equation, we need to find the sum of three months by substituting in 5, 5, and 7 for the number of phones sold each day in month 1, month 2, and month 3. $(360 + 110(5)) + (360 + 110(5)) + (360 + 110(7)) =$ $910 + 910 + 1,130 = 2,950;\ \$2,950.$ At the end of three months, Danielle will not have enough money to purchase the motorcycle. **Partial Credit** will be given for the linear expression OR an appropriate explanation. **No credit** will be given for an incorrect answer.
B	2	**Full Credit:** Roberta's base salary is $90 per week, so her base salary per day is $90 \div 5 = \$18.$ Their combined income per day can be written as $(20 + 5.5x) + (18 + 5.5x) = \$38 + 11x$ To determine how much is made per week: $5(38 + 11x) = \$190 + 55x.$ $190 + 55(4) = 190 + 220 = \$410.$ Therefore, Marcus was correct. **Partial Credit** credit will be given for the linear expression OR an appropriate explanation. **No credit** will be given for an incorrect answer.
C	2	**Full Credit:** Sample answer: $b + 0.15x.$ Marcus's salary would be $20 + 0.15(200) = 20 + 30 = \$50.$ Marcus would make $50 that day.

Part	Max Points	Scoring Rubric
		With Marcus's plan, the more an employee sold in a day, the larger their paycheck. If an employee wanted to make more money, they could work harder to sell more phones or accessories. **Partial Credit** will be given for the linear expression and Marcus's salary OR an appropriate explanation about the effect on employee pay. **No credit** will be given for an incorrect answer.
D	2	**Full Credit:** Plan A: $29.95 + 0.12m;\ 29.95 + 0.12(500) = \$89.95$ per month Plan B: $95.20 per month Plan C: $49.95 + 0.05m;\ 49.95 + 0.05(500) = \$74.95$ per month Plan C is the best plan for Cho based on 500 text messages per month. If she had 1,000 text messages per month, Plan C would cost her $99.95 per month. So if she thinks that the amount of text messages might double, she should choose Plan B. **Partial Credit** will be given for a correct recommendation based on 500 text messages OR a correct recommendation for 1,000 text messages. **No credit** will be given for an incorrect answer.
E	2	**Full Credit:** Sample answer: Plan D: $115.20 per month, unlimited text messages, 5 GB of data. This would be $20 more than the monthly fee for Plan B, covering Cell City's additional cost but charging the customer less than the $15 per GB overage cost. The student's plan should charge more than $5 for each additional 1 GB of data but less than $15 per GB and should not include additional charges for text messages or phone service. On Plan B, if a customer uses 9 GB of data per month, he or she would be charged the $95.20 monthly fee plus $15 for each of the additional 7 GB of data. The monthly charge would be $95.20 + 7(15) = \$200.20.$ With this Plan D, the customer would only pay for an additional 4 GB of data at $15 per GB: $115.20 + 4(15) = \$175.20,$ saving the customer $25 each month. **Partial Credit** will be given for a new plan that meets the criteria OR an explanation of how the plan will help the customer using 9 GB of data per month. **No credit** will be given for an incorrect answer.
TOTAL	10	

Performance Task Rubrics

D	1	**Full Credit:** $\left(\frac{2}{7} + 1\frac{3}{4}\right) = 2\frac{1}{28}$ acres mowed on Saturday before it rained. Noah will have to mow $3\frac{1}{7} - 2\frac{1}{28} = 1\frac{3}{28}$ acres on Sunday. No credit will be given for incorrect answer.
E	2	**Full Credit:** $\frac{5}{4}\left(1\frac{1}{3}\right) + \frac{16}{5}\left(2\frac{1}{2}\right) + 3\frac{1}{7}\left(1\frac{5}{16}\right) = \frac{331}{24} = 13\frac{19}{24}$ acres over the next three days. $13\frac{19}{24}$ acres will be mowed by Noah's brother. Partial Credit will be given for correctly calculating the total acres to be mowed, but failing to give the number of acres Noah's brother will mow. No credit will be given for an incorrect answer.
F	1	**Full Credit:** First property: $20\frac{1}{2} \div 3 = 6\frac{5}{6}$; 7 bags of mulch. Second property: $3\frac{1}{4} \div 3 = 1\frac{1}{12}$; 2 bags of mulch. Third property: $9\frac{3}{7} \div 3 = 3\frac{1}{7}$; 4 bags of mulch. No credit will be given for an incorrect answer.
TOTAL	9	

Page PT7 Summer Job

CCSS Content Standard(s)	7.NS.1c, 7.NS.1d, 7.NS.2a, 7.NS.2b, 7.NS.2c, 7.NS.2d, 7.NS.3, 7.EE.3
Mathematical Practices	MP1, MP2, MP3, MP4, MP6, MP8
Depth of Knowledge	DOK2, DOK3

Part	Max Points	Scoring Rubric
A	1	**Full Credit:** We know $\frac{1}{2} = 2\overline{)1.0} = 0.5$ and $\frac{16}{5} = 5\overline{)16.0} = 3.2$. He mowed $0.5 + 3.2 = 3.7$ acres on Monday and Friday combined. No credit will be given for an incorrect answer.
B	2	**Full Credit:** Noah is correct. Sample explanation: We know $\frac{5}{4} = 1\frac{1}{4}$ and $\frac{16}{5} = 3\frac{1}{5}$. Our sorted list Sorting the list, we get $\frac{1}{2}, 1\frac{1}{4}, 1\frac{1}{3}, 2\frac{1}{2}, 3\frac{1}{7}, 3\frac{1}{5}$. Our sorted list becomes Monday, Thursday, Wednesday, Tuesday, Saturday, Friday. Therefore, Noah will need to use more gasoline on Friday than on any other day because mowing more acreage will use more gasoline. This tells us that Noah's opinion is correct. Partial Credit will be given for a correct ordered list without an explanation. No credit will be given for an incorrect answer.
C	2	**Full Credit:** $\frac{1}{2} + 2\frac{1}{2} + 1\frac{1}{3} = 4\frac{1}{3}$ acres Monday through Wednesday $\frac{5}{4} + \frac{16}{5} + 3\frac{1}{7} = \frac{1,063}{140} = 7\frac{83}{140}$ acres Thursday through Saturday Since it takes more gasoline to mow a greater number of acres, Noah will need more gasoline for the second half of the week (Thursday through Saturday). Partial Credit will be given for the correct answer without an explanation. No credit will be given for incorrect answer.